COLIN JACKSON

COLIN JACKSON

THE AUTOBIOGRAPHY

BOOKS

David Conn, who helped Colin with the writing of this book, is an award winning journalist, author and broadcaster. He has written and contributed to several sports books, and writes a sport column every Saturday in *The Independent* newspaper.

Published by BBC Books, BBC Worldwide Limited, 80 Wood Lane, London W12 0TT

First published 2003. Copyright © Colin Jackson 2003
The moral right of the author has been asserted.

ISBN 0 563 48738 0

Commissioning editor: Ben Dunn
Project editor: Sarah Emsley
Designer: Linda Blakemore
Copy-editor: Mandy Greenfield
Production controller: Arlene Alexander

BBC Books would like to thank the following for providing photographs and for permission to reproduce copyright material. While every effort has been made to trace and acknowledge all copyright holders, we would like to apologize should there have been any errors or omissions.

All photos courtesy the author except:
Empics section 1 p6 (all); section 2 p1, p2 (below), p4/5, p6, p7; section 3 p2 (below), p8 (below). Getty News and Sport section 2 p2 (above), p3 ; section 3 p8 (above).

Set in Berling and Requiem
Printed and bound in Great Britain by The Bath Press
Colour separations by Radstock Reproductions, Midsomer Norton

CONTENTS

If I were to thank everyone by name who deserves a mention here, I would need another book – but all of you out there know who you are.

Hopefully you will not mind me mentioning some special people who, without a doubt, have had a massive influence on my life. I would like to thank my mother, my father and my sister Suzanne, and also my coach Malcolm Arnold without whose continued help I would not be writing this book today. I'm going to leave the name-calling there in case I miss someone!

My memories will always be with my grandfather, Dee, who died in 1998, Ross Baillie who died in 1999, and Rhys Davies who died on the day of my final race. Each one of them played a special part in my life. So to you guys, until we meet again, thank you.

Thanks should also go to all at BBC Worldwide who worked on this book, especially David Conn who knows me inside out now! A special thanks to you, Dave.

INTRODUCTION

I began to work on this story of my life – my 18 years' competing in international athletics – in Cardiff, where I have always lived, in my house staring out at the bay, the cranes, the new apartments constantly going up and the Millennium Stadium, perched opposite, across the water. Sitting alone with a minidisc recorder and microphone, I wondered where to start, what to include – from my happy childhood as a bundle of mischief, always running and jumping, in Llanederyn, a new council estate on the outskirts of Cardiff, to my status now, having retired in March 2003 after one of the longest careers of any modern British athlete, with what they tell me is a record-breaking hoard of 25 major championship medals, tucked away in a glass cabinet in my parents' home.

I thought of the people who have been important to me and my journey, from my grandfather, Dee, who arrived in Wales from Kingston, Jamaica, in the 1950s with nothing and built a proud life, through to my association, friendships and occasional bust-ups with some of Britain's, and the world's, greatest athletes.

Some of it was easy; my parents, Ossie and Angela, and big sister Suzanne, successful in her own right as an actress, have always been there for me. Malcolm Arnold has been my coach throughout my 20-year career, since I was 16, when he came to my house and told my mother and father that if I worked hard enough, I had a chance of making the British team for the 1988 Seoul Olympics. I always laugh at him for that astounding prediction; I made the team all right, then went to Seoul and picked up the silver medal. He hadn't quite seen that coming. But he won't give an inch: 'Well,' he scoffs, 'I was right, wasn't I?'

I wanted to talk about how athletics really was: the sacrifice and dedication – obsessive many might say – to reach the top and remain there. There have been many laughs too: great friends, training partners, entertainers born as much to fill the hours of hanging out on the circuit as to perform in their events. And I wanted to describe the toughness of the life, the mistakes and misjudgements that must figure in 18 long years but which are disasters in their own right and have to be fought and overcome or they may end a career. My life as an adult was about winning – which brought relief more often than sheer delight – and trying desperately to avoid the gnawing emptiness and shame of defeat.

It was also about negotiating the business of athletics, the towering egos, the clashes between performers and the bureaucrats who run the sport; the money, which brought envy and corruption with it, as it always will. Drugs: what I have seen, heard, and what I have been assumed to be taking. What the public sees – eight fit young men in sponsored kit running in neat lines – is the shop window, not the reality.

Putting my thoughts into words was a stop-start affair; I'd remember some crucial incident or person, then muse on who or what to talk about next. There was my friendship with Linford Christie, and the unhappy story of the promotions company we founded, Nuff Respect, which I had to leave eventually, for the sake of my health. I'd remember, stop, come back, make another note, start again, gradually piecing together the story of my life and career.

But when it came to the races, there was no hesitation. I flew off the lot in one sitting. Since my first major championships, my memory has been crystal clear for all the details: where the championships were, almost every meet, who lined up, the weather, where I finished, who won if I didn't. And times – tenths, hundredths of seconds – were the currency of my business. I remember them as solid facts: heats, semi-finals, finals, everything.

I sat down in my house with the microphone and, in a single take, reeled them all off, from the European Junior Championships in Cottbus, East Germany, more than an athletics generation ago in 1985, to the World Indoor Championships in Birmingham, when I finally said goodbye, in March 2003. I remembered the great champions I competed against in my early years, whom I was realistic enough to know I couldn't yet touch, the Americans Greg Foster and Roger Kingdom, how Roger breezed to the gold in Seoul in 12.98, an Olympic record, and how happy I was to land the silver, three metres behind, in 13.28.

Along with the times, the circumstances of each race flowed back; whether the difficult responsibility of being favourite, or the more intense pressure of coming back from defeat or disappointment, and having to prove myself all over again. The injuries, illnesses, all the twists of fate that conspire to thwart even the finest preparation for an event which lasts 13 seconds outdoors, just over seven seconds indoors.

Some times are etched in records anyway: 12.91, set in Stuttgart when I won the World Championship in 1993, still a world record a decade on. The world indoor record, set in my golden year of 1994, 7.30, in Sindelfingen, Germany, which most athletics people believe will last for many more years before somebody finds what it takes to run faster.

As in any career, some times didn't bear too much remembering, and why in my case they had to coincide so often with Olympic years is a question I still have to answer. But when I retired, finally leaving track behind, Michael Johnson, the great American 200m and 400m champion, said I was 'the greatest sprint hurdler ever' – which was kind of nice.

Only one of my 25 major championship medals was from a relay, the rest I won as an individual. I finished with a record-breaking four European Championships, won in a row from 1990 to 2002. I was the world junior champion in 1986; I picked up two Commonwealth silvers and two golds; one silver and three golds in the European Indoor Championships; three silvers and a gold in the World Indoor Championships; one Olympic silver; two gold medals, a silver and a bronze in the World Championships.

I made it to be double world champion and double world record holder – not bad, if I say so myself, for the kid who grew up in Llanederyn with his mother, father and sister.

From the age of 18, I dedicated everything to hurdling. My life was body posture, training phases, a specially designed diet, early nights, stride patterns, starts, centimetres over hurdles, tenths and hundredths of seconds, dipping over the line, and that extra killer's edge of competition, the extreme focus of running an individual sport but needing to crush the other guys in the race. We all have to finish some time, and I wanted to retire when I could still perform at the top, go out in a world final, health and happy. In Birmingham, my old friend Sally Gunnell told me she was jealous that I hadn't had to make my exit clapped-out, injured, exhausted, as so many athletes do. I was pleased with that, delighted with the affection beaming out of the British athletics fans, and the glowing praise of the press, who I feel did not give me the recognition my achievements deserved throughout my career, for whatever reason. And now, at 36, I'm free, ready to blast out again and attack my next series of barriers.

CHAPTER ONE
DAYDREAM BELIEVER

I was, my family say, born running. At least, I was walking at nine months, which is ridiculously early, running at 12 months, running strongly three months later. They remember me constantly running, climbing onto the highest and most dangerous places and jumping off. They spent their lives trying to keep me from serious injury. My sister Suzanne once put me in hospital trying to protect me: she was always shutting doors to keep me in, and this time I was too fast for her; I was halfway through the door, and she slammed it on to my fingers. As far back as I can remember, all I ever wanted to do was run fast. I loved it. Even at the end of my professional athletics career, as a grand old man of track, when I hit it right, I still felt that pure elation. It is like flying, like nothing else on earth – like freedom.

I was born on 18 February 1967, at home, in 200 Mackintosh Place, Roath Park, an area of Cardiff whose tall, white terraced houses are part of student-land now, but back then were first homes for working families like ours. My mother, Angela, used to tease me, saying it was lucky I was born at home, because that way she knew for certain I was hers. Otherwise, because I was such a bundle of mischief, she would have sworn they'd swapped me in the hospital for somebody else's baby. She was just teasing – so she says.

My father, Oswald – known by everybody as Ossie – was working as a bus driver when I was born, about to move into engineering, in which he would spend the rest of his working life. He has a son from his first marriage in Jamaica, Gerald, who grew up in the US. At home in Cardiff, I was raised with my sister Suzanne, four and a half years older than me. She's an actress now, perhaps best known for playing Mick's wife in *Brookside*, but with a long roll of credits to her name. She's always been my wise older sister, seemingly ever there with the right guidance at

11

crunch moments, still trying to protect me and usually doing a better job than she did with that door.

I don't remember too much of my earliest years, to be honest. They were just happy, full of playing and laughter. We grew up really close to our cousins, Wayne, Rose and Samantha, the children of my mother's sister, Winsome. We were very similar in age, too close for our parents' comfort; we were terrible when we got together, which was all the time. When I think of what we used to do – jumping off the highest trees we could climb, roller-skating down the steepest hills – I can hardly believe we survived. Looking back on my childhood, I seriously do think it is a miracle I made it through unscathed. I believe in fate, and seeing that one badly broken leg could have scuppered a whole future athletics career, I can't help thinking I was in some way protected.

As kids, we had no idea of how we had come to be there in Cardiff, a family from Jamaica making its way, nor did we particularly think about it. My grandfather, Dee, was somebody I loved and always admired; he was a special kind of person, gentle and friendly, and so many people knew him. But his story, the family stories, of how we got here, came out when my mother and Winsome would get together and tell us about life in the old country. We'd sit around all cheeky, shaking our heads, going: 'Yeh, yeh, yeh, you poor things, life was *so* hard in those days…'

Cheek wasn't always a good idea in our house; my mother had a good line in traditional Jamaican discipline and we would get our backsides tanned for naughtiness. Mainly it seemed to be for leaving a mess around the house, although bare-faced cheek was never advisable. My father is laid-back – he just wanted everything to run smoothly. It was never 'Wait till your father gets home'; he left it to my mother (the dragon, as he jokingly called her) to sort us out. My mother had a saying, 'Children who cannot hear, must feel', which doesn't leave too much to the imagination.

Dee was only five feet four inches tall, and my mother used to tease him, saying he was small because his full name was so long: Everil Emanuel Augustus Dunkley. He and my grandmother, whom I never met, had lived in various parts of Kingston, the capital of Jamaica, latterly in the suburb of Rollington Town, with my mother, Winsome and their older brother Tony. The way they tell it, Jamaica was lovely: hot and sunny, green, friendly, orderly, a paradise for children. My father went back a couple of years ago and was shocked by the crime and the slums, the fear people are constantly in for their safety. Any idea they had of going back there to live at some point disappeared with that visit.

Dee was a snappily dressed guy in his suit, hat and brogues, and he had a little business restringing tennis rackets, which took him to the establishment parts of Kingston, such as the sports clubs and tennis courts of the police and the civil service. Unfortunately they weren't as keen on paying him as they were on chatting to him; my mother and her brother would be sent at nine and ten years old to chase up the money, only to be fobbed off with excuses. They ended up stubbornly trailing the tennis coaches around, refusing to leave without being paid.

When my mother was four, her mother left for Panama – lots of Jamaicans went there and to Cuba to find work on the canal or in construction. My mother's grandfather had gone and fallen ill there, and her mother went out to look after him. She tried to bring the children over, and asked the Salvation Army to help; my mother remembers a visit at their home in Kingston. But the Salvation Army reported back that they should not be moved because they were happy children. Otherwise I could have been born a Panamanian – which might have made it difficult to represent Wales in the high hurdles! My grandmother wrote letters and sent presents to her children every week, parcels of American clothes, which seemed glamorous to them, but when my mother was 13, her mother fell ill and went into hospital and they never heard from her again.

My grandfather, looking after the kids, was always struggling with his cashflow and the late payers of Jamaica's establishment. At the same time, the British Government was advertising all over Jamaica for people to move to Britain to work. There was reasonable prosperity in the UK after the war and a shortage of people to do the menial jobs in the 'dirty' industries, the health service, the buses. According to my mother, in 1955 Dee was struggling with his business and he just decided to come over here and try his luck.

He arrived, like the vast majority from the West Indies, in London, but he never liked the capital, and after six months he left. Nobody knows why for certain, but Dee was a friendly guy who liked to pass the time with everybody, and London then – like London now – is not the place for a man like that. Quite why he came to Cardiff, they're not sure, but he probably heard there was work going on the docks, or in coal or steel, which were then massive employers in Wales.

He came determined to build something, to make a mark for himself, and he worked hard to do that. Two years later he was settled enough to bring my mother over, and when she arrived from sunny Jamaica, she found that her father's job was delivering great bags of coal around the homes in Cardiff. The first day she saw him he was covered in coal dust, his hands were hard, his skinny body like granite; she couldn't believe her father was doing that for a living. He did this for a couple of years and then in 1961 the huge Llanwern steel works opened in Newport. Dee landed a job there as a fitter and he stayed for nearly 30 years.

It was grey that afternoon in 1957, my mother says, when she arrived, aged 15, at Dee's first house in Constellation Street, Adamstown, Cardiff. It was cold and miserable, and she cried non-stop for a fortnight. Eventually Dee turned round and threatened her: 'If you don't stop, I'm sending you back!' And she bawled: 'Please do! Send me back! I want to go!'

She didn't feel comfortable calling him Daddy because she was so much older now than when she had last seen him, and he was different, so she shortened it to Dee, and it stuck. She missed her friends terribly, and it took a long time for her to settle, but eventually she did. The Labour Exchange sent her to various places to work before she decided to go to training college and become a nurse.

It was at this time that she experienced the first of only two incidents of racial prejudice in her whole life in Wales. She'd been sent to work as a seamstress in a dressmaking factory, but the woman in the Labour Exchange said there might be 'some sort of problem' from the workers there. Dee marched my mother straight out and told the woman to forget it. The other incident occurred much later, just a few years ago, when she was coming to the end of her working life as a sister in the Heath Hospital in Cardiff. A man was dying from cancer, and she was putting a scope in as part of the examination when he said: 'Get your dirty black hands off me.' Everybody was shocked, the doctors and her colleagues didn't know what to say, but my mother said she was fine. Later she told us: 'I knew the man would have a painful death, if he had that much hate still in him at a time like that, towards somebody who was trying to help him. So I said nothing.' But in a lifetime she can remember only those two racist comments.

My father cannot recall a single incident of prejudice in his whole 42 years in Cardiff. If we had lived in London or elsewhere in England, perhaps it would have been very different. In my life, I've never experienced any specific incidents because I'm black. At school I had white and black friends and we pretty much ran the show when we were older. British athletics, in my time, has been full of black athletes, including some of our great champions: Daley Thompson, Linford Christie and a string of top competitors. Listening to some of the stories from London, I felt that life was certainly edgier there than it was for little old me, growing up in cosy Cardiff. Nevertheless, prejudice is there, unspoken much of the time, but you can see it in people's faces, and I've always wondered if I would have had more accolades for my athletic achievements had I been a clean-cut white boy from England.

My father had a steady office job in Kingston, but he too decided to try his luck in Britain, and came over aged 28, in April 1961, with a plan to become an architect. His friend, Neville McLean, had already left for the UK and had hooked up with their mutual friend Trevor Seal. Trevor's cousin, Donald Stewart, worked closely with Dee and the four of them used to hang out together. When my father left Kingston for England he had Dee's address as a point of contact.

The classic family story is how my Uncle Tony and Neville were supposed to meet Ossie off the train at Paddington Station, but missed him. He flew in from Kingston to Gatwick Airport, took the train to Paddington, looked up and down the station for them but they weren't there, so in the end he made his own way to Cardiff, clutching Dee's address: 23 Constellation Street.

Dee's home was one of a row of terraced houses, and on this cold, grey day, all the chimneys had smoke coming out from the fires that were lit within. My father's taxi pulled up outside and he looked at this long, solid brick building with all the smoke and the series of doors and windows, and he thought it was a factory. He thought his friends had given him their work address. The shock, arriving from Jamaica, was massive.

But he and Dee hit it off straight away; Ossie could hardly believe how accommodating Dee was to new arrivals, and anyway he'd found the way to my grandfather's affections with a flask of Jamaican white rum that he'd brought with him. That's how my mother and father met: through my grandfather, a generous man and a port of call for the new arrivals from Jamaica.

The Labour Exchange sent my father down to a rubber factory, where he worked night shifts making oil seals. He enrolled on a correspondence course in draughtsmanship, but it was tough to study while he was working nights. My mother's brother, Tony, was working in the bus company, and he suggested that Ossie might find it easier there because there were no shifts, and that's how my father ended up first as a bus conductor, then a driver. The route his life was taking was towards becoming a bus inspector or working in the civic offices – not quite what he'd had in mind, and he stepped off the buses in May 1967, just after I was born, to do a sheet-metal course.

By then they were married. My mother had qualified as a nurse in December 1966, and they had bought their first house, in Mackintosh Place, a deceptively roomy terrace. My father found a job in a small engineering company and then moved by recommendation to Nuaire, a good company in Caerphilly that made air-conditioning systems. He worked for Nuaire for more than 20 years until he retired in 1991 as a service supervisor.

My father worked days and my mother nights, for seven years. They passed us to each other like handing over the baton in a relay. My mother barely slept for years; Suzanne used to say she never saw her in a good mood. In the morning, when she came home from a night shift, she used to go to bed and lock us in the room with her, telling us to play while she slept. She says I was pretty good, except for the running and jumping.

I was a handful. I ran off when I was three, got clean out of my pushchair in Littlewoods, even though she'd strapped me in, and it took her ten minutes to find me, sobbing, on the steps of Boots. She gave me a clip on the leg, then sat down and we both bawled our eyes out. She took me to an interview once – she had no choice – in the operating-theatre section of the hospital, and I spent the whole time jumping on the floor to make the automatic doors open. The nursing officer, who is still a good friend of my mother's, had to take us on a tour of the hospital to keep me occupied. How my mother got the job, I'll never know.

We moved to Llanederyn in 1971. It was a new estate of grey and brown breeze-block homes, built by the council on the outskirts of the city. Now it looks shabby, there's litter everywhere and Fort Knox-style security at my old school, Llanederyn High. Then, to a child's eye, it was heaven. All I remember is green: fields and woods, a stream and a lake. Now it looks like a few forlorn trees and scraps of grass, but it was a huge world to us; we'd be out all day in the long summers, in the woods, climbing trees, jumping streams. I think I got my power training from a game I played with my cousins and street friends, jumping across streams. If you put a heel in the water as you landed, you were out. We took turns to be the leaders, and I always chose the most obscure and highest ways to jump the streams. That was me always: athletic – and out-and-out competitive.

There were only eight families when we moved there, mostly young with kids like us, and everybody was so friendly. My parents never deliberately lived with other black families – they took the view that in Jamaica you chose where you lived, and who you lived alongside, and they weren't going to live in a predominantly black area just because they were in Cardiff. So it wasn't deliberate either way, but we never lived in mainly black areas; we were always among white people, and we never had any problems from anybody in Llanederyn. I think the Welsh are a lot more tolerant because everybody comes together to collectively hate the English!

We used to walk everywhere from when we were tiny; everybody felt safe. I remember that, when I was six, I used to call for a girl, Samantha Webb, who lived round the corner from me, and we'd walk to infant school together, which was quite a long way, about a mile. The funny thing was, we never actually saw each other during the day; we just used to walk to school together, do our own thing in our own classes and at playtime, and then, at the end of the day, hook up and walk home. I don't suppose you'd see many children being allowed to do that now; parents would fear too much for them, and kids seem to have lost their freedom. It seems sweetly innocent, thinking back. I saw Samantha not long ago and she looks virtually the same, with tons of blonde hair.

Even then, at five or six years old, at Springwood Infant School, I can remember consciously wanting to run when I grew up. There was a patch of tarmac in the playground, which looked – at least to my imagination

– like a huge foot, a giant's step. I used to lie in the middle of this step and daydream of one day being a runner. I dreamed that if I lay back on the step gazing up at the stars, the steps would make me fast, quick and strong. Before every school sports day I used to go and lie there, and it was *my* step; if anybody else came up, I'd tell them to keep off it. I giggle now when I think of it. To me it's bizarre that I felt that certain so young. So, whatever the gruelling demands of professional athletics and the often cut-throat business of the sport, when I run I really am fulfilling my childhood daydreams.

I won my first athletics trophy at junior school, in the 60m dash. Being Mr Competitive, when the local inter-schools sports day was coming up, I used to run round the school twice, for training. I think I won my age group twice, and came third twice.

Like the estate itself, Llanederyn High was a new school. Somehow it had a bad reputation, as if we were hard kids, but although we could look after ourselves – we were street kids – I don't remember any violence, certainly no bullying. We wouldn't have put up with it. The facilities at the school were, at the time, superb; it was a world of opportunity. Besides all the academic subjects, we could do woodwork, metalwork, design, technology; we did needlework, cookery, pottery. We had a chance to try everything.

I was good at the sciences and decided I wanted to be an electrician, but had a bit of a problem because for some reason I struggled at maths. I was hopeless at the creative arts: I learned I couldn't paint in the juniors, but I seemed to have a gift for cookery, which continues today; I can taste something and reproduce it pretty well. By the time I was nine, I was cooking breakfasts for the family at the weekend – egg, bacon, toast for four.

At school we were encouraged to play a lot of sport: athletics, basketball, cricket, and there were a huge number of pitches for rugby and football. We had two gyms, lots of tennis courts; it was phenomenal. We were county champions of basketball, which I played, and I was also good at cricket. Glamorgan picked me for the under-15s; I opened the bowling and batted number 5. The winter sports (football and rugby) I hated, but they wanted me to play because I was quick. We had a really fast back line at rugby; I played stand-off, and we used to cream other teams. At athletics I was an all-rounder and could do everything reasonably well – but I wasn't the fastest runner, even in Llanederyn.

At home my father was a sports enthusiast, and sport was always on TV. We used to gather round the set watching boxing, football, athletics, always the Olympics. My interest in athletics thrived in that environment, and I would be glued to the TV in our living room, usually cheering on the top Jamaican athletes, like Don Quarrie, the great sprinter who won the gold medal in the 200m at the 1976 Olympics and the silver in the 100m.

Looking back, I was feeling my way into the sport that suited me best, then narrowing it down to my event: high hurdling. I believe I chose track, even at that age, because I am so driven to a challenge, to win, and in track you are responsible only for yourself. In a team game you can play your best and lose, because the other team members have had stinkers. I never wanted that. Equally, in track, you can never coast and still win, as you can in team sports. It's individual. You have training partners, friends, and at championships you're in a team, wear a British vest, but it's really nonsense: you're on your own, every time. At most championships you don't even see the other people in your 'team'; you don't stay in the same sites as them. You line up alone against seven people who want, metaphorically, to destroy you. You want to come out on top, to ice them. You win for yourself. Lose, and the pain and recriminations are for nobody else: just for you. And that's how I liked it.

Then, it was more a process of elimination. I liked athletics, was good at many events – I was good enough to represent the county at long jump, hurdles, high jump, even the javelin – and I felt comfortable with the people, the atmosphere. I didn't much like rugby and you got needlessly smashed up playing the game. The only fun was playing stand-off and lobbing hospital balls at your mates if you were getting your own back on them for something they'd done at school. At cricket I never liked the people running the clubs and playing it, for there was a snob factor. I was a summer boy anyway – and I liked basketball, because you did that indoors – and gradually I began to take track more seriously, competing in school championships, graduating to county and national trials.

What I was ultimately best at in school, however, was mischief. Chatting, cheek, entertaining the class – I was great at that; the prankster. There was a little group of us knocking about together:

Gary Parry and Gary Headley who were black, and Geraint Thomas and Robert Jones who were white, so it was a good mix. Another friend, Neil Parsons, came all the way from infants' school with me, but stopped knocking about with us because he thought I was a bad influence, which was no surprise as he wasn't far wrong.

When we got older we used to kind of run things at school. We used to have what we called an office, in the girls' toilets. It was the safest place to be – in all our years, no teacher ever went in there. We used to send the girls out to make sure the coast was clear before leaving. Our little posse controlled the cigarettes, because Gary Parry had a newspaper round and he used to pocket a few packs of fags while the newsagent wasn't looking, for us all to sell at school. I never smoked myself, ever, but it was the number-one commodity and we made the most of it.

I had a brace on my teeth around then, and I picked up a pile of appointment cards from the orthodontist's reception. For a small fee, I used to write them out for people so they could skive off school. If you timed the appointment right, it would mean just about a full day off. We got up to scams and pranks like that, but nothing heavy; I was never into violence, never in trouble with the police, and I never got caught. I'd return to the scene of the crime like the classic villain, but I was cheeky with it and my smile could get me out of situations. Imagine a boy with a tiny little afro and a permanent cheeky grin: that was me. One time I remember a teacher grabbed me, furious, from the back and said: 'Jackson, I'm gonna get you!' I turned round and laughed straight into his face: 'In your *dreams*!' I said, and walked off. Needless to say, he never got me.

My sister left home for Warwick University when I was 13. Older brothers and sisters have it easier – they just go, they don't think too much. The younger ones are left behind, alone with their mother and father, and I felt a sense of responsibility. In a way I felt I had to look after them, and I had to be good! All their attention was on me. They were both still working very hard; my mother had moved up the hospital hierarchy and worked days, and I used to cook dinner for all of us, ready for when they got home. I used to get up to some pranks, and probably got away with more than they knew, but at home we were respectable. There were values and standards to be kept. Both my parents worked hard and I suppose, although I didn't realize it, that was my role model, my example: you got nowhere without working hard. We weren't rich, but with both parents working at good jobs (for Llanederyn) we were never too short of money.

By 14 I was joining a group of junior athletes training on Mondays and Thursdays at the Maindy stadium in Cardiff. My father used to take me. Later, when I started training every night, at Cwmbran, sometimes indoors at Swansea, he'd faithfully run me around to all the sessions. At 14 it was social, but I had a coach, Mike Jones, and graduated from the purely Welsh scene to British junior sessions and squads. I was still an all-rounder, and quite late there was talk of me doing the decathlon and trying to emulate Daley. But I did like hurdling best; it's more interesting than sprinting and anyway I never had the raw power for straight sprinting. I could throw a javelin well, but it used to strain my shoulder. I could long-jump pretty well, but I hated always landing in the loose sand and getting it in my shoes. Gradually I narrowed it down, deciding that hurdling was far and away what I liked best.

My father would come home from work, often have no time to eat, and take me straight out in the car to train, frequently giving other boys a lift too; then he'd sit high up in the stand, watching, and drive us all back. The coaches – particularly Malcolm later – loved Ossie because he was supportive but never pushy. My parents never were; they watched and helped me, but they never cajoled me into doing track, or keeping at it. In fact, it was the opposite; one parents' evening the teachers told them I was being disruptive in class because I was too interested in athletics, and my mother and father threatened to stop me running unless I improved at school.

My father was quiet at that time, he didn't say much; I suppose he was always tired out. But gradually he began to help me with hurdling. He'd write my times down in my training drills, clock me sometimes up to the first hurdle, or from the second to the third, and so on, then we'd go through the record at home and I'd work out where I might need more effort. I was always methodical, calculating what I needed to do to improve my performance. Later I went through a stage of slowing up between hurdles seven and nine, and in training my father would clap his hands, give me a 'Come on' at the seventh hurdle and wake me up so I would maintain the pace.

He took me everywhere. In the summer we had competitions locally every week, then regional trials, and finals in Birmingham or Crystal Palace, which was like the Olympics to us – huge and glamorous and you'd see the big stars there. Daley Thompson was a hero. He was an Olympic gold medallist, he had class, he was lippy and he took absolutely no nonsense. I admired him so much. Some of the coaches would be bending my father's ear about me, telling him how good I was, that I could be better than Daley – he used to brush them away, ever so nicely of course. But he always remembers one coach who told him, quite casually, that I had what it took to be a champion. It was not simply to do with speed or performance; it was my attitude. He'd noticed that at meets I'd be laughing and joking, in the thick of all the banter – I was always the same, right up until I retired at 36 – but an hour or so before a race I'd take myself completely away and begin to prepare, to focus on what I was going to do. This guy – my father can't even remember who – said that this mental approach was the sign of a winner.

It might never have happened, though. I was still planning to be an electrician, and had enrolled on a college course. Then the two Garys, my two mates, went and left me. Looking back, this was a very important factor in my athletics career. Gary Headley was a good cricketer, good enough for the MCC to sign him on, and he went up to Lord's to take that up. He stayed on the cricket scene for a long time. He played in Barbados and I used to see him from time to time.

Gary Parry left school at 16 and went up to London with his brother. At this stage I was already a senior GB athlete – I got my first vest at 17; I'd competed in the European Junior Championships. I'd been on TV, I was known round Cardiff. But I still might have gone with them, gone to London to try my luck, live like 'normal' teenagers do. The temptation was there.

But I didn't go. I was dedicated, serious, focused, too much so to risk any of it. When they left, I stayed. But then I was floating about with no real mates to lark around with. They'd gone and left me, the sods. Also, when I was 16 my parents decided we were moving house. They came home one night to our house in Llanederyn and some kids were burning tyres in the middle of the road. On the spot they decided that was it, the area was going to the dogs, and we moved to another area, Birchgrove.

'Oh, come on,' I complained, 'it's just starting to get interesting round here!' But we were off.

I didn't know anybody in Birchgrove, and my mates had gone. I was on my own. It was a pivotal moment for me, mapping out my future course, fateful that I stayed in Cardiff and didn't leave. In some ways the focus on athletics presented itself, made itself very, very plain. I was becoming established, I had a talent for it, I enjoyed it and I was extremely competitive and naturally ambitious. I don't know why; it's not something I have questioned. Whatever I did, I wanted to be successful, to win.

Looking at it another way, there was nothing much else to do, because everybody had gone. So although I was ranked fifth in the country at 17 – the first year you are allowed to do high hurdling – it was still partly by default that I dedicated myself completely to it. It might also, of course, have had just a little something to do with the fact that the best hurdling coach in the world happened to be working right there in my neighbourhood.

CHAPTER TWO

COACH ARNOLD

Malcolm Arnold was the national coach of the Athletics Association of Wales, and was at the time coaching Nigel Walker, Wales's champion sprint hurdler – later a Welsh rugby international and now doing rather well for himself as BBC Wales's Head of Sport. When we were 16, Jon Ridgeon and I (the top two juniors in the UK) were invited to join a national hurdle squad at Lilleshall to train with the top under-20s and seniors. Mike Jones had helped me to reach these national standards in my age group, and I had no personal problems with him, but I could see the progress Nigel was making, pushing into medal contention in international championships and heading for a place in the Los Angeles Olympic Games, where he made the semi-final. Graham Knight, the coach in charge of the hurdle squad, told me that Malcolm was Nigel's coach, and that was all I knew: I wanted him to do the same with me.

My father and I approached him and asked him to take me on, and from then until I retired 20 years later, Malcolm was my coach. It was an unusual – if not unique – partnership, lasting from the time I was a skinny, cheeky kid in a Welsh suburb, daydreaming of success, along the whole relentless journey into major professional sporting competition, right through my years of performing at the top. We're very different: Malcolm is steady, granite-faced at times to people who don't know him, not given to non-stop chat and larking about, like me. But we have huge mutual respect and we've been through so much together that we have formed a special relationship.

Looking back, the low patch of my career coincided with me spending less time with Malcolm; the golden times were when we were working closely together. Throughout my career Malcolm was a brilliant technical tutor in athletics; a truly expert teacher who helped to give me all the physical and psychological skills needed to achieve excellence in my event. And from the first, though he's a bluff northerner who can make an art out of grumpiness, he has been my friend.

At the time when we approached him in 1983, I didn't know about Malcolm's background and credentials. He was the national coach, his speciality was hurdling and I could see what he had achieved, technically, with Nigel. I felt that I was not progressing with Mike as quickly as I could have; I was fast, I was a natural hurdler, but I wasn't improving enough, not moving on to the next level. I discussed it with my father, and we decided to ask Malcolm to take me on as one of his athletes. Malcolm said that it wasn't permitted for any coach to talk to an athlete unless they were finished with their current coach, and told us that we would have to write a letter of request to him. Only then could he consider it. In order not to upset Mike, and to play it all correctly, we decided to ask Mike to stay with me, but work with Malcolm.

We played it by the book, but that was my first education into the ways and meanderings of athletics bureaucracy, which so often means that things for athletes are not as easy as they should be. It was fair enough that there are rules to stop coaches poaching each other's athletes, but that wasn't what was happening. We went to see Mike at his house and said that I wanted to work with Malcolm as well as him. Malcolm, as the national coach, wasn't always going to be around because he had the whole country to cover, so we suggested that Mike could work with me too, according to Malcolm's programme. It could have been a learning opportunity for Mike too, because he would get to work with Malcolm, but it was as if he wanted me all to himself; perhaps he wanted the glory, I don't know. Anyway, he refused and said he couldn't work with another coach.

My father is gentle, calm and everybody likes him. But there is steel underneath; there had to be for him to arrive in this country with nothing and quietly build a life for himself. Perhaps I inherited my certainty about decisions and ruthlessness from him. His attitude was clear: 'You're giving me an ultimatum now, which is unfortunate, because Colin is not going to be happy with you now. Thanks for the memories, Mike.'

We wrote to Mike thanking him, saying that we wanted to leave him. Then we wrote to Malcolm explaining that we were leaving Mike and asking if he would take us on. Malcolm agreed, and I thought that was it. I was just looking forward to starting the training. But then we were hauled into a meeting of the Welsh Athletics Federation's coaching committee, at Sophia Gardens, the headquarters of the association – heavy stuff – where Malcolm was accused of poaching me from Mike. My father had to go to the hearing too. It was, as Malcolm tells it, 'all rather sad.' We had the letters, and we'd tried to be polite and do things properly; I only wanted to better myself. Eventually Mike gave up on it; he actually told Malcolm it was all getting silly, and apologised for causing him trouble. When the meeting finished with no action taken against Malcolm, my career started seriously, with my coach officially approved: Malcolm Arnold.

If I have some criticisms of the British sporting system, then it has its good sides too. Malcolm is one of the best products there is of the classic sporting education. He grew up in Northwich, Cheshire a hotbed of semi-professional football, and played for the youth and reserve teams of several of the historic football clubs up there, like Northwich Victoria and Hyde United. As an athlete he was a moderately successful triple jumper, ranked fourth in the UK in 1962. He developed an interest in coaching at the traditional sporting academy, Loughborough University, in the 1960s and was inspired to become a sports teacher. But it isn't all about training and technique with Malcolm; there are some aspects of him – his principles, his morals, his belief in the value of sport and disdain for the money that he believes has tainted it – which I think are innate to him. That's Malcolm: bluff maybe, but true, unshakeable – mostly shaking his head these days at the business of the sport in which he has spent his life.

When he left Loughborough, he worked as a PE teacher at a couple of middle-of-the-road places: Marple, near Stockport, and Mangotsfield, near Bristol. It's amazing to think that he went from there directly to his next job, in 1968 – as the national coach of Uganda. He's adventurous, in his matter-of-fact way, and says he just saw the Uganda job advertised, applied, went for an interview at the Ugandan High Commission in Trafalgar Square and got the job. Next thing his wife Madelelyn knew, they and their two children (Helen, then four, and Andrew, two) were packing up and moving from Bristol to a flat in Kampala, in the middle of Africa.

Even at 16, I quickly found out that while Malcolm was there, working in a poor African country with scrappy facilities, no structures or resources, he unearthed and developed an Olympic champion at 400m hurdles, John Akii-Bua. Now, as an adult, I've talked to Malcolm and heard the stories of how in Uganda just getting one square meal a day was a major achievement, and I can appreciate what Malcolm provided to shape John Akii into the world's greatest athlete in his discipline. Generally I have a profound appreciation of Malcolm, so profound that I can even understand when and why he's getting on my nerves!

Akii-Bua's victory in Munich was particularly noted in Britain because in the final, when he broke the world record, running 47.82, he beat the favourite, Britain's own David Hemery, into third place. Hemery lost with grace, and paid tribute to John Akii and his coach. So Malcolm – not that I fully realized it at 16 – came with a huge pedigree, and Wales must have been well chuffed to snap him up. And although Wales in the 1970s hardly compared to the African country he had left, with Idi Amin in charge and slaughter beginning, nevertheless Malcolm does suggest a parallel between the two. There he was, stuck in the sticks, finding a talent he could hone into top quality.

Just a few years ago he found out more, when John Akii-Bua presented him with 12 notebooks painstakingly setting out his life story in longhand English, which was his third language. I haven't read the notebooks, partly because Malcolm hasn't suggested it, partly due to my own ego: I don't look to anybody else as a model, I concentrate on my own work. The only athletics autobiography I have read is Daley's, which I read when I was young and found inspiring.

But I do know some of the detail, some I've picked up from Malcolm and from his wife Madelyn; and don't get me wrong, I have the utmost professional respect for what John Akii-Bua achieved. And I recognize the connection between me and what I achieved with Malcolm, and John Akii, who came before me.

Famously, Akii-Bua was one of 43 children whom his father had with nine wives. A couple of his brothers were athletes too, and like me he was an all-rounder who had a talent in several events. If one square meal was a problem in Uganda, there was certainly no money for kit or equipment, and a pair of spikes would have cost a month's salary.

The athletics was structured around institutions like the army, prison service and police, and John Akii, as a policeman, was given time off to train. He lived on the floor of a hall attached to the police barracks, just dossed down alongside dozens of others, in a draughty building with windows missing and constant noise and bustle. Even approaching the 1972 Olympics, Malcolm was feeding John Akii himself, paying for the most basic resources. At the Games themselves, the athletes found their daily allowances weren't enough even to eat properly. This kind of puts into perspective our grumbles about the old cinder track and training gear in my early days in Malcolm's group in Cardiff.

Malcolm had to do everything in Uganda, from setting up some sort of structure for athletics – he set up a national league, coaching coaches – to fettling tracks on the African scrub. The Ugandan athletes were also suspicious of him, this serious-looking white guy suddenly appearing on the edge of training sessions, unsettling the established coaches – trackside rivalries that seem to be the same all over the world, at whatever level. They struggled to pronounce his name too, so they settled on a nickname: 'Mzungu', Kiswahilli for 'white man'.

John Akii said Malcolm kind of wore down their hostility eventually. I can imagine him doing it. He played the long game, offering advice, quietly changing structures, until the athletes came to appreciate the qualities he was offering, the acuteness of his technical knowledge, and fell into working properly with him. Part of Malcolm's job was to identify John Akii's event, as he did with me. John fancied himself in my event, the 110m high hurdles, but Malcolm believed he didn't have the explosive speed required, more the flat-out endurance needed in the 400m hurdles. They had a row because Malcolm wouldn't take him to the 1968 Mexico Olympics as a sprint hurdler. Then in the 1970 Commonwealth Games in Edinburgh, Malcolm persuaded John to enter the 400m as well as the sprint hurdles and see what happened. In the 110m he went out in the semi-final, but in the 400m he qualified for the final. Another of Malcolm's Ugandan athletes, Bill Koskei, won silver behind England's John Sherwood, but John Akii-Bua surprised himself by coming fourth in the 400m final, running 51.1, one second off a medal.

Malcolm had revealed John Akii's ideal event to him and from then on they dedicated themselves to the 400m hurdles. Malcolm says John was a great talent, and he says, as he does of me: 'His head was right. He wanted to be successful. He could see what he needed to do, and he was prepared to do all the necessary hard work to get there. Like Colin, you wouldn't call him academically brilliant' – cheeky now, Malcolm – 'but he was astute, like Colin. They both had what I call excellent sporting intelligence.' That's nice.

Malcolm worked with Akii-Bua on the 400m hurdles, building the physical combination of speed and endurance necessary, and the techniques of the event: the numbers of strides between hurdles, how to take them, starts and finishes. He did all this in the scrub of Uganda, which had by then fallen to Amin, the date of 25 January 1971 being etched into Malcolm's mind and that of all Ugandans. Armed thugs were beginning to commit murder and atrocities that would later claim members of Akii-Bua's family and cause him to flee Kampala. Malcolm stayed on to see his work through after the coup; in fact he says Amin was always friendly to him because he was very keen on sport, particularly boxing and football, and saw it as a path to glory for his country. There was Malcolm, dodging the bullets, at times literally, in the cause of grooming his athletes to excellence.

John Akii completed his final training in 1972 on proper tracks in Germany. He was by then a favourite for a medal, had competed on the international stage, and so had been paid for races and earned kit and shoe sponsorships. He made the final, but was drawn in lane 1, the worst. 'The prima donnas now will refuse to run if they're drawn in lane 1,' Malcolm scoffs. 'They insist on a change. Not John.'

David Hemery was the race favourite, drawn in lane 5. Malcolm and John Akii planned their tactics, as we do now. People are always amazed at how much goes on in a race that lasts, in my event, under 13 seconds; under 50 in John Akii's. But hurdling is a highly technical event and you don't just go charging out. You have to be aware not only of how best to maximize your own performance, but also what to do about the others in the race, the danger-men. Months of work and preparation go into being able to perform to the optimum at exactly the right time. And in a race so much happens; it can take 20 minutes to talk it through, even if in reality it happened in the blink of an eye. According to Malcolm, John Akii-Bua was the same as me: afterwards he'd talk races through in minute detail, the tactics, what happened at each hurdle, how he reacted, where the others were.

In Munich, John Akii recorded in his notebooks that he could remember what Malcolm drummed into him before the race, like 'computer-stored data'. I liked the parallels when Malcolm told me what he wrote:

> I had known Arnold for six years as Uganda's national coach and above all as my personal coach as well as a friend. He coached me up to the last minute, reminding me of the stride patterns, when to switch from 13 strides between the hurdles to 14. He used to remind me with a kind of artist humour.

> He used to say: 'Hey, don't just go and play around.' Then he would conclude with: 'Come on.' He rarely wished me good luck.

So Malcolm never changed much; that's him to a tee.

> With ten minutes to go, this man said one sentence I will never forget, overcame all my nervousness and fear. In one uniform voice, Mzungu Malcolm Arnold said: 'You are in the final, and it's useless not to think of something. One of them is yours.'

> He never mentioned the word medal.

David Hemery made his attack earlier than expected, at 200m, between hurdles five and six. John wrote in his notebooks that he immediately changed his stride pattern from 13 to 14 strides. Then he attacked the tenth hurdle with a new 15-stride pattern. He came right through, far in front of the field, blasting and coasting. He wrote that the finish was the easiest part of the race. After he won it, he carried on running round and took the first hurdle again, just to show he had reserves of energy left – a nice, flamboyant touch.

He said he looked up and there was a blinking light next to his name and it was only then that he realized he had run 47.82, a new Olympic and world record. He said in the notebooks that he met 'the Coach Arnold' by the stand after his lap of honour, and when he saw him he broke down and cried. Malcolm said to him: 'It's over. Let's go.' Typical!

Malcolm doesn't show his emotions too much and likes to keep you on the ground in his gruff way, but he feels it; he just hides his depths.

He describes the showbiz and press of athletics as 'a bit annoying', and when John Akii won, the BBC discovered that Malcolm was English and interviewed him too. We may have been watching it, back in Cardiff, Suzanne, my father and I – I don't remember.

At the press conference, David Hemery took his defeat with dignity. He said he had lost to a 'better-trained man', a great tribute from an athlete to a coach.

Malcolm left Uganda shortly afterwards, because the political situation was worsening into a bloodbath, and Helen and Andrew were coming up to secondary-school age. The last time he saw John Akii for years was at Munich, where they said their farewells. John Akii had to face the horror of his country, and the loss, in the anarchy, of all the money he had earned in athletics. Malcolm says he was going to build himself a house – investing it in property, as I mostly have – but the building materials were all stolen from the ground where they had been laid out ready, and John Akii lost everything.

Malcolm came back to England, taught in Hull briefly and then in 1974 was appointed national coach of Welsh athletics. He describes Wales at the time as something of a wilderness in its own way. Rugby was in its brief prime, with Gareth Edwards, J. J. Williams and all the other famous players beating all-comers – not like now, when Wales lose to Italy but the players are still swanning about Cardiff in their flash sponsored cars with their names on the side. If it was me, I wouldn't show my face after dishing that up, and I think they'd seriously benefit from having to earn their money the hard way, but that's another story.

At that time, in the 1970s, athletics didn't get much of a look-in. Facilities were poor; there wasn't much beyond the cinder track at Jenner Park in Barry, and Malcolm had to do it all over again: put structures in, coach coaches, build a presence and a system. He lived in a little place in the valleys near Bargoed, north of Caerphilly, so he could cover north and south Wales without too much trouble. He spent years putting the basics in place before Nigel Walker and others came along in the early 1980s and became the first really promising athletes he'd had.

I was aware of him as a kid in the way you are of a headmaster, not knowing much about him except that he's the boss and a bit strict-looking. He remembers first coming across me when he was giving out the medals and cups at the South Glamorgan Schools end-of-term presentations. He says I was 'a cheeky little bugger, nodding and winking at the back', so it must have been me. He'd heard of me, that I was a decent all-rounder, and when he watched more of me, he began to see I had some promise. Although my physique wasn't outstanding – I could have been taller or more powerfully built for a sprint hurdler – he said he could see that for all my larking about, my head was right, my attitude was there. I wanted to win, loved to win, but I could also see what it took to do it, that hard work was involved. And I was prepared (eager in fact) to do it, right from the beginning.

Once I was in his group, I began to learn the methods that Malcolm had applied and refined to make a champion out of John Akii-Bua and an Olympic athlete out of Nigel Walker. He has a quietly steely way of working personally with his athletes, but he's also a student, a reader and teacher of athletics, and the author of the definitive coaching textbook, *Hurdling*, which has been translated into any number of languages. He introduced me to the science of athletics, the careful application of training principles to get the body, its responses and the mind at peak fitness and sharpness for the moment of the final of a championships.

It doesn't always work: you can be scuppered by injury or illness – as I seemed to be whenever the Olympics came around. But as much as you can, you plan to be right, you prepare. The coach knows about the body and what it needs, what it can take. So much of the training in other sports is still based on lack of knowledge; I don't understand why the top footballers are constantly being injured, unless they are doing something seriously wrong.

Our training is based on what Malcolm calls (very teacher-like) the periodization of the year – which is a posh way of saying that you break the year down into various periods. Overall, it is made up of strength development, to make the legs and the body strong in particular ways, to make it explosive.

You come back after an autumn break to start training, usually in mid-November, to build your preparation up for the championships to come at the end of the following summer. It is done in separate phases, creating the foundation of strength, power and endurance on which to build the speed work closer to the championships. It's progressive, too; as you go on, the year's work builds on the level you managed to reach in terms of fitness and speed the year before. I didn't do any serious, heavy weight-training until I was 20 or 21, and by then I had been with Malcolm for four years.

In the first weeks back, I'd do basic fitness work, not much different from what the average person does: weights, various types of circuit training, endurance runs. My aerobic state, my stamina, wasn't great in the early years and I've never much enjoyed long, steady road running. But I had to do it to build up my heart–lung capacity. Eventually when we were living in Birchgrove my father used to come out and cycle alongside me, timing me. Malcolm jokes that he hoped my father had a big stick with him; Malcolm kind of relishes the memory of me not being good at it and having to work so hard. Of course, Ossie didn't whack me, just offered his quiet encouragement, and we got through it.

Later on I'd do road running, skipping, aerobics classes, weightlifting, circuit classes, swimming and cycling. I'd do that for four weeks, to get a basic level of physical fitness, where my joints would start working again, have a sense of flexibility and range. Only after that would I be ready to do any proper training, do my conditioning; this first phase is almost pre-conditioning-conditioning.

The conditioning phase involves weightlifting and running, at higher volume, low intensity, to build the foundation of endurance and strength. I'd do weights at the David Lloyd centre in Cardiff, running at the track at Leckwith stadium in Cardiff or, in later years, at the University of Bath. A typical session would be 1, 2, 3, 2, 1 – a 100m sprint, 200m, 300m, then back down again, with just a short recovery of two and a half minutes between each one. The following day I would do weights: standing lifting, bench, cleans, squat, an upper body circuit, an abdominal circuit. The following day's running session might be 3, 2, 1, 3, 2, 1 – more 300m sessions with a shorter recovery. It is building up speed with endurance, before the sharper work to come as the season draws closer. You're always pushing yourself, but you also have to be safe, be very aware of the phase you are in, the level of fitness you're working with, taking care not to overstretch and get injured.

I'd start with hurdles in December. Nothing intense: just skill stuff, ticking over, making sure my legs could hurdle because later I'd have to force the speed.

That conditioning phase lasts around six weeks, then you move into the preparation work for four weeks. You reduce the volume and increase the intensity, so the weights change to sharper lifts. In the running I'd begin to work less on speed endurance than on shorter distances, perhaps ten broken 100m: build up to speed for 20m, hit it hard for 30, relax for 20, hit for 30. It becomes more event-specific, and we'd begin to work more on hurdling, this time concentrating on technical endurance, so I would hurdle over 12 and 10 hurdles to make sure my technique was coming right.

I'd start competing in races in this preparation phase, but indoors or early-season stuff, working up to peak form before the final preparation phase when I would do the training to become razor sharp. Then the high-intensity, lower-volume work kicks in: everything down to a minimum, but really quick. Short, sharp drills. Do them quickly, then repeat. Take the hurdles to the side, first with the lead leg, then the trailing leg. Short high steps in between the hurdles. Practise starts. Then take five hurdles, no more than that, at full pace. Some sprints. You've now done basic fitness and endurance, built up technical endurance and done preparation. The final phase is aimed at getting really sharp, training for the nervous system as much as the muscles.

Malcolm is very keen on having no distractions in the final phase of preparation. We'd go away to a warm location and concentrate solely on training and getting totally focused on the championships, hammering away every day, with longer recovery periods. He stressed the importance of rest too, to give the muscles, and the mind, time to recover, so that they can take the next phase of work.

I never particularly enjoyed final preparation; it was always the most nerve-wracking time. I always felt I hadn't done enough, I'd always be looking back and thinking that I should have done more work, I could have been better prepared, and the championships would be pressing and there was no hiding place. It's just like going into an exam feeling badly prepared, that you haven't done enough revision, you're going to flunk it – the same dread and guilt. And because the training is so keenly worked out, and because it works, every phase is as important as the next; if you haven't put the conditioning work in, you can't do the speed training. So throughout the year the guilt is there: you have to train.

This is the hard work of track, the months of effort alone, training in all conditions, which are vital building blocks for the championship performances that entrance the public on television or in the arenas.

Usually I would do it because I wanted to; at my core, I never found it an effort. It was the work required to take me where I wanted to be and I was always prepared to do it; I wanted to do it. If ever I did struggle with motivation, if I was ground down by injury problems or personal strife, if I was hurting deep in the gloom of November, I would think of the target, the date and time of the major championships coming up the following summer, and I'd say to myself: if you think this feels bad, well, fourth place will feel a lot worse. And I'd also think: somebody – some opponent – is getting it for this.

In my teenage years I was very lucky with the group of athletes who had come through under Malcolm in Cardiff. Nigel Walker was the pick and he was very good to me when I came into the group: helpful, encouraging, welcoming. There is a fine tradition in athletics of senior athletes helping, not envying, the young kids coming through. When I was established, I was more than happy to work with athletes in whom I could see desire, talent and application. I never had much time for those whose heads weren't right.

Nigel was excellent, and the others in the group were welcoming too, and we became great friends. A few of the long-stayers were Rhys Davies, Kay Morley, Paul Gray, Sallyanne Short and Carmen Smart, an established international sprinter who has become my great friend, personal assistant and backbone to my life in Cardiff. As a group, we had everything important. We worked incredibly hard, we helped each other, we were competitive, but we had fun.

There was no indoor facility in Cardiff as there now is at the superb, grandly titled High Performance Centre at the University of Wales Institute. The only indoor facility we had was literally about 60m of track at Morfa stadium in Swansea, so sometimes my father would take me up there. Mostly we hammered round the cinder track at Jenner Park in Barry, every evening, 6–8.30, in all weathers. The changing rooms were always filthy because Barry Town football club used to play there. We had no training tights; they hadn't been invented. We wore baggy tracksuits or wetsuits, which let the rain in and ended up drenched. We'd stretch out there in puddles, do sprint repetitions and end up pebble-dashed from kicking up the cinder. Then we'd go indoors and do circuit training, which was nothing short of dangerous for our health. Then we'd lie back on the benches, absolutely exhausted. I can remember Kay

Morley, the women's sprint hurdler, nearly beating Nigel in a race because he was so knackered. And then, the following evening, and every weekend, we'd all be back, together, doing it all over again. Malcolm was only with us on Mondays, Tuesdays and Thursdays, so quite often we would be on our own. And with our group he used to say he always knew we'd do it. We didn't need telling to do it: we'd be there. It was a great initiation for me, a great lesson for my whole career in track. I was always the same: Malcolm knew he could give me my training programme in November, not see me for three months and I'd follow it to the letter.

It helped because we all liked each other, gelled as a group and had great laughs. Sallyanne was generally wrapped into most of the pranks; she was the glamorous leggy blonde of the group, sashaying about in high heels, fancying herself – we used to call her Gladys. It was a laugh seeing her covered in gravel at the end of a session. She and Carmen, who's black, were salt and pepper, or tit and nipple – sorry, but it's true. Sallyanne, the good-time girl, bunked off training once, I remember, because she wanted to go clubbing. Malcolm pulled her up on it and she just looked him in the eye and told him she'd been training at Cwmbran: 'Ask my mum,' she said, straight-faced, 'she'll tell you I was there.' Malcolm just looked at her and said: 'I was at Cwmbran all day, coaching, and I didn't see you.' She didn't even blink, just said: 'OK, OK, you've caught me out.'

I took to it all with no problems; I was never overawed – never, at any phase of my career in fact, was I nervous about stepping up a level. I wanted to be there, and I took to it hungrily. I was a little shy, though, until I got the measure of a group, which Carmen mistook for cockiness. Her tale is that she gave a group of us a lift back from an indoor meet in Cosford in 1984, when I was still only 17. She dropped me off – miles away from home, as I remember it – and I said thank you, very polite. Then she reckons when she saw me next with my father a few days later, he said hello and I blanked her. She's got to remember she'd been a Welsh international since 1974 and to me, at 14, these people were giants, I didn't know you could just go up and start talking to them. But she mistook this for arrogance. Then she had a go at me one time when we were fooling around, when I'd lost my inhibitions. She said: 'I've never seen anybody laugh at his own jokes as much as you, Colin.'

Which may or may not be true, but it's not the sort of thing you want to go around saying to me if you want a quiet life.

We got to know each other through her job. She worked for a firm of accountants and, even at 18, I had a shoe sponsorship with Adidas and had to file a tax return, so Carmen offered to help me. It was the start of a beautiful friendship. I turned up at her house one evening with my paperwork, rang the doorbell, then it took her ages to let me in. It turned out she was knitting. She was terrified I'd see her, then the rest of the group would hear about old nanny Carmen sitting doing her knitting, and they'd murder her for it. She was, of course, fully justified to fear this.

Anyway, we chatted and watched TV and she realized I was OK; it's all part of me, the joking about in a group; I never stop. She says now that I've never changed, throughout my long journey from the beginning in that early training group right up to now, which is nice.

We had technical work to do in training too, another of Malcolm's particular gifts. Hurdling is a complicated, technical event. As he puts it: which perverse character decided to put ten metre-high barriers in the way of a 110m sprint? The idea is to clear the hurdles as efficiently as possible so as not to break up the speed of the run.

Starting is technical in itself and the subject of constant modifications to the position of the blocks. It's eight strides to the first hurdle, and you have to compromise your initial speed because if you hurtle full pace at the first hurdle, it would end up around your neck. The take-off point has to be very accurate, seven or eight feet away. Then, when you go over the hurdle, you have a lead leg and a trail leg and your trunk has to dip to make sure your centre of gravity doesn't fly up too high, which would lose you speed: the aim is to clear it almost as an extension of the sprint momentum, rather than leaping up and over.

You've then got three strides between each hurdle, but all three strides are of different lengths. The first one, when you land, is a recovery stride; the next one is the only proper sprinting stride; the next is preparation for take-off into the hurdle. Through the race, the stride patterns constantly change; as you get faster, take-off is further away from the next hurdle and you land closer to the hurdle on the other side. And as you slow down towards the end of the race, the take-offs get shorter and the landing points longer. Body posture is vital to clearing the hurdles at the fastest possible speed, to take them low and flat and dip your body to maintain momentum. The difference in strides and speeds throughout the race demands constant changes to body posture too. Then there are the technical aspects to the finish: landing after the tenth hurdle, going all out for the line, and the dip, which I developed into the best in the world in my event.

I know all this now – it was my life, I learned it, worked at it, perfected it as far as I could. Malcolm said when I finished my career that I knew more than him because I was the one who actually did it. I don't think that's true; he's the expert, but I do know what he means. There are some things about doing it which even the best coach doesn't know, which nobody else can know except the person going through it, particularly the mental part of competitions: how to go out and apply it all, win a race, under pressure. Back then I was the wide-eyed pupil, eager to learn, as he applied his knowledge to honing my natural ability into accomplished technique.

When I started, Malcolm felt my posture was poor: too hollow-backed and splay-footed. Malcolm's eye for posture is clinical. As we developed together and I became experienced, we formed a deep understanding and his job was almost to be an extra pair of eyes, there to watch me train and point out if anything wasn't quite right, rather than a coach teaching me technique. At the outset it was different. There were constant basic corrections to make: to stand up straight and straighten my back, point my toes up, make my posture more correct.

I absorbed knowledge from everybody around at the time, particularly the senior athletes. We went to summer sessions at Lillieshall and I loved listening to Daley when I met him there and on the circuit. I can remember turning up at a meet and Daley's Porsche was parked outside and one of the officials grunted: 'It's supposed to be an amateur sport, this.' Daley was quite flash, and he had plenty of attitude, but he had worked very hard for his name and his achievements. I wanted to emulate him. Let me be clear about this: I didn't covet his Porsche. Yes, I was a kid from Llanederyn, where we were never poor but never rich; I wanted to make money, but my prime motivation was to emulate his achievements in track.

I also learned by watching people. Training in Cardiff, I watched Lynne Davies, one of my female contemporaries, take the hurdles so smoothly and efficiently, with an elegant stride and low dip over the hurdles, and I decided I wanted that technique. So I copied her. The technique that took me to world championships and world records, my signature posture, which people have admired, pundits and commentators have described as close to perfection? It was Lynne's.

When good people gave me advice, particularly Malcolm, I listened and found I could put it into practice, could absorb the lessons. In short, the training, and our relationship, went well. He saw my ability, but he also recognized I had hunger and dedication. We worked well together from the start – once I got used to him being a man of few words. Most of the time he says nothing. You do some drills, clear some hurdles, and he says nothing. You do some more, and he says nothing. In later years he'd chat about any old thing – his wife, that he'd bought a new part for a car – not even mentioning the run I'd just done. I used to say: 'How come you're talking to everybody else and barely speaking to me?' And he'd reply: 'You don't need it because you're doing very well. The others need me to help them.' He talks when something needs looking at. If he sees anything wrong, then he's all over you, working on it, looking to rectify it: the lead leg, trailing leg, posture, stride pattern, start, whatever. At sessions Carmen says he 'prowls around', watching, attending to things only where necessary.

When I was still 17, Malcolm came round to the house and famously told my parents I could make the British Olympic team in the 1988 Seoul Olympics. He also told my father I was good enough to retire my parents – in other words, that I would make enough money to support them in retirement, but I never knew that at the time.

In his wilderness years in Wales, Malcolm had kept his spirits up partly through his admiration of another Lyn Davies, the male long jumper, winner of the gold medal at the 1964 Tokyo Olympics. He was an icon in Britain and his native Wales, and Malcolm has huge respect for him, knows him as a tremendous athlete. All those years, slogging away in the shadow of rugby, putting a basic athletic and coaching infrastructure in place, Malcolm had hoped that somebody else of Lyn Davies' stature would come along in Wales. He says that after he'd worked with me for quite a short time as a teenager, he believed I could be of that class. Ask him why and he says, always, that it was in the mind, not the body. There were other athletes – still are – with more natural raw material than me; quicker, more powerful. But he says he saw in me as a teenager, underlying my cocky, prankster ways, the attitude of a potential future champion. He also believes the values instilled in me by my parents, of hard work and a deeply held respectability, provided a stable foundation for all the hard work he knew lay ahead.

Ask him whether it wasn't strange in a way, seeing a willowy kid in an ordinary house in Llanederyn and believing he could perform at the very top of the world stage, and Malcolm shakes his head: 'An experienced coach can spot potential. It doesn't matter where people come from, it's where their aspirations lie, and how you can inspire them. Good sportsmen have come from everywhere all over the world.

'If I could find John Akii-Bua living in some bloody hovel which passed for a police station outside Kampala, why should it be at all strange that I believed I had a future champion on my hands, living with his mother and father on a grey estate on the outskirts of Cardiff?'

CHAPTER THREE

ALWAYS MAKE THE FINAL

Ambition can tip over into recklessness, and it was something of a gamble when I decided, aged only 18, to quit my electricians' course and devote myself full-time to athletics. Malcolm was horrified; he thought I was completely wrong, and tried to persuade me to stay on at college, qualify as an electrician and have something to fall back on. That was the sensible view, from a shrewd teacher of young people. But, with respect to Malcolm, it wasn't how I saw things at all.

Athletics was changing. Like most sports at that time, it was changing because of television. Satellite TV was on its way and paying big money to land the rights to sports that could bring in the viewers. That meant sponsorship money was going through the roof as well. Athletics was breaking out of its long amateur tradition, which was already compromised when I started, and was on the way to becoming a fully professional business. Many, including Malcolm, feel that has eaten into the core values of the sport and the things that motivated people to do it, coach it – the pure striving for excellence that drove young people to devote their lives to it. I believe I always retained the original motivation – just wanting to run fast, to excel, to win – but professionalism worked for me. I was truly lucky to have come into the sport when big money was washing through it. Even in the last few years of my career, the bubble had burst, and young athletes are now struggling to make a living in the sport. But as an 18-year old I could see that if I gave up everything to concentrate on track, the financial rewards were there to be had, alongside the personal fulfilment.

That was still some way ahead, and I still needed my parents. They were steady, my father working his way up the departments of the air-conditioning engineers Nuaire, my mother bustling through the NHS hierarchy as a midwife. They were never exactly rich, but nevertheless they said they would support me financially until I was 21, when the Seoul Olympics shimmered ahead. We'd see what had happened by then, and whether I was going to be able to make my living in track.

My first full-time year, from 1985, turned out to be hugely significant, mapping out in several crucial ways my future career as an athlete, although of course I didn't have a clue it would last so long.

Major challenges lay ahead: first the European Indoor Championships, my first major adult championships, then, in the outdoor season, the European Junior Championships. The following year I would graduate to the seniors, and was intending to be at the Commonwealth Games in Edinburgh, the European Championships in Stuttgart as well as the World Junior Championships in Athens. If I was really going to establish myself in the sport, put the name Colin Jackson up there in people's minds, then I had to begin to make my mark internationally straight away.

Looking back on my career, that first major race at the European Indoor Championships in Athens in 1985 had an enormous impact on all that came afterwards. Although it appears to be a negative, it turned out to be a landmark.

Going into these championships competing against seniors for the first time, I was never overawed. I just wanted to get in there as soon as possible, beat up everyone in my event and be the champion. I was scared of no one.

In the early days Malcolm was never keen on us running indoors: the meets interrupt winter training for the summer outdoor championships; you have to get race-sharp at an awkward time in the schedule. Indoor high hurdles is a tough race: 60m, five hurdles, doesn't allow much time for skill; it's a blast-out, not for the faint-hearted. Senior athletes enjoy the break from training and the competition, but the priority for me was to train to break through into genuine senior status outdoors. But in 1985 I qualified for the European Indoors and Malcolm decided I might as well compete, for the experience.

His attitude was totally different from mine. I was only the third-ranked British hurdler, behind Nigel, the senior athlete and British champion, and Jon Ridgeon, who was just four days older than me and my major rival in the juniors. Malcolm was saying: 'This is your first competition at a major championships, you should watch, learn, be observant of what's going on. It should be a valuable learning experience for you.'

Well, nuts! In my mind, I was going there to win, to lay waste the field. Even back then, learning experiences were never exactly what I was after. I had no right even to think of being the best in Europe when I was only the third best in the UK, but that was my aim when I went to Athens. I wasn't going there to look around and taste the atmosphere – in fact, venues and crowds never bothered me; I was always focused on the business of the races.

I qualified from the heats in 7.83, not far off my personal best indoors of 7.78, which was fair enough. In my semi-final I had Nigel, Romuald Giegel of Poland, who was the defending champion, and Gyorgy Bakos of Hungary, major European names of the time. There were only six lanes, and three to qualify for the final, so I was up against it with those guys. The gun went and everybody blasted off; I was already behind at the first hurdle. The race went on with the whole field in front of me; we came across the line and I was fifth. The only guy I beat was Giegel, whose best days were behind him by then.

Nigel qualified and Jon Ridgeon also made it through from his semi. I was out. It was so utterly disappointing. I was gutted, and when I say gutted, I mean it: sick to my stomach, with the spirit knocked out of me. I felt personally humiliated, coming fifth in a semi, forgotten, bringing up the rear. I just wanted to hide away. When the final was on, with Nigel and Jon in it, I crept up into the stand, far away from everybody else, watched the race and just burned away.

You might wonder at me feeling so bad, so young. Malcolm certainly wasn't disappointed. He was pleased we were there; he thought fifth in a semi was a decent base to build on, at 18. I didn't run badly – I ran the third-fastest time I ever had indoors. I'd have had to beat Nigel, run a massive personal best and nearly break the British record to qualify for that final, none of which was realistically possible at that time. If I'd thought about it rationally, I'd perhaps have understood that as I was not near the top six in Europe, my name wasn't going to be on the sheet for the final. So there was no need for me to be hiding up in the stand, with my tracksuit top practically over my head to disguise my identity, internally combusting over the fact I'd gone out. But I couldn't take it. I watched the final; Nigel was fifth and Jon got a bronze, with Bakos taking the gold in 7.60, and I was absolutely gutted. I looked down on them and so desperately wanted to be in that final; I felt so alone and excluded – God I wanted to be in there.

And sitting there, I promised myself that I would never, ever fail to make a final again. I never wanted to feel like that again, useless and beaten, so I would never go out in a semi-final again, ever. I would never sit up in the stand at a major championships watching the final of my event. I would always be in it.

Why did I react like that? I don't know. I don't know why I have always been so driven to win. Perhaps if I questioned it, I'd stop being so consumed by it. I'm the same whatever I do. My family tease me; they remember the excesses of my competitive urge, that even if we were about to play Boggle or Scrabble, they'd find me up in my room with a dictionary, memorizing words. I have an almost photographic memory and I'd come down and remember the words, especially the awkward little ones you need for Scrabble. My father would challenge me, and we'd get the dictionary out and they'd see that I was right. I just want to win at everything. Isn't everybody the same?

That disappointment in 1985 turned out to be significant because I had experienced defeat and had the motivation never to taste it again. And, looking back, I kept the promise: a record you don't see in the cabinet of medals. Barring injury, I never after that, in a major championships, went out in a semi-final. I didn't always win – that wasn't possible, although it always burned me when I didn't. But I never again felt the humiliation of sitting in the stand watching other people fill the lanes.

In a practical sense, it was fantastic, because I could always plan for a final. People would ask me what time I was racing and I always told them the time for the qualifiers and the time for the final, because I knew I'd be in it. It felt good, as time went on, part of my growing experience and confidence. When I finally retired in 2003, I would have liked to win a medal at the World Indoor Championships, but for me at the end of my career there was still satisfaction that my last race was in yet another final of a major championships.

Back then, there was an awfully long way to go. I wasn't even the number-one junior sprint hurdler in Britain: Jon Ridgeon was ahead of me. It was a typical athletics rivalry, in many ways. Later, as I progressed into racing the world-class champions of the sport, rivalry was balanced by a more level mutual respect. At that age, though, it burned badly when Jon beat me; I felt it bitterly and was desperate to beat him next time. Personally, though, we never had a problem; we were always friendly and had respect for each other as young athletes.

But in my mind, at the time, I felt there was more than pure sporting rivalry going on: not with Jon, but in the athletics establishment. A number of coaches and agents that I met along the way seemed to be more interested in Jon than me. I felt that although Jon and I were so close, in age and ability, Jon was given all the attention, all the plaudits, and I was treated in a lesser way. I couldn't help but feel that it was something to do with me being black and from Wales: the scruffy kid from the sticks. Jon, on the other hand, was white, blue-eyed, fair-haired and not only English, but a student at Cambridge University. He, I saw, was the great white hope for hurdling; everybody seemed to want Jon to succeed. Perhaps he was their embodiment of the perfect English athlete. I was in his shadow.

This wasn't in my imagination, it was clear as day to me. As I've said, I never experienced overt racism and it is not my style to imagine or invent it. But ask Malcolm and he says the same: 'I think it's right. Look at Jon, a blue-eyed, fair-haired Cantabrian, so in the English context it's probably true that Jon was favoured. But athletics only reflected society then. There was prejudice, there was an idea that black athletes were naturally fast, rather than that they had worked damn hard at their sport, while a white athlete who was good was regarded as a hero. Daley Thompson had much to do with breaking the mould – I'm not sure we had any really great, immensely popular black athletes before him.

'Mind you,' Malcolm smiles, 'there can't have been prejudice against Colin. He got the best coach, didn't he?'

On the track, I'm not arguing, Jon was ahead of me at the time. He beat me in the second major race of my career, later in 1985, outdoors, in the European Junior Championships in Cottbus in East Germany. Again I ran quickly, 13.69 for second place, equalling the Welsh national record at the age of 18, so it was a successful run. But Jon was two metres in front of me all the way, and his time, 13.46, was a new European junior record and just three-hundredths off the senior British national record – a major achievement for Jon as a junior.

Still, I had a silver, my first major medal, but I felt it was lost in the accolades to Jon, the blue-eyed boy. I felt my recognition was zero. Looking back, it wasn't simply because Jon beat me in my race that I came low in the list of plaudits. Britain enjoyed a great haul of golds in those junior championships – it seemed as if the country had years of success stretching out before it. A guy called Elliott Bunney won the 100m sprint, Ade Mafe won the 200m, the Welsh athlete Helen Miles won the 100m, Roger Black won the 400m, and John Hill won the high jump. It was a great championships for Britain, so I suppose it was easy for my silver to be forgotten.

Look at the names now, though, and it puts my career into perspective. All of them finished competing years before I did; they really represent a former generation. Several, including Jon, were dogged by injury or lost their form, which highlights the longevity of my career. I really shouldn't look back and complain at missing out on all the attention when I went home from Cottbus with my silver, but at the time it did burn badly.

One thing that does stand out in my mind is a fashion item. I wore these very long tubeless socks and everybody was taking the mickey out of me, saying I looked like an overgrown schoolboy. We had to wait all these years for my fashion statement to be vindicated – Paula Radcliffe wears them now and they're all the rage. Ho-hum, that's me, ahead of my time in the fashion stakes, as ever.

Still a mischief-maker and non-stop chatterer while hanging out with the other athletes, I was deadly serious about the sport, which was my full-time job. Not that we trained all day; we still trained in the evenings in Cardiff with Malcolm and our intrepid group. During the day I used to hang out, go up to my Auntie Winsome's and chat to her, put the world's wrongs to rights. Wednesdays my mother never used to work, so we would go out. Other days I used to go into town and have lunch with friends who were working, mostly Lynne Davies, the athlete whose technique I copied.

But already my diet, lifestyle and all my habits were focused on being an athlete. Going out late, drinking, smoking – none of it was for me. I even listened to my mate Gary Headley, who said I should steer clear of the girls, because if I was going to be successful I didn't want to make a mistake one night and land some girl with a baby.

The further and more deeply I went with Malcolm, the more progress I made. Ranked fifth in the country at 17, in 1985 I moved up to third behind Jon and Nigel, and by 19 I improved my personal best and began to beat Jon and Nigel in domestic meets, finally making it to number one in Britain.

In 1986 we were preparing for a major season of three champion-ships. As I was ranked first, I was the favourite for the World Junior Championships, again in Athens. This brought with it another pressure: the responsibility of meeting expectations, of winning when you are predicted to. My winter training and race preparation went very well indeed, building on the serious training I had done with Malcolm and our group for a couple of years, and I came into the season in really good shape. My early races were slick and smooth and I had a cracking run in the AAAs (Amateur Athletics Association), effectively the British National Championships, which I won for the first time in 13.51, beating Nigel who came in with 13.65: a big margin in sprint hurdling.

Racing was coming easily. Experience teaches you that this is when you have to be careful; when it's all going well, something's bound to go wrong, but I was too young and foolish to know that yet. All summer in 1986 I was nagged by a slight hamstring strain, and Malcolm advised me not to race in a domestic meet, the Peugeot Talbot Games, because they were too soon before the World Juniors.

Being Mr Headstrong, I would not be told, I knew best; so sure enough I went and raced and pulled my hamstring seriously. The injury ruined my final training and preparation schedule for the World Juniors. I couldn't train at all, and spent ten days in Athens literally sitting on a pack of ice, hoping that my hamstring would make it, that I'd somehow qualify and get through the championships. A physiotherapist called Terry Newsome looked after me very well, working the hamstring and doing a grand job to get me fit enough to compete at all.

Meanwhile the team management got together and suddenly realized that nobody had seen me doing any training at all, so they pulled me out of the 4x100m relay, which I'd been selected for as well. They said I could only possibly be fit for one event, which was obviously the hurdles.

When the championships finally came round and we lined up for the heats, I was so nervous I nearly didn't qualify. I sat back in my blocks, terrified that my hamstring was going to snap when I started; I hardly moved up the track and only just made it through with a time of 14.10, way below my natural times. But I felt no reaction and settled down a little, then in the semi-final I ran 13.72 and felt like I'd walked it. It was easy, comfortable; I had my rhythm going and was much more confident about the hamstring. At that stage I knew that actually I was going to run very quickly indeed.

In the final I went off really fast, with no inhibitions about my hamstring or anything else. I was out in front, gliding the hurdles, came over the tenth, finished with my dip (which was coming on nicely at that stage) and was way out in front. I ran 13.44, which was the second-fastest ever by a junior, only one-hundredth off the UK national record, and a new European junior record. In a reverse of what had happened the previous year, Jon was second; he ran 13.92, so I absolutely hammered him in comparison to what he had done to me in the European juniors.

That race in Athens will always be one of my favourite races, when I look back, not only because I came out on top in my early rivalry with Jon. I see it as a map of what I would have to do, throughout my career. There was pressure, tremendous responsibility, to win as the favourite in front of the world. I had nagging injuries that had interrupted my training at the end and which had to be surmounted, physically and mentally. To win, to come through triumphantly, to be a champion, you have to overcome those tests many times. When I consider my career, that World Junior Championships gold is one of my most memorable races.

I'll always remember it because it had all those ingredients I would need later to be a champion: to come back successfully from adversity and live up to the responsibility of being a favourite. I made some mark on world athletics then – and the 13.44 run put paid to any lingering questions of me emulating Daley by going into the decathlon. Fittingly, I suppose, being on the rostrum at the World Junior Championships set a definite mark and meant that I'd grown up – as an athlete at least. Growing up as a human being is not something I've ever been sure I wanted to do quite so quickly.

CHAPTER FOUR

WHEN IN ROME

We came straight home from the 45°C heat of Athens – a city that was always good to me after that first European Indoor disappointment in 1985 – to the grey and cold of Edinburgh and the Commonwealth Games. But it was really exciting to be representing Wales; the Commonwealth are one of the few times at the top level internationally that you get to wear the Welsh vest, not the GB one. Our group was still very much together in Cardiff and we were there in force in Edinburgh: Sallyanne Short, Carmen Smart, Karen Hough, me, Nigel Walker, Kay Morley.

Not that Sallyanne, Karen or I were in the Welsh team picture. We were the juniors of the team, but Karen had won the AAAs in the javelin, Sallyanne was the 100m and 200m UK sprint champion, and we had come back from the World Juniors, so we were all quite pleased with ourselves. Not at all in the mood for immediately having to line up sombrely for the official photograph.

Look at the picture now and you won't see us in it. We were at the back playing this silly game: having to hold a coin, drop it, then catch it with your hand still on top – the kind of game you dream up to while away the hours when you're a junior athlete on tour. Anyway, Karen was absolutely focusing on catching this coin – she was very intense about most things – then, as she bent down to catch it, she let out an almighty fart. Everybody in the back row spun round to see who had done it. Sallyanne and I just looked at each other. We were rolling on the floor laughing and going: 'Did she just do that?' and poor old Karen burst into tears. So we made the games, but not the picture – blame Karen for that one.

Of course, all the old fellas of the Welsh association were horrified at our six-year-old pranks, but when it came to the sport we were deadly serious. In the hurdles Mark McKoy, the Canadian, was the defending champion and I was the up-and-coming young guy, and I looked at it realistically. People around me were telling me I could win it, but at the time he was far superior to me in his experience and speed and I genuinely didn't think I could be any real sort of challenge to him.

Only a couple of times in my career did I decide that winning was not a genuine target, and in a couple of very important major races I did plan for a silver. It might seem defeatist, but in a way it's highly professional. Winning isn't about psyching yourself up to believe you can do the impossible. It is about doing the work, the training and preparation, starting months before, knowing yourself and understanding how good you are and can be, and what you need to do to be at your best. Then, mentally, you focus everything on the day, at the allotted time, to achieve the best you can. At no stage in Edinburgh did I think that at 19 I could beat Mark McKoy and become the Commonwealth champion, and in my mind silver was my attainable goal, the best I could do at that time.

It was about the first time I had met Mark properly, and I respected him hugely as an athlete. We were to become great friends and training partners for three years running up to the Barcelona Olympics in 1992; he came over and lived with my parents and me in Cardiff, and we trained together with Malcolm. Mark was one of the great champions of hurdling in my time, along with the Americans Roger Kingdom and Greg Foster, and later Allen Johnson – the genuine giants.

Mark won the gold medal in 13.31. My time, to take the silver, was 13.42, which would have been a British record, but for the fact that the tail wind was over the legal limit. So I took the silver, running the fastest hurdle race ever run by a Briton, even if it didn't legally count as an official record. Nigel Walker was fourth, Jon Ridgeon fifth. I couldn't be disappointed, having run faster than ever but lost to a true champion. The challenge was to work hard enough to bring my performance up to and beyond his, to work to get better.

At home in Wales, silver was cool. I was big news. My father was keeping scrapbooks of cuttings, starting from my first mentions in local papers and the Welsh paper, the *Western Mail*, in junior county races. Now I was the world junior champion and had the Commonwealth silver, my first senior international medal. Wales's hunger for sporting success – something to cling on to in the shadow of the English and the painful decline of rugby – meant that my early triumphs seemed to have cheered up the whole country.

I was still living at home with mother and father in Birchgrove. My father had a couple of medals to keep safe for me, and I was earning some money; I had a £15,000 annual retainer from Adidas to wear their shoes and kit, and was being paid £1,000 by the British Athletics Federation to compete in eight domestic races. The appearance money didn't amount to much, but it was money: enough for me to have to see Carmen and do a tax return, when she put her knitting down. My mother used to say of my hurdling: 'How on earth are you making money from doing *that*?' But it was still early days.

My father had found his niche in the service department of Nuaire, where he got to have a look round and a good chat with customers out in the field. The company's owner, Brian Moss, always took an interest in me and the managing director, Terry Pardoe, became a family friend who'd invite my mother and father to parties. 'They seemed to like me,' my father shrugs, nice and quietly. 'I wouldn't know why.'

They knew me at the company; Suzanne and I had been taken along to Christmas parties when we were little, so when I started to have a bit of success in track, live on TV, appearing in the papers, I was the talk of the place. My father would go to the plant in Caerphilly, behind the Miners' Hospital, and everybody wanted to talk to him about me – they'd all watched me race.

After the Commonwealth Games the new managing director, Michael Hunt (who'd replaced Terry Pardoe in 1985), called my father in. Michael sat him down and said, 'Colin did pretty well in Edinburgh didn't he?' My father said: 'Yes, he did all right, even though he's carrying a little injury.' Then Michael explained that the financial director, Gwynne Jenkins (still a family friend today), had been following my career and had been looking into ways in which Nuaire could help me. They had decided to sponsor me with a car.

It came out of the blue. My father, always understated and diplomatic, nodded: 'That'd be appreciated.' But it was a real break, a genuinely valuable sponsorship. It might be hard to believe, but it was the only sponsorship I had from any company in Wales throughout my 18 years of flying the flag for the country. My father used to sit at home, painstakingly writing letters asking for sponsorship from the country's biggest companies, and he was constantly knocked back. We needed it – travel to training, to meets, to domestic championships, to airports was a big hassle and major expense. Track is all travel, and I couldn't be cadging lifts from my father, Carmen, Nigel, Malcolm, whoever, all my life. But every company my father approached – British Gas, Nissan, Panasonic, everybody he could think of with a major presence in Wales – replied saying they had their quota or they didn't sponsor athletes. He had a thick wad of rejections and never stopped trying. Then he walked into work one day and they handed him a car for me.

He'd asked for sponsorship from Nuaire before, for my sister, who had finished her degree at Warwick University and decided to be a drama queen – sorry, an actress – at which she has been a great success. My father asked his company for sponsorship for her to go the Webber Douglas Academy. Brian Moss had smiled and said: 'Ossie, come on, I'd love to get the company to sponsor my own son through university, but we can't do it.' Now, without him asking, they were offering to sponsor me.

It turned out that the support for me, among the 450 or so people now working at the company, went deeper than we realized. Because many of them had known me since I was a kid, because they knew my father and he was widely liked and respected, the staff at Nuaire were almost living my career with me. They were like rugby or football fans supporting their club – more so because they knew us personally. And my performances were having a similar effect on the place as victories for the rugby clubs in the Welsh valleys traditionally had on the coal miners. Terry, the MD, said to my father, 'Keep Colin winning, won't you, Ossie.'

'Why's that?'

'Because when he wins, everybody's up, and so is production. When Colin loses, production goes down.'

It's a shame that companies a great deal bigger than Nuaire did not have the vision or confidence to sponsor me as an athlete. For me, it was incredibly useful and I think Nuaire felt they had some value from me. They gave me a company car – my father made sure it was nothing too fast for a speed-merchant of a teenage son who'd just passed his driving test – a Ford Orion. They didn't splash the company's or my name on the side, but they paid for my petrol, all the servicing and my phone bill. My end of the deal was to turn up at exhibitions and be associated with Nuaire, which I was more than happy to do.

At the end of the year, they changed the car for me, and I crept up a grade, having a Sierra, a senior manager's car. It wouldn't be long before my career took off financially, to the point where I bought a Mercedes and had my own number plate, but as the Nuaire car was for running around in, I'd sometimes lend mine to my father to drive to work. It caused him a bit of a problem at times: that I had a car equivalent to the directors'. Senior managers would be a bit peeved that they couldn't even get a car of the quality I was using as my second car. But my father paid no attention, brushed it off in his own way, quietly shrugging: kids, what can you do?

My hamstring was still troubling me; it was really sore throughout the season and I couldn't get enough range or extension clearing the hurdles. It was also affecting my ability to train, which frustrated me – and Malcolm, who was harrumphing about 'all that hamstring nonsense'. My knees were also giving me problems, as they would do throughout my career.

Eventually in Stuttgart, at the European Championships, the third big event of that year, my poor hamstring couldn't take it any more. It was so fragile that I pulled it in the warm-up for the heats, and it packed up. My year was over – a good one for me, a huge step forward, but I was still burning up that I couldn't race in Stuttgart, because I thought I had a good chance of a medal. Ten days earlier I'd come second in the Zurich Grand Prix, absolutely hammering some of the biggest names in hurdling, including Stephane Caristan of France, who ultimately won in Stuttgart.

Sitting up there in the stand with my wetsuit on, in the cold and bluster of Stuttgart at the tail end of a European summer, my own misery briefly melted away as I watched Heike Dressler, the great East German athlete, running the 200m. I was enthralled seeing her absolutely fly round the track; it was inspirational. She took the gold in 21.71, equalling the world record, the first I had seen live and one of the most impressive sights I have ever witnessed. Later, as I matured, Heike became a colleague, but then she was a giant. Like Daley and the other greats, she showed me true excellence, where I wanted to be.

We had our post-season break, then came back to training in Cardiff on our good old cinder track. I was acclimatizing to the rhythm of being a full-time professional athlete; the job of honing the body to do what it had to do to perform. I've often wondered whether we would actually have been better if we'd had the facilities, and Lottery funding, to which athletes now have access. I'm not sure. Not that it was good to have it tough, but we had such a solid group of committed athletes who pulled each other on that it's difficult to think we could have done better.

I managed to have a major strop and fall out with Nigel because one day they started training without me. I suppose it shows how extreme I was – I didn't talk to him at all for eight months afterwards – but I was furious because I was always at training; everybody knew I could be relied on absolutely, and I was almost never late. For 18 months prior to that, everybody in the group had been late at some stage and we never started without them, so why, why on this one particular day, the first time I was ever late, did they start without me? It cheesed me off completely.

I couldn't understand why Nigel would do that to me. I went perhaps a bit over the top; it was quite bad, with people caught between two groups. That's me, though: little slights gnaw into me and I'm not easily given to forgiving and forgetting if something is clearly wrong. I didn't have a conscience about it because they should have waited for me.

Malcolm wasn't sure whether I should run indoors at all in 1987. I was struggling with my hamstring and we weren't sure whether to interrupt my training with preparation for an indoor season, given that the outdoor World Championships were coming up in Rome in the summer.

On balance, we decided I'd go for it, prepare myself, get sharp, and the experience of the European Indoor Championships in Lieven, France, would do me good. Nigel and I both made the semi-final; I won it and he came second, so I came back down, stopped and we shook hands. Carmen was watching, and she was like: 'Oh my God, they're talking!'

My hamstring was killing me, constantly; I hated it, but in the final I got a silver behind Arto Bryggare of Finland. Nigel and I came across the line together in 7.63, but the photo showed that I had just beaten him on the dip. It was still a little frosty between us, and we never actually cleared the air, but two weeks later the World Indoor Championships came up in Indianapolis and we were sharing a room, so we started mucking in and getting on again. For eight months I blanked him, just for starting the circuit training when I was 15 minutes late.

I struggled in Indianapolis; my hamstring was giving me hell and I suffered seriously from jetlag. It was the first time I had experienced it – you didn't really get jetlag driving from Cardiff to Cwmbran in your Nuaire-sponsored Orion. It was awful, I felt drained and shattered, and never switched into the competition, couldn't clear my head or prepare my body. Then Greg Foster equalled the world record in my heat; he ran 7.46, astonishing. I was a way behind with 7.60, but I finished second with that and qualified for the final.

It was one of the strangest finals ever – quite dramatic. Mark McKoy got out to a tremendous start, as he always did, he was one of hurdling's great starters. Greg Foster started running him down, then boom! Greg hit the hurdle and pushed into Mark, who nearly broke his neck as Greg landed on top of him. We all carried on taking the hurdles, with the two favourites – the top men in the world – on the floor. And still, where did I finish? Fourth. I couldn't believe it, still can't when I remember back, that with two guys flat out on the floor behind us, I couldn't win a medal. What made it worse was that Nigel beat me this time and got a bronze. He was Britain's only medallist in those championships and I shouldn't begrudge him it after all these years. But I still struggle to believe what happened in that race.

Hurdling, like all track, is a non-contact sport, but you still have to stand up strong and have some courage when the race is on. Hurdlers tend to be big men, the lanes aren't wide and we're hurtling down there, over six feet of packed muscle, at 25 miles per hour. You have to have some trust in the people alongside you, because if they so much as nudge you, you can go flying and really damage yourself.

We came back to Britain for an invitational event at our indoor venue, the rough old Royal Air Force base in Cosford, and I won. I beat Tony Campbell, who'd won the World Indoors, and Mark McKoy, and ran 7.52, breaking my own previous national record of 7.60.

To try to get myself right for the outdoor season and particularly the World Championships, I went to Lanzarote to train. I'd heard it was a good venue for training, and I've since used it many times. My parents came out too. They had a bit of a holiday – there are all sorts of snaps in my mother's album of the two of them clambering rocks and taking in the sea – while I attempted to get fit and concentrate on the championships.

That was when I first hooked up properly with Linford Christie, who was trying to make his way in the 100m and 200m. For various reasons (mostly because he lived in Shepherds Bush) he was a bit of an outcast from his north London training group, and seemed to spend most of his life out in Lanzarote. I'd been training on my own quite a bit because of my row with Nigel, so I guess we immediately had something in common: outcasts.

I bumped into him at the airport, and we spent a lot of time training, hanging out and getting to know each other. Things were cool. Claude Moseley was out there too. To me, Claude was a star; I loved him to bits. He'd been a 400m runner and a high jumper, and was an awesome athlete, one of the most talented Britain had at the time. Of all the young guns around, and the coming generation of British black athletes in the early 1980s, many fancied Claude, who had the natural talent, raw power, to be the best. Linford wasn't thought to have as much potential as Claude, and didn't win too much in the early years.

But by the time we met Claude in Lanzarote, he had hung up his spikes and was just hanging out. He'd struggled with injuries, left his famous Haringey training group and, knocking about in London, had become a bit of a hardcore gangster. He'd been slashed on a tube train in Brixton in 1982 and still came back to compete in the AAAs one month after leaving hospital.

Claude was special, but he was a bit of a wild cat. Some of the stories he would tell used to blow me away. One time he said he was in a nightclub and he didn't like the way a guy was looking at him; he thought he was sizing him up. So Claude decided to play with the guy. He went into the deepest, darkest corner of the club, took out a thick wad of cash and sat there counting the money. The guy started making his way through the club towards Claude and came too close for comfort. Claude said he took out his 'piece' – his gun – and put it on the table. 'The guy just turned right round and walked out.'

Little old me from Llanederyn could hardly believe it: that Claude's life, where he was from, was like something you would see on a film. I remember watching him running superb 400m races at domestic meets when I was a kid of 14, and here he was telling me how life was.

I remember in Lanzarote we were out shopping with my mother and he picked up a knife, a huge Rambo-style dagger. My mother said to him: 'What the hell do you need a knife like that for? You only need a knife like that if you live in a jungle.' And Claude turned to my mother and said quietly: 'Mrs Jackson, where I live *is* a jungle.' We all kind of coughed and swiftly changed the subject.

Rome was the first stadium that really impressed me – and the last. After that great old Olympic venue, nothing could make the same impact again. But I wasn't in much of a state to compete; my left hamstring, my trail leg, was in constant pain, and I was on a daily dose of six paracetamol and six aspirin, something I wouldn't advise anyone to do; it's a wonder I've still got a liver. Analyse what you are doing and it's quite scary, self-destructive: taking paracetamol to kill the pain, aspirin as an anti-inflammatory, damaging your insides so that you can go out on a track and damage your body some more. Not always healthy, the lengths that sport drives you to, but I was desperate to be in the World Championships.

My hamstring was still killing me, but in the heat I ran my season's best, 13.37, to come second to Greg Foster, who broke the championship record with 13.20, a fair start for him. I came only fourth in my semi, and would have finished third with the same time in the other one. I just thanked the heavens that there was a day off before the final, otherwise there was no way that I could have raced. It gave my hamstring just a little time to calm down and my body time to switch off and relax, so I was very fortunate.

I had no thoughts of getting a sniff of a medal. Perhaps, if I ran really well, I reckoned I might come in fifth or sixth. My main worry when I got on the line was that my leg was hurting me so much. I think the fear factor of trying to perform under these circumstances is what made me run well in the end; I was so worried my leg wouldn't make it through that when the gun went, I just took off. Greg Foster was the defending champion, he'd won in Helsinki in 1983, and he went into this race with three of the four fastest times of the season.

Early in the race, though, I was just about level with him, and I thought: this is weird, I must be running half decently or he's having a nightmare race, because I should not be this close to Greg Foster – no way. I just kept going and as I came off the last hurdle, I ran in, absolutely legged it, dipped, looked across and saw Jon Ridgeon there, but nobody else really around, except the American Jack Pierce. And I thought: well, he's behind me, definitely; I might have got a bronze here. I absolutely couldn't believe it. I waited and looked at the scoreboard, and it came up and I thought: yes! I got a bronze. I was so, so pleased because I got this bronze out of nothing. I'd had no season to speak of, then I went to the championships, my 13.37 in the heat took me to another level, then I somehow managed to pull out a bronze.

Greg Foster won the race in 13.21, recovering from what had been a slow start. Jon Ridgeon, yet again, finished in front of me: a great silver for him, with 13.29, a new UK record. I managed to run 13.38 for my bronze, really quick and a great performance for a 20-year-old, but once again Jon seemed to get all the accolades. I felt completely forgotten, strangely down after getting my medal; it was all an anti-climax.

Malcolm came to find me afterwards and he was quite intense. 'I need to speak to you,' he said. 'You and me are going out for dinner tonight. What do you want to eat?'

'Er, I don't know. Pizza?'

Pizza was certainly achievable in Rome, so off we went to find a pizza place. We sat, ordered and chatted about what had happened, how the race had gone, and I was pretty miserable because I was behind to Jon again and felt I was some kind of afterthought to the media. But Malcolm looked at me intently, his blue eyes staring into mine.

'Now,' he said, 'you're going to have to look after yourself from now on. You're going to have to have your wits about you, be very careful and carry on doing exactly what you've been doing. Don't change or be distracted.'

I really didn't have the first clue what on earth he was talking about.

'You've just won a bronze, a medal, at the World Championships,' Malcolm insisted. 'And that means your whole life is about to change completely.'

CHAPTER FIVE

SEOUL SILVER

For all the deflation I felt, munching my pizza, grumbling about the plaudits all going to Jon Ridgeon again, Malcolm was trying to tell me that he could see the reality: I had arrived on the world stage. He'd been around and he knew what came with performances at that level. Suddenly people in the sport would want to know me. I had kudos, in my event, worldwide. I was a draw, a big name for a race; I'd be flooded with invitations to meets in obscure places I'd never heard of. Malcolm was warning me: 'People will try to take advantage. Just be yourself. Don't change.'

It didn't take me long to realize what he was getting at, just until my very next race, the Grand Prix in Brussels. Then it became clear: he was talking about money. Remember, I was on £1,000 for eight races only the year before. It wasn't proper money; my living came from the shoe deal with Adidas and the car from Nuaire. Then, in this first race after my World Championship bronze, just for turning up and taking part, they paid me £5,000. I was still only 20. It would not be too long before I was commanding £12,000–£15,000 a race, and with one or sometimes two races every week, and an average of 18 meets a year, there was big money there just in fees on the racing circuit. Sponsorship deals became much easier to get and increased overnight. In 1987 my boot deal nearly tripled, from £15,000 to £40,000.

With me suddenly in the big money, agents were coming at me from all sides. They'd get 10 per cent of an athlete's fees, so after the World Championships, Colin Jackson was a name that could make them some money. I didn't understand that part of the business then and hadn't ever dealt with an agent. My focus had been on my body, training, diet, preparation, technique and championships, on reaching the top in my event. Malcolm might have had a strange way of expressing it, but the essence of his warning was: big money is coming your way, and with it temptations, distractions, hangers-on, people who will want to exploit you. He's a purist, an athletics coach, a teacher who does it because his satisfaction comes from seeing young people achieve their potential; he's not interested in the glitter around the sport. He'll say straight that it's 'all crap', and he believes it's a problem and a trap. So that was why he'd taken me out after my race in Rome and told me, along with a mouthful of pizza, to be myself: 'Don't change what you do this for, what your spirit is all about. Just stay the same, son.'

I brushed him off because I didn't feel he had any need to worry. Sure, I was cocky at times, but fundamentally I was still driving for the top, I knew I was still far from being the best in the world, and I was committed to doing the work necessary, in all areas of my life, to get there. I just said to him: 'Malcolm, I don't know what you're talking about, but I'll just get on with it anyway. I only want to run fast.'

As for agents, I was bemused. I hadn't the first clue how it all worked in the big-money league – how to deal with agents. So I approached Andy Norman, the head of promotions and meets at the British Athletics Federation, whom I'd known since I was starting out and who'd always taken a shine to me. He organized races and also organized the athletes to participate in them, and he handled the money, for the Federation, and for the athletes. When in 1986 I got my £1,000 from the Federation for eight races, it was Andy who handed out the cheque.

'Andy,' I said to him, 'there are all these agents telling me they want to look after me. What should I do for the best?' And he said: 'Well, don't you be worrying about that because we'll be looking after you.' And that was it. That's how naïve I was.

Don't get me wrong; Andy did look after me, very well indeed, thank you. He became a controversial figure and in the end the Federation got rid of him in 1994. They said he had made accusations that had contributed to Cliff Temple, the *Sunday Times* athletics journalist, committing suicide, but I was never convinced. Temple's problems, in my view, were his own; Andy hadn't caused them. Yes, Andy had serious rows and run-ins with people and he was a straight-talker, blunt without doubt, if you were on the wrong side of him. If he thought you were a bastard, he'd say it straight out. But if he thought you were good or had run well, he'd say that too. To me, and many other people, the Federation wanted him out because when the big money came in, he was sitting there organizing all the meets, paying major money to these new superstars of athletics, so he held the purse strings and, from their point of view, too much power.

I can see that as an agent for the athletes, he was a bit of a double agent – there has to be a conflict of interest if you're organizing the meets for the Federation and looking after the athletes' money. But he did his best for both the Federation and us. For me, Linford and others there was no problem; he looked after us, we raced at the right meets and we made serious money. Andy was also steeped in athletics, he loved the sport, and so career-wise, for our development, he knew where we should be racing at what times. Some people, I know, he didn't look after, and he had the power to freeze athletes out, which was terrible if you were on the receiving end. But I never had a problem.

The first time I met him I was 17. He phoned my house and said: 'I'd like you to run in a Great Britain versus USA match. Can you get a train and come up to Cosford?' So I got my stuff and went straight up there; actually my father took me. I raced and came home and that was my first real association with Andy Norman. He was always in a rush and almost never wanted to talk about anything beyond where you were going to be and when, but it was always properly organized and the set-up was always right. And he took a shine to me from the beginning; because he knew athletes, he could see what I was about, that I was serious about getting somewhere in the sport. He also had an eye for who was going to make it; his first major athlete from his own area was Steve Ovett, the great middle-distance runner of the late 1970s and early 1980s. Andy saw me as the sort who was going to be good. If I was good, then I would be good for him too, and I was aware of that. I was a little investment for him, so Andy was going to look after me. And he always did.

He and Malcolm would sort all my races out at the beginning of the season. Andy would drive down from Francis House in London, or from Birmingham later on, when the Federation's HQ moved, and they'd work out my itinerary from a racing and training point of view, then Andy would sort the money out.

Malcolm had no real need to warn me not to lose my head. I'd set myself the goal of becoming the best in Britain (which I'd done), then to be the best in the world (which I was heading for). Physically and technically I was achieving what I'd known I could, and I was loving it. I loved racing and took to the sport at that level as I had when I was a kid and first started holding court with the senior athletes. Because I was a lover of racing, of the whole athletics scene, and not a lover of money for its own sake, I would always choose the meets for racing reasons: go for the fast tracks, good facilities, an impressive field, not for the money. If people were offering big money to race on crap tracks, I wasn't running.

The year of 1988 was a huge one for me, still only 21 and coming up to my first Olympics, in Seoul, where I fancied my chance of a medal if the preparation was right. By now I'd been with Malcolm for five years. We had been through the early regime of building the physical foundations for power and endurance; I'd developed a more muscular physique, and more explosive power for starts, to go with the posture and hurdling technique, which people on the circuit were always cooing over. I had worked at it, studied it, watched videos of myself and other people, and been over it relentlessly with Malcolm, to perfect it. I was young but gaining experience now, with the confidence of the World Championship bronze behind me.

In the winter of 1987 and spring of 1988, we missed the indoor season completely; we didn't want any interruptions to training and preparation for the Olympics in the summer. In the winter I went to Norway, where a physio called Bjorn Forsan worked a miracle on my hamstring and completely fixed me up. I can remember the feeling of it coming right, and I still love him to bits for it.

Linford and I started to train together more often in the run-up to Seoul. He had his own coach, Ron Roddan, but he worked with us on every aspect of training, according to Malcolm's programme: weight training, preparation. Particularly in the later stages, Malcolm worked with him on preparation, starts and other speed aspects of his sprinting. Linford had been around for a while, but hadn't really taken his sport seriously until he was 26, when he won the European 100m gold. He had become British champion and record-holder, but missed out on a medal at the 1987 World Championships, where the Canadian Ben Johnson had won the gold with a new world record.

That summer we went warm-weather training in Nice, and Linford and I did huge sessions together. We were working really hard; we were both hungry for the Olympics and it was really fantastic. I enjoyed all

My grandfather Dee (*left*) emigrated to Britain from Jamaica in 1955. He left London for Cardiff a few months later and my mother joined him there in 1957. My family has lived in Cardiff ever since and I was born in the Welsh capital in 1967. *Below* First ever photo of my sister Suzanne and me, taken in 1967. Suzanne was six and I'm about five months.

Opposite A photo taken at Springwood Infants school when I was about six. *Above* Happy childhood memories – growing up in Cardiff during summer 1976 (left) and winter 1978. *Left* On my marks in the garden. My parents encouraged me from a very early age and have always been incredibly supportive.

Opposite top My sister, me, my mother and my father on board a pleasure boat in Brixham. I was about eleven at the time.
Opposite below Taking part in an inter-schools event in 1981. I represented Llanederyn High School and I was captain of the Welsh schools' athletics team.
Left With cricket trophies won as part of the Schools' County Championship, 1980.
Below Running against Daley Thompson in 1984. I'm on the far right lunging for the tape, Daley's second from the right.

Top left A silver medal at the 13th Commonwealth Games, 1986. On the rostrum with Mark McCoy who beat me to the gold.

Top right Bronze at the World Championships, Rome, 1987. Jon Ridgeon took silver.

Above Winning my heat at the Seoul Olympics, 1988. Unbeknownst to me, winning the silver medal in the final was to be my only Olympic success.

Above World Junior Championship semi-final run in Athens in 1986. Even though I was slightly injured, I remained confident that I would go on to win the Championships.
Overleaf Colwyn Bay 1989, visiting schools on behalf of the Milk Marketing Board.

this mega-training with Linford so much. And we began to hang out, too, and became pretty much inseparable, and always at the heart of everything going on in any camp. He was like a big brother to me at that time; he made me laugh, he was always game for everything and he was protective of me, too.

We stayed in the most awful hotel in Nice, truly disgusting. It was close to the track and the sun was shining, so we weren't complaining. But Nice was hot, and this place was smack on a motorway – and I mean right on it, as if the A4 was rolling out in front of the window – there was no air conditioning, and Linford's window was broken. The only way we could function was to open both our bedroom doors and let the air whistle through the corridor.

Malcolm was staying there too, and one night he was woken up by the hotel manager screaming at him in French, steaming into him. It turned out he was shouting: 'Where's my wife? Where are you hiding my wife? I know she's in here.' Poor old Malcolm – the guy had walked into the wrong bedroom!

We moved from there to the Olympic preparation centre in Nihon, Japan, the holding camp for the whole British Olympic team. The US team were staying there too, which was cool; I particularly remember meeting Florence Griffith-Joyner, one of the great stars of athletics, who was about to win three golds and a silver in Seoul. She was a lovely woman, a fantastic competitor; her husband Al was telling me she was the type of woman who, if there were 300 sit-ups to do, was doing 400 if you did 350. She was always intensely competitive, a great athlete, and it was a desperate shame and sad loss to athletics when she died in 1998.

We had a great time in holding camp. I was lucky not only with the money in the sport, but to come through at a time of great characters and good friends. Kriss Akabusi, a lovable rogue before he got God – although he was always a kind person – was one of the good guys. If Kriss asked how you were, how you were racing, he really wanted to know and was genuinely concerned for you. Dalton Grant, one of my favourite people in athletics, was coming through. Tom McKean, the Scottish middle-distance runner, was another: he was sound and down-to-earth. We had a good group atmosphere going on in track, which helped us all to be successful.

Linford was always at the centre of everything, the ringleader, the mouthy one, and that never changed. He was always an amazing story-teller; he'd be holding court with all his tough, hard, fabulous London stories, mainly about going out, the parties he'd been to, the people he'd known and hung out with. I can remember Sally Gunnell, the hept-athlete Joanne Mulliner and me just hanging on all these stories – although after a few years they did always seem to be the same and we'd be saying: 'Hang on, we've heard that before. Doesn't *anything* new happen in London?'

One night Linford and I decided we were going to frighten the living daylights out of the girls. Sally was sharing a room with Kim Hagger, another heptathlete, and one night Linford and I swiped one of their keys, let ourselves in and hid in their wardrobe. Kim and Sally came up and started to get ready for bed, chatting their girly talk, then got into bed and turned out the light. We started scratching, ever so lightly, at the wardrobe. So of course, as in every good horror movie, one of them decided to get up and investigate. Just as they approached the wardrobe, we burst out and threw ourselves on them, and they just screamed and screamed the place down. They didn't recognize us for ages in the dark and went on screaming, which brought the team manager, Joan Ellison, hurtling in from next door to find out what was wrong. We looked at Joan, a serious character, wearing the tiniest, skimpiest negligee ever invented. She screamed when she saw Linford and me – and we just started ripping into her, telling her what a tiger our team manager turned out to be, in this little skimpy number.

The group of athletes we hung out with were like a big family. Training was serious and we were dedicated, our minds tuned right into the Olympics, but outside working hours it was playtime. In Seoul we were young, running at world-class standards. I had enjoyed preparation so much and was in great shape, and we had a brilliant group of people to hang out with – loads of fun, the sun was shining, we met athletes from other countries; I loved it, loved the whole Olympic experience.

Then the press was full of a huge story that Tessa Sanderson – another of the good people – was having this humungous affair with Linford. It was all over the papers: Tessa's and Linford's 'romps in the woods' in Tokyo. Now in some of the pictures, I knew I had been standing right next to them, but I wasn't in them; they'd cut me out and left it looking suggestive, with just Linford and Tessa there. That taught me to be wary of the press generally, and of their interest in celebrities' private lives, and I kept them at arm's length throughout my career. My life was mine, and the people I loved – my family and friends – were mine. I never saw them as fair territory for the press and certainly not the sports press. I wanted to be judged on my performances alone, and to have fair coverage for that, nothing else.

It was very important for me to perform well in Seoul, for this was a huge chance to make my mark properly on the world stage. For Linford too it was a crunch competition; he was 28 and had to make his mark there. We shared a room – a poky, awful little room as it turned out, but that's not unusual. We also shared hopes and dreams. Having trained with him for a year on and off, I knew how hard Linford worked, and had huge respect for him as an athlete. We were both willing each other to do well.

My target was silver again. It was another time when realistically I didn't believe I could beat the top athlete, Roger Kingdom, who won the Olympics in Los Angeles in 1984 with an Olympic record and was seriously flying in 1988. Silver was not only realistic, but by now I was established, and Malcolm was insistent that I had to go there and come back with a silver. He said: 'Look, you are the second-best hurdler in the world, so your reward for that will be to win the silver medal in the Olympics. It's very important you go and do it.'

I can remember that I had a problem with my spikes; I had requested some new ones from Adidas and they didn't arrive, so I had to compete in a really old tatty pair I'd had for ages. I qualified for the final, although Malcolm was upset with me because I eased up and finished third, which meant that I had a pretty poor draw for the final in lane 2.

I don't remember too much about the build-up. Obviously I was nervous and felt the pressure; I always did, although when I was young and establishing myself I had less to lose, so there was less pressure than later on when I was expected to win or defend titles. All I can remember about the call room (the holding area where we are taken to contemplate our destinies before being led out on the track) is the sheer, outrageous confidence of Roger Kingdom. While the other athletes were all alone with their dread, he was singing: 'We're off to see the Wizard, the wonderful Wizard of Oz' constantly, all the way to the track.

'We're off to see the Wizard, the wonderful Wizard of Oz...'

And I was looking at him, thinking: that's so unfair, he's just so much better than anybody else.

I planned to play it safe because ,if I ran as I could, I was a metre faster than everybody except Roger. That meant, over ten hurdles, that I could afford to lose one-hundredth of a second on each – a big margin at the pace we run – and still win the silver. If I'd gone too fast and blasted off, I could have hit hurdles and ended up with nothing. I thought that the next Olympics, in Barcelona, would be mine, when I would have years of experience and I presumed Roger would be finished, so silver would do me fine in Seoul.

Roger, like many of the people I admired, was good with me and looked after me on the circuit. I respected the people who performed at the highest level, admired that skill and tried to home in on it, see what made them win, learn from them. Perhaps they saw that in me, so I got some respect in return when I was making my own way.

Roger wasn't a great starter, but he was an amazing finisher, so I used to know when I raced him that if he got out of the blocks with me and was level at the first hurdle, it was all over – he'd kick my ass by the finish. In the final I ran 13.28 to achieve my aim, the silver medal, and sure enough he was metres ahead, running 12.97, breaking his own Olympic record. He was a great athlete, a champion, but for me it was just so cool to be on the rostrum.

As a 21-year-old Welsh athlete, it was phenomenal to come home with an Olympic silver. It gave me ammunition against Malcolm for the next 15 years of our time together, after his wild prediction to my parents that I might just make the Olympic team that year. Tony Campbell, of the USA, won the bronze and two other Brits were in the final, a great record: Jon Ridgeon, my old rival, and my new competitor, Tony Jarrett, who came in fifth and sixth.

It was a huge experience. Everything had gone well for me in athletics, except for some niggling injuries. I was flying. I had a little way to go before I could break 13 seconds, but I was confident I could do it. I'm sure I thought a string of Olympic medals would naturally come my way. But I was too young to know that nothing runs so smoothly and that plenty of challenges would rear up to test me. I'd have been truly surprised to be told that 1988 would turn out to be my one and only Olympic medal, but that's how the cookie crumbled.

Linford got himself a medal too. He came third in the 100m, behind Ben Johnson and Carl Lewis, but then Johnson was disqualified in that infamous race for using steroids, and Linford was upgraded to a silver behind Lewis. Linford set a new British record of 9.97, the first European to go under ten seconds, and he was absolutely overjoyed with it. I was really pleased for him because I had lived and prepared with him and knew how much it meant, how deep his commitment was. And he, likewise, was delighted for me.

And then doom and gloom hit. We were coming back from dinner in a pizzeria, a whole group of us, and one of our team managers, Mike Turner, pulled Linford aside. I went with him, but Mike sent me away. I didn't think anything of it at the time. Then Linford didn't come back, all night. This was seriously unusual and I was worrying.

He turned up early the next morning looking drawn. He looked at me: 'Colin: do you think I take drugs?'

'Sorry?' I was shocked.

'Do you think I take drugs?'

'Well, I've trained with you all this time. I've seen what you do, and how hard you prepare. If you take drugs, well, I must do too.'

Then he just blurted out: 'They've accused me of taking drugs!' And he burst into tears.

'Linford,' I was saying, 'what are you on about?'

'I've been dope-tested positive,' he moaned. 'They've accused me of taking drugs.'

I really did struggle to take it in. Sallyanne wandered into the room, saw Linford in floods of tears, asked him what was wrong and Linford turned to her: 'Sal, do you think I take drugs?'

'No way,' she said.

'Well, they've accused me of it,' he said, and Sallyanne just burst into tears, too.

They were hugging each other and all three of us were devastated. I said: 'Come on, we're going to have to sort this out. There is no way you've taken a drug. What's the story?'

He'd tested positive after his race for the performance-enhancer ephedrine, a stimulant. 'Right,' I said, 'let's go through all your tablets and find anything you've taken which I haven't: vitamins, aspirin, everything.'

So we went through all his medicines, but there was nothing there that was illegal. Then Linford pulled out this little bottle of ginseng, which he'd bought in Korea for a pep-up after he'd had a cold. I still have that very bottle.

'Is that the only thing you've used differently?'

He said, looking me in the eye: 'Yes.'

Soon the Olympic doctors came into our room and cleared everything out – every multivitamin, every mineral. It was a horrible, nerve-racking time for both of us.

Sure enough, it turned out to be the ginseng, which had a trace of ephedrine in it, that caused Linford all the grief. Then we had to wait for the Olympic committee to decide what to do – the worst time for Linford in his life. Finally it came through, in his favour, just: they were going to give him the benefit of the doubt. The decision confirmed that the ginseng contained the banned substance. Linford could keep his silver medal and also his place in the 200m final, and the 4x100m relay. He went on to help Britain to a silver medal in the relay, and that chapter was over.

I remember thinking how an episode like that reveals who your friends are. Clearly Linford didn't have too many, because plenty of people – fellow team members – who knew I was close to him said they believed he was a user of drugs and that he deserved to get caught; it was about time. I put their comments down to envy and jealousy, an integral part of athletics, where the sports are individual and, really, the winners take all.

I returned to Cardiff a big name. I'd made some money, too, and it was time to move out of my folks' house and buy one of my own. Athletics was still in its uneasy compromise between amateurism and professionalism. We were paid for racing, but because we were, strictly speaking, amateurs, the money went into a trust fund, which we could draw on when we requested it for our legitimate expenses. But there was never a problem; we needed somewhere to live, a means of getting around, so we could buy a house, a car, anything, with our earnings. We'd have to write to the trustees and say how much we needed and for what. It was never questioned, and a cheque would arrive three or four days later.

Andy Norman wouldn't tell us in advance how much we were getting for a race – nobody is paid for running the Olympics or World

Championships; the money is made on the Grand Prix circuit and at organized, promoted meets. I'd race and Andy would give me some form and ask me to sign it, then he'd send the money into the trust fund. Later, when athletics turned fully, openly professional, he'd put a cheque in my hand. He was just a businessman about it: 'You raced well, here's your money, off you go.'

So I bought my first house out of my trust fund, in Roath Park, Cardiff – note the 'Park', because Roath itself is rough, Roath Park is posh. It was a three-bed semi, and I bought myself a Mercedes to go in the drive. Now I realize I must have looked ridiculous: a 21-year-old wallowing around in this saloon and rattling around a big booming house. When I met my new next-door neighbour, he asked me when my parents were arriving. I still looked like a teenager, and he couldn't believe I was moving in on my own. He probably thought I was a drug dealer.

Three of my old teachers from Llanederyn High lived on the same road. I used to get in their faces about my new success and wealth; I'd pull up outside their houses in this huge Mercedes and just smile and wave slowly: 'Hi there.' They'd look out of the window and see cheeky Colin Jackson beaming at them from behind the wheel.

'Thought I'd stop to say hello,' I'd call out to them. 'I'm just off down the road. To my new *starter home*.' Cocky sod, they surely thought, but in Wales, in Cardiff, from my family to my friends, old schoolmates and teachers, to people on the street I'd never met, everybody seemed pretty pleased for me, patting me on the back and calling out to me in the street, the silver medallist from Seoul.

CHAPTER SIX

THE PEERLESS
PRINCE OF WALES

The year following my silver was one of the most enjoyable of my life. Everything was coming right, I was reaching my target of making it to the top in track, and back home I had my new house, which became a drop-in centre and crash-pad to seemingly every scruffy person I knew who wanted somewhere to party at all hours of the morning and night. I never went out because I was always training the following day, and drinking and late nights weren't for me. So my friends would be turning up at two or three in the morning, mostly when I was in bed, and making full use of the facilities. It was a ball! Most liberating for me, there were no major championships to prepare for in 1989. It was the first year like this, and it would turn out to be the last. It was an oasis.

All I had to do was appear in meets of my choosing all over the world, and run fast. I didn't have the pressure of preparing and the dread of the final build-up to championships. Looking back, it was a year of freedom.

I was hanging out and training, really hard, usually with Linford. I seemed to spend most of my time with him. I did my winter training at home with Malcolm and our group, then spent the whole summer season with Linford in London. After the Commonwealth Games in Auckland in 1990, Carmen finally retired from athletics. She'd been plagued with awful, ruptured Achilles tendons, and she'd first called it a day in 1988. Malcolm had seen her there with swollen tendons and he'd told her she had to think about how she'd be later in life – whether she would walk. We used to tease her, tell her that if there was a fire where we were staying, she'd never get out – which doesn't sound funny, but it was dark humour because it was pretty much true. The following year she seemed a lot better, and I suggested she come back. Carmen said: 'OK, but who's going to be there to mop up the tears?'

She came back, but just did strength training, then in the summer of 1989 she amazed everyone by winning the Welsh Championships and qualifying for Auckland. Malcolm still uses her as a case study in his lectures to show what a huge part power training can play. She reached the semi in Auckland, but her injuries came back. Then she decided she couldn't go on any more. It is an emotional business, and many tears are shed when people are pushing themselves to the limit, especially if they are ripping their bodies apart at the same time. Carmen was devastated, but she had to quit.

All the while Linford and I were just having a good time, messing about like kids. We were suddenly big sporting celebrities because we were Olympic medallists, the new hot stuff in British athletics; it was an amazing experience and an amazing time. It was strange to go from nothing to so much in such a short space of time.

We were settled into our relationship, with me as the guy behind. Linford was always going to be up front – he was the 100m man, loud and boisterous, the one everybody wanted to talk to. I didn't want to be a superstar at all; I just wanted to run fast – I wanted to be the best hurdler in the world. It is one thing for your performances to be appreciated, and I always enjoyed meeting high-achieving people from other walks of life, but celebrity status is never something I have managed to get my head round – why the public needs a piece of me, an autograph, although of course I sign them if people ask, in the right circumstances, politely.

On the track Linford had an awful year because he suffered a nasty injury, a dislocated toe, in an indoor race, so his performances were down. I saw him through much of it and I understood what he was going through. We were like brothers, really, and we trusted each other.

I was improving all the time and mercifully free of injury, and Malcolm and I set a personal target for me to break 13 seconds for the first time. My preparations were geared to that, to run as fast as possible. In the winter I competed in the European Indoor Championships in The Hague, which I won – another medal to join a nice little collection for which my father was having to find room. It was all happening, and it was awesome.

I managed to run under 13 seconds for the first time in a meet in Birmingham; just ran the race smoothly, fast, in rhythm. The time was 12.99 and I was truly happy, although the tail wind turned out to be over the legal limit so the time didn't count officially.

Then in the World Cup in Barcelona in 1989 I came second to Roger Kingdom, breaking 13 seconds again by running 12.95, although again that turned out to be wind-assisted. Legally my best race in the year was 13.11, equalling the British record. But although officially they didn't count, the fact was that I had run sub-13 seconds twice, and it was pretty special. It meant I could do it, and that I could do it again.

I invited Mark McKoy over to train with us at the end of 1989. It was fate. I knew Mark as a great hurdler and a cool guy; Ghanaian originally, he now lived in Toronto and raced for Canada. I'd taken his Commonwealth record off him with my 13.28 run in Seoul. He was one of the giants when I came into the sport, but he'd always been kind, and now I had my Olympic silver I felt on a par with him. I liked and admired him both as an athlete and a person.

My sister was touring Canada in a show called *Our Country's Good*, so I said that while she was over there she should get in touch with Mark. I gave her the card he had given me when I'd last seen him, when he had been working downtown in a real-estate company. Suzanne phoned the number, but by then he'd left and a woman answered and said: 'There's no Mark McKoy in this office.' But somebody happened to be walking past who heard her say this and knew where Mark had gone; she put Suzanne on to him at his new office. She phoned that number and Mark was out, but they gave her his mobile number and that was the trail Suzanne followed which led to Mark.

They met up and it turned out that Mark was in a bad way. He'd been in Ben Johnson's training group in Toronto, and when Johnson tested positive after he won the 100m Olympic final in Seoul, Mark became caught up in the furore. He didn't test positive himself for any drugs, but in the Canadian public inquiry he admitted having taken steroids. In Seoul he'd left the Olympic village without permission and the authorities had banned him, so he wasn't racing. Back home, the Johnson training group had fallen apart, so Mark wasn't training either. Plus, he had injury problems, so now he had no group, he was banned, nobody was helping him and he'd pretty much given up.

Suzanne and Mark got talking and she said: 'You should give Colin a call. He's just bought a house; if you need to train, you should just go and stay with him and train in Cardiff for a bit.' Seems they talked it through, then Suzanne phoned me from Mark's house and said: 'Mark wants a word.' I chatted to him and I said: 'Sure. If you want to come and stay here and train with me, just come. It's not a problem.'

Malcolm had his doubts. He felt that Mark was one of my major rivals in the world, so why should he come over and work with us and learn all our secrets? 'Are you sure about this?' he asked. But in my mind, Mark could help me. Working with an athlete like him every day would improve my work. He might take 90 per cent of what we could give him – which he did – but if I just had 1 per cent from him, that could be a phenomenal boost, perhaps the final extra to take me to the top in the world.

So Mark packed his bags in Toronto and came over to Cardiff. He stayed with me in my house in Roath Park, and we trained and hung out together. He became my partner in my working life, and part of my family too, and I developed the utmost respect for him.

When he arrived he could barely walk, let alone train. He had a horrendous Achilles problem and was giving himself laser treatment on his foot every day. Just sitting around the house, he had the laser permanently on. He'd try to do some running, then he'd ice it, come home and get back to work with the laser. He worked really hard to get himself back, in all areas of athletics and in his life. Malcolm might have been worried about what Mark would learn from us about training and technique, but I learned a lot from seeing Mark's deep commitment – that he was prepared to uproot himself and come to live so far away, in the search to get back on track in athletics.

He couldn't race at all in 1989 because of his Achilles, and the following year he only raced once. He didn't come back properly until 1991 when he forced his way into the World Championships in Tokyo.

For me 1990 was a big year, with plenty of pressure lurking. We had the Commonwealth Games first, and as they were in Auckland, New Zealand, they were scheduled to start in late January, when normally we wouldn't even be competing outdoors at all and would only be starting on speed preparation. Then there was a long stretch until the European Championships in Split, in August. The timing made it a really awkward season, which I pretty much hated, because it disrupted any sensible training and preparation schedule. As I was the second-fastest hurdler in the world behind Roger Kingdom, who wasn't racing in either of those championships, I was the favourite for both. So I had the responsibility to win, in conditions that were not favourable.

I always knew I was fortunate having Malcolm for a coach, but in 1990, when he had to design a programme around an outdoor championships in January, then one in August, he really showed his quality. With Malcolm, the preparation was never going to be a problem, and sure enough he reorganized the preparation diary so that I was race-sharp in Auckland.

Linford and I were each planning to make our mark, and we went to Narrabeen, a beach resort in New South Wales, Australia, to train. We prepared really hard, and as usual there was plenty of interest in the two of us. It was fun, but I remember a little incident there that was quite revealing. We were just hanging out and decided to have a game of tennis. Now, neither of us is any kind of mean tennis player at all; in fact we're both lousy, but I'm a natural ball player. I was good at cricket and have got pretty decent eye–ball coordination. Linford, love him, wasn't blessed with the same skills, and I was beating him.

The game went on, then he called one of my returns out. No way, I said, the ball was in. He insisted it was out, so, being me, I picked up my racket and walked off the court, leaving Linford looking an absolute lemon. I told him I wasn't arguing; I wasn't interested. The ball was in. If he was telling me it was out – not a problem, we could leave it right there. Perhaps I was being a bit of a kid, but it unsettled him. Linford was a big guy and when he got upset, he frightened people. Lots of people ate humble pie with him, but not me, which used to unsettle him. He knew, underneath my cheeriness, that I had an edge.

It was freezing in Auckland, and it's not my favourite venue, but I went to perform and do my work. In my heats I equalled the European record. In the final I was confident, in good shape and I attacked from the gun, flew over the hurdles in front of the field and took the gold. I ran 13.08, the fastest time in the world that year – very pleased with that. When I watched it back home on video, I heard Ron Pickering getting all excited on the BBC commentary, watching me win that medal, and as I dipped over the line to take it Ron said: 'Colin Jackson really is the Peerless Prince of Wales.' Which I did like, I must admit, and people remember the phrase. Dear old Uncle Ron, he was a top man.

When the real outdoor season began I ran quite well, but my fortunes took a sudden turn for the worse when I tore some cartilage in my right knee, the first of what became a catalogue of injuries. The knee niggled at me during the long stretch towards the Split championships, the pain worsening through the season, and I struggled in some of the Grand Prix meets. The result was that I was under a huge amount of pressure to perform well in the European Championships. In fact, the pressure bore down on me more than at any other time previously, and perhaps since. My rise to the top had not been effortless – I'd put a lot of hard work in since my teens – but my progress had been smooth and uninterrupted. Yet here I was, the favourite, weighed down by expectations, plagued by injury and coming off a terrible last in a Grand Prix race in Zurich. Emotionally, it was almost too much; suddenly I was completely wrapped up in all this pressure. It was horrible. I felt I was almost dying.

It was a major test, but somehow I did manage to come through it. In the final I set a European Championships record of 13.18. Tony Jarrett was second, just behind with 13.21, as he had been in the Commonwealth Games, so our first-second rivalry was just starting then. After the race, I broke down. Not in front of everybody, but I went into the bathroom in the athletes' area and cried and cried. There was a small pinch of joy, a handful of pleasure, but mainly just a huge, rolling wave of relief. Relief and release, the pressure drained away in my tears.

When you win as a champion, relief is the dominant emotion. Joy is for the early races, when you're breaking barriers, when it's all new. On the rostrum at the 1987 World Championships I was pretty pleased with myself, even if Jon Ridgeon's silver took the attention away from me. But even by 1990 I was expected to be on the rostrum, and if I hadn't made it, it would have been a calamity. So I stood on the rostrum in Split feeling only profound relief and a professional sense of a job completed – along with a searing pain in my knee.

In October Mark McKoy got married to Yvette, and the Jackson clan was over in Canada for the happy occasion. But after the winter break Mark was back at my house, and we were back into serious training, preparing for another big year and the World Championships of 1991.

At home Mark was low-maintenance; he didn't need anything, he was happy in his own company, or we used to go out and meet people. He was just cool, easy. He had sorted out his Achilles and we were training well in the mornings with Malcolm. After his initial doubts, when I said that I wanted Mark to be with us, Malcolm had taken him on as one of his own athletes. He coached Mark properly, not just off the cuff. Malcolm worked out his training programme for him and, when Mark began to come back, his racing schedule too. Malcolm loved working with great athletes and good people with the right attitude, and Mark had all of that.

We went through the endurance phase together, lifting weights, building our power and strength, and then towards the end of the year began to work on speed. Mark was coming back. His strength was there, his hurdling technique was superb and he was always a phenomenal starter. Linford, who trained with us in Cardiff throughout the winter, would be well behind Mark at 60m on the flat before he ran him down.

Mark's progress was an important lesson to me about drugs in the sport, which I always knew were rife. I was always the biggest accuser, because I couldn't see how people could possibly beat me – they had to be on something, to my mind. Then when I started winning as a senior, people said the same about me. They were obsessed with my body and thought it could only be so conditioned because I was using stuff. The fact was I never took anything, but then I never had to. If I was struggling, I wouldn't like to say whether I might have been tempted. But I know I wouldn't have slept at night – I had enough doubts about my performances (whether they were good enough, whether I trained hard enough) without having to live with the knowledge, as users do, that the whole of your life is a lie.

But Mark's journey back to greatness taught me that drugs might not do much for people, if they were anyway doing the wrong training, in the wrong group. In Ben Johnson's group, Mark might have been using steroids, which are a performance-enhancer, artificially aiding the body's muscle development, but he wasn't doing the right kind of training for a hurdler, so he was an also-ran. With us, he was clean, but he was also doing the best training possible for a hurdler, and he was on his way to the very top. So the sad thing is that people put their lives and careers on the line for drugs – and it was rife; I knew many people who were doing it, and since people thought I must be too, they'd talk openly to me about it – but most of the time it wasn't doing them much good.

One thing Mark and I did in training used to really bug Malcolm. In hurdling drills we'd finish level, because I didn't run past him. It wasn't intentional. Mark was a great starter, so he'd get out miles in front. Then I'd begin to run him down over the hurdles, so Malcolm used to say:

'If he gets out so quickly, run him down and run past him, don't just stay there.' But I just seemed to find myself running in level with him. Obviously in races I'd run past him and win, but in training I used to stay alongside him – I don't know why. Malcolm used to hate it; he called it synchronized hurdling. Or 'synchronized bloody hurdling'.

In 1991 I collected another knee problem – surprise, surprise. It was a miracle I got to Tokyo in the World Championships, although I had run 13.09, which was the second-fastest in the world behind Greg Foster. I could still have gone into the championships with a chance of winning it, but to top the bad knee, I pulled a muscle in my back in the semi-final. Everything just sucked. It was a stupid year, really, faltering and frustrating.

For me, the worst thing was watching in the stand with the crowd as Tony Jarrett won the bronze. Mark managed to come through in fourth place. I hadn't changed, and never would throughout my career. I wanted to race, to win, and if I couldn't, I hated watching what should have been *my* race, and other people (whoever they were) winning what should have been *my* medals.

Linford was fourth in the 100m and Sally Gunnell was second in the 400m hurdles, both pretty glum. We went out to the Hard Rock Café all miserable and I said to them: 'Listen, next year is Olympic year and it's all going to be different. Trust me: it's going to be different for all three of us.'

Which, of course, would turn out to be true – 1992 was going to be very different. But the intense, almost unbearable pressure of 1990, followed by the injury and disappointment of 1991, made me look back and realize what a joy life and athletics had been in that oasis year of 1989. Just running fast, with everything in my favour. No championships. A blessed life. My first year of freedom – and, as it turned out, my last, until I finally retired, 14 turbulent years later. Ever since, my memories of 1989, the training and friendship with Linford, and the fast races, have lingered as special times, when life was good and I was 22. It became part of my being: 22CJ, my car number plate, almost my signature. I like to think of it as my perpetual age, the part of me – a big part, I think plenty of my friends will say – that has never grown up. In many ways I like to consider myself forever 22, a gilded year when I was young, successful and free. And nothing really bad had ever happened. That was yet to come.

CHAPTER SEVEN

BARCELONA

In 1992 I was all set to become Olympic champion: the pinnacle of my dreams and all the work I had devoted myself to since lying back on that giant's step at Springwood Infant School, Llanederyn. I was 25, close to the peak age for any hurdler, with a silver medal from Seoul behind me and years of experience, training and improvement added since. I was now the number-one hurdler in the world, had arguably the best coach and was training with Mark McKoy, probably the second best in the world.

Our training was exceptional. We were two sub-13-second hurdlers, going at it together, with maximum commitment, to a programme tailored by Malcolm to have us at our absolute peak at the Olympic final in Barcelona the following summer. I'd concentrated with the doctors and physio on getting my knee right after the problems of 1991, and soon enough it was giving me no further trouble. Malcolm worked the training schedule from the chilly days of November 1991, through the power and endurance phases of winter training, into the spring of 1992, when we would attack speed and sharpness work, all of it geared to the final in July in the Spanish heat.

Linford went to Australia, training in Melbourne for the winter. He tried to drag me out there but, as this was so important a year, I felt I really had to stay with Malcolm during the winter. Linford and I believed we were going to be Olympic champions in 1992: we'd proved we could win championships, and we had done the work to be the best in our events. We began to talk about forming our own promotions company, to manage our own commercial affairs on the back of becoming Olympic champions, rather than go with an agency and have to give them a 10 per cent cut, or just get lost in a huge register of big stars. They were ideas we would pick up when the Olympics were over.

At home, my father had finally retired from Nuaire, with a pay-off that could have been a bit more generous. He'd worked there for more than 20 years, having started on the shop floor and made his way up the hierarchy. In 1990 they were suffering in the recession and had withdrawn their sponsorship, which was fine because by then I was making money and could manage without it. When Dad retired, I decided to repay my parents for all the support they had always given me and make sure they would be sorted financially. Malcolm's prediction that I could be successful enough in athletics to 'retire' them had already turned out to be partly correct.

I could have paid their mortgage off for them, but we all decided that instead I would buy a big house, sell mine, and we'd basically all live together. I was away racing so much of the time that my father was always having to go to my house and look after the bills dropping through the letter box, so it made sense. I bought a big new house in Rhoose, just out of Cardiff. It was theirs really, but I had a sort of wing of it, with a large wide space upstairs as my own play area, for me to hang out in, with my TV, music, a pool table, couches and cushions.

When we moved, the McKoy family moved too. Mark moved right in with Yvette and their new baby, the lovely Isys. So there we all were, living together – my mother and father, me upstairs, and Mark and his family. My mother loved having them, Yvette had the best help on hand with Isys, and Mark and I just got on with our preparations.

Malcolm decided we didn't need to run too many Grand Prix races, because we were performing so well in training. He thought Mark's preparation would work best with just six choice meets. Malcolm was strict; he told Mark he raced too much, with about 16 meets a season. 'I think you burn out, so I don't want you racing.'

By the time the outdoor season came round, even before we had raced at all, we were truly sharp. When we did starts in training, it was better than any race practice could give us anyway. We were doing some wonderful sessions, fast times, lovely hurdling. Malcolm could see what we were doing; he didn't need to put it to the test too much.

Mark finally ran his first race in Germany on 24 May, where he did a personal best and set a new Canadian record of 13.11. Not bad at all. He didn't win, though; Tony Dees, the top American at the time, beat him. I hadn't started my racing programme yet; I was in the wings, watching Mark, and the opposition. I saw Dees and one or two others beat Mark, but I really didn't think we had much of a problem. I said to him: 'Mark, don't let them beat you. Trust me, if you lose to them again, when they come up against me in a race, I'm going to spank them.'

I always felt I was better than Mark, so it was simply not going to happen, their beating me, and when I raced against Dees in the Grand Prix at Crystal Palace, I just beat him. So I was looking at Mark, saying: 'See, don't worry about him, we've got him covered. Come the Olympic Games, I'll slap him up all the time.' Mark shook his head: 'Well, I'm glad you're so confident, because you only just beat him.' Which was true – it was only by three-hundredths or so, but who cared? I'd won it, that was all that mattered.

Malcolm decided that we were going to Monaco for warm-weather training, and we went down there and put in some absolutely phenomenal times. We hooked up with Linford again, and the three of us trained together, with Malcolm, for the rest of the summer in the run-up to the Olympics.

Mark's starts were just fantastic. He would come off the blocks absolutely light-years in front of us. Linford would have to run really hard to run him down on the last 40m, because Mark was shifting. When you think that Linford did go on to win the Olympic title at 100m, it gives you some idea of Mark's speed, especially his starting speed. With hurdling, though, Mark wasn't a problem for me; he'd always get out phenomenally quickly, but I'd get out and my technique and finishing meant that I'd run him down in a race. All three of us were at our peak as athletes. We were working with a masseur, Mark Zambada, and he was keeping us in tip-top shape; we were honed, all-round. It was incredible and as the Olympics approached I was in the best shape I have ever been in my life.

Mentally I was well prepared too: confident, focused, loving the training and preparation, working with great athletes who were great friends, too. I was so excited, I had almost a breathless feeling: here I was about to fulfil my dream – how many people have the chance to do that? How lucky I was.

When the time came, Linford went to the Olympic village first. Mark and I left a few days later, arriving in Barcelona together. I remember having this massive smile on my face when we arrived. Mark went off with the Canadian team and I went on my way with the British team. It was the first time we'd been separated for years.

I went over to see his room and it was awful. So often at these great major championships, the accommodation for the athletes, the stars, is dreadful: student halls of residence or barrack-like blocks where you have to share rooms. I just gawped: 'Is this where you stay?'

He said: 'I know; our blocks are terrible, it's so hot. We've got no air conditioning, they haven't even given us a fan.'

Mind you, our place – I was sharing with Linford again – was pretty rough, too. Claustrophobic, no air conditioning, sweltering heat, tiny – there was no room for our luggage, our kit or equipment – awful. There was a kitchen on hand, but we didn't use it, except to chuck some stuff in the fridges. To think we had to go out from there and compete, in front of the world, in the greatest sporting competition on earth. We were lucky we arrived just two days before the heats, so we didn't have long to spend there. That is the glamour of the Olympics, for the people who have to do the business.

Linford went out and won the 100m. He was up there on the rostrum with his gold medal and the national anthem playing – this guy who didn't even take track seriously until he was 26; this guy, my friend in athletics, who worked with me and Malcolm, worked so hard, improved his training and technique so much, powered through to world-class performances, and there he was on that rostrum, aged 32, getting his reward. I was so pleased for him. He'd done his final preparation with us, we knew just what he had done to take him this far, and I was delighted he had pulled it off. I was thinking: yes, please, it's my turn next.

Our heats were early in the morning, nine o'clock. Mark and I hardly did anything in the warm-up, because we didn't need to. We hardly did any drills, we hardly sprinted; all we did were some stretches with Malcolm, just so that we were loose and supple. Malcolm asked: 'Do you want to do some drills? 'And I'd say: 'Nah, not really.' And he turned to Mark: 'Are you doing any hurdling?' And Mark was like: 'I don't think we need any.' The rest of the opposition were killing themselves, hurtling up and down, sprinting, doing their drill work; we were just sitting, talking and laughing.

I just wanted to get on with it. Malcolm was his usual blunt self:

'Well, you haven't done anything for four days, so get out there and just run.'

We went out into the stadium and there was hardly a crowd there at that time in the morning. All I can recall is spotting Fatima Whitbread and Andy Norman sitting in the stand, and Fatima standing up and roaring: 'Go on, Colin!'

I was in the first heat, so ready for it. The gun went and I just took off. My start was really quick, powerful, I was already ahead at the first hurdle. I took it smoothly, then three fast, rhythmic strides and I was up, dipping my torso, flying over the next one. Three strides, gliding the next. I was way ahead, and it felt so smooth and easy. I took the last hurdle nicely and was so far ahead that I pretty much stopped running and almost walked over the line. The clock stopped: 13.10. 13.10!

I just looked, and I laughed: 13.10 in the heat! Nobody, I knew it, was going to run 13.10 in the whole Olympics. I'd even lost a couple of metres easing up before the line. So I knew then I could win the Olympics, and break the world record while I was there. I felt this with certainty – not arrogance, but the clear knowledge of a professional who had done his work.

Malcolm came over. 'Happy?'

Really good, I told him. Easy, good conditions, it felt great. We stayed to watch Mark's race. He cracked it, no problem, at 13.23. Mark and I had a chat; we were happy with the track.

'Yeah,' he said, 'but we've got to pray for a head wind. We've got so much leg speed, if there's a tail wind we'll be going too fast and wrap ourselves in the hurdles. Pray to God for a head wind, every round from here on in.'

The second round was the same afternoon. 'Go back and get ready for that,' Malcolm said. I went back to the barracks, had some rest, then got up and did my stretching, there in the village, before coming back to the stadium.

'You know what you're doing now,' Malcolm told me. 'You've run a really fast time, you've let everybody know you're here. Just make sure you qualify from this one.'

I decided to conserve energy in the second round, just do what I had to do to qualify for the semi-final. I'd take it easy and get through. And that decision is what scuppered my whole Olympics.

I started fine, but I wasn't committed fully to the race. I should have just taken off and torn into it, but I didn't. In trying to run more easily, I ran unnaturally; in fact I ran badly. I caught one of the early hurdles; my trailing leg snagged it and it jarred me, twisting me round. My trunk was heading over the hurdle, but my hips were now facing the other way. In trying to correct this, I tore my oblique – the muscle in the hips, which, in less athletic bodies, is covered by the love-handles.

At the time, I didn't realize. I came in second and qualified for the semi. I wasn't happy – it didn't feel natural to ease up in a race, and I knew I'd clattered the hurdle. My side felt a little strange, but I didn't know immediately that I was injured, so I could still hardly wait for the next day, the day of the semi-final and final.

I kept cool that evening, hung out, ate my food, relaxed and went back to the room. I'd hardly seen Linford at all; he was the Olympic champion and he was all over the place, giving interviews to the press and TV, celebrating; everybody wanted to know the 100m champion. He just pushed his head round the door at some point: 'Wicked run today! I'll see you later.' Oh yeah, I thought, whatever ridiculous time you decide to roll in. Some of us are still working here.

As soon as I woke up the next day I knew I was in serious trouble. When I tried to roll over, the pain in my side felt as if somebody was stabbing me. It was searing. I couldn't believe it was happening. I thought: this is stupid. It's the day of the Olympic final. I can't be in such a bad way. It's not possible. I got up to test it but when I moved to stretch, the pain was there again, ripping down my side. I couldn't believe it.

My physio had gone home. Mark Zambada had gone straight back to England from Monaco – we'd been in such great shape, there was nothing for him to do. And here I was now, standing on the floor of my bare room on the day of the Olympic final, with a sodding pulled muscle.

I assessed that the muscle could give me only one race, but I had two to face that day. If there were only half an hour between the two, I thought, I might make it; I could keep the muscle warm in between. I didn't care – I was happy to rip my oblique to shreds if it meant I'd win the Olympic gold. But two hours were scheduled between the races and it would surely seize up in between and I'd be in no shape at all for the final.

86

I didn't even tell Malcolm. Mark was in my semi, and I had a word with him before it: 'Mark, my muscle's absolutely caned. I can't move to the side, not at all. Can you work on it, can you stretch it for me, get me through the semi-finals at least?'

Mark gave me some massage, some stretching. Then we went into the semi-final. Mark took off in his usual lightning-quick style and won it, 13.12. I came in and qualified, 13.17. It actually felt quite comfortable, easy.

But as soon as I crossed the line, my left oblique started to seize up and I knew I was in big trouble. Mark asked me how it was and I told him: 'Mark, you're going to have to stretch it for me. Only you know how our masseur works. I'll get ready with all my stuff and you're going to have to stretch it for me between the semi and the final.'

By then I was depressed, because my dream had gone. My whole world was folding in front of me and all I could think about was the injury. I wasn't concentrating on the race any more: the Olympics, the medal with my name on it, waiting for me at the finish line. I was just thinking about a stupid rip to my muscle.

We went back, rested a little and did some stretches, then came back to the stadium for the final. By now the stands were packed, not that I noticed much. For athletes, there isn't too much glamour in the stadium. The warm-up areas are functional places, and changing rooms are the same everywhere. Then we're taken to a small place in the bowels of the stadium where we have to wait until we're summoned out: the call room. This is the time athletes hate most, shut up silence in these soulless rooms in Barcelona, Budapest, Birmingham, stewing in silence and nerves. Thinking of everything, which piles on further pressure: the world watching on television, family, friends, everybody at home, expecting us to perform cleanly and win.

I knew what would be happening back at our house in Cardiff. My mother and father and Suzanne would be on the sofa in front of our nice telly, camera crews jostling outside on the drive, waiting for their reaction when I won. Our whole family would be glued to the TVs in their houses, and all my friends would be frozen, petrified, waiting for me to run. They say it is a major stress, waiting and watching. They're worried for me physically, and they're twisted up emotionally because they know how much it has meant to me, and how much can go wrong.

My mother says she always knew when I was injured, even if I'd been telling them everything was cool. She says she'd look at me when the camera focused on me, and she could see in my eyes if I was carrying an injury. My Auntie Winsome would get so nervous she couldn't watch. She used to hide in the toilet while my race was run, then come out to find out what had happened.

What was happening in the call room in Barcelona's Olympic Stadium was Mark McKoy, bless him, frantically giving me massage. I was lying on my side on a narrow bench and Mark was stretching me and massaging my oblique, hoping I could get it to move.

'How's that?' he'd ask, 'how's that?' And I told him it didn't feel that bad.

'Is there anything else I can do?'

I shook my head: 'Come on, Mark, you've got to run yourself, you've got your own work to do. Leave me now. I'll just get on with it, don't worry.'

But I was thinking: I can't do this today. It's not going to happen.

We lined up for the race. I was in lane 5 and I started to try to persuade myself: if we get out first time, I might be OK. I'll put everything into my first push out of the blocks, and just keep going; it'll just be a rhythm thing after that, and with the shape I'm in, I could just do it.

So we got down on to the blocks, set, and somebody finally put paid to my chances by doing a false start. The start is the most explosive part of the race: you blaze out of the blocks, you can't wait to see if it's a false start. We'd gone out over the first hurdle by the time we were called back, but pushing out, trying to accelerate, was all my oblique was going to take and now, Jesus Christ, I could feel it.

Who turned out, to my fury, to be responsible for this false start? None other than Hugh Teape, the third English guy in the final, alongside Tony Jarrett and me. Now Hugh-bloody-Teape's got no chance of winning, so why, I thought, is he so eager as to do a false start? You're going to do nothing in this final, you're sure to be last – which he was – so what are you false-starting for? Later Tony Jarrett told me the only reason Hugh did the false start was so that he'd get on the TV. Whatever, I had little chance before, and now I was really gone.

I knew it wasn't going to work. We set ourselves up, got ready to go again. Mark was on my right and I knew he would get out fast, flying out off the blocks. It was always part of my plan; Mark would fly out and I'd focus on the barriers, on running him down and hammering everybody else in the race. He'd be the race leader until I went past, and when I did, that'd be the race won – no doubts. We'd done it over and over again.

We got down again, set, the gun went and I came out and started to work. Mark was out in front already, but I was the next-best starter and I didn't see anybody. I began to chase. I was thinking: oh God, this is hurting. I got to another hurdle and it was really hurting now. Concentrate. Concentrate!

I couldn't lift my leg high enough because of my pulled oblique. I smacked into the next hurdle, absolutely crashed into it, and it pulled me right back, put me off my rhythm so that I smacked the next one. I fell over on to Mark's side and was practically on the floor. I looked up and I saw Mark going zoom, speeding up the track ahead of me. I thought: there, it's gone, it's over. I thought I might stop, but then I decided: hell, no – run! Go for it! I was half-taking Mark's hurdles because I'd pitched over so far, and I started running hard again, praying he wouldn't hit any because that would disrupt my hurdling. I ran hard, gave it everything and got into overdrive. Suddenly I was flying past people left and right and I was thinking: I can catch him, I'm still good enough to catch him, I'm actually gaining on him. And if I catch him, I'll surely go past him.

He was approaching the last hurdle and I was thinking: Mark, do not hit that hurdle, just don't. As I thought it, he lashed it. The hurdle rocked away from me, and I had to shift back left into my lane to take my last hurdle properly; my rhythm, my rolling rhythm, which was on song and ridiculously quick again, was completely shattered. I smacked into the tenth hurdle and literally fell – just stopped still. I looked up and saw Mark cross the line and others coming past me, lifted myself up and finished. Seventh. I ran 13.46, stopping twice after clattering the hurdles, so that tells me I was in absolutely incredible shape. But I'd lost.

Mark crossed the line, threw his hands in the air, then turned straight round and looked for me. 'I'm so sorry,' he said, putting his arms round me.

'Don't you worry about it,' I said. 'You've won, man, you enjoy it.'

'Colin, I am so sorry,' he repeated, then he took off for his lap of honour, the Olympic gold medallist. It was half-hearted, because in a way he was gutted that he won when I was injured; he said later he'd have got more pleasure out of winning silver, if I'd been fit and won gold.

For me, it was important that Mark enjoyed it and appreciated it. He felt that other people – in our training group, friends – resented him his victory, but I never did. He'd won; it had nothing to do with me, stumbling in seventh. He was a great athlete and a cool friend, and nobody knew better than me how hard he'd worked. He deserved to succeed. More importantly to me, the fact that Mark won meant that all our preparations had been right, spot-on. We prepared so well. Mark's time: 13.12. So, as I knew when I ran 13.10 in my heat, nobody would run faster in Barcelona. I'd run faster in my heat than Mark did to win the gold, but I went away with nothing.

Afterwards many people commented on how gracious I had been in defeat, saying that if anybody was going to win besides me, I'd hoped it would be Mark and telling the press he was a great champion. For the press, it was an unusual story: Mark was staying in my house, we worked together, and then when he won I showed no bitterness whatsoever. Even at the time I could separate my disaster from his triumph. It's an individual sport: Mark ran as well as he could and he won it. I was able to be genuinely pleased for him, while in shock myself. I didn't feel as if we had given Mark all our secrets and he had robbed me; I knew that if I hadn't been injured and had run well, I'd have beaten him.

The world's sports press gathered round the new champion and his great story – how he had come back from drug use and his two-year ban, put his life back together and made it to Olympic gold. I've often reflected on how it came about, because it was so vital to Mark that he came to Cardiff to work with Malcolm and me. I think of my sister chasing him round Toronto just to pay him a visit; and if that woman in his old office who knew where Mark was hadn't happened to come past at that particular moment, Suzanne would probably never have found him. Or she might just not have bothered to take time to look him up; she could have been too busy, anything. Then Mark and I would never have spoken and he would never have come over to train, and his life and our lives would have been so different. You have to believe in fate, I'm telling you.

For me, fate meant that it just didn't happen in Barcelona. I was numb. I felt as if disaster had struck, that I had let everybody down. But out there, still on the track, there are things to do: you have to get your stuff, get out of there. There is plenty of time ahead to stew.

I went to pick up my clothes from where I had left them before the race, at the trackside. The long-jumper Mark Forsythe was there, and Kay Morley, my friend from our Cardiff training group. Kay's reaction was the worst thing that day. She was absolutely bawling. It was as if somebody in the family had died. Her eyes were red, blood-red, from crying. So I put my arms around her and I said: 'It's OK, you know, it's only the Olympic Games. Don't you worry yourself.'

She was devastated. Mark Forsythe just had his head down, looking at the floor. I had to keep myself together: 'Listen, I'll see you lot later, don't worry about it.'

Then, to add insult to my injury, the first four in a race are dope-tested and one random number is drawn – and guess which one came up? Seven. Little old *moi*. So I had to trudge into doping, sit there for ages with all the guys who'd picked the medals up.

People were coming up to Mark, and giving him congratulations. I sat on my own. I didn't want to talk to anybody and I certainly didn't want to be with all these people. But it had been really hot and I don't drink much water at all when I'm racing, so it took me an absolute age to be able to pee for my sample.

At one stage Malcolm came in. 'Bad luck, son.'

'Yeah,' I mumbled. 'I tried.'

He knows better than to try to talk about anything when an athlete's on the floor after a defeat. Anyway, he knew me better than anybody, and I was not interested in conversation.

Finally – it must have been two hours later – I managed to pee. All the other athletes, and everybody milling round them, had gone. I came out of the dope-testing room underneath the stadium, into a long, concrete tunnel. There, sitting on some cold stone steps, was Linford. He was just in his normal stuff, cycling shorts and a vest, and he'd been waiting all this time for me to come out; Lord knows how long.

He looked up, he saw it was me; he didn't say anything, he just stood up. He put his arm round my shoulder, and we walked up that long corridor together. He walked me back to the bus, and all the way back to the village.

'Do you know what?' he said. 'I've won the Olympics here. You don't want to win it when I win it. You win the next one – it's only four years away, and you know you can. You win it on your own.'

And then I was crying. I was weeping and bawling, walking back with Linford. What moved me most was that he had waited all that time for me, just to console me. He was the Olympic champion; I'd hardly seen him because he'd been so busy, and I was so touched that he waited so long just to walk me back to the village.

Back there, nobody knew what to say. I was just telling people: 'It doesn't matter, don't worry about it.'

Then I called home, from a phone box in the village. I talked to my sister and she was devastated for me: 'Are you all right?'

'Yeah, I'm fine. How's everybody at home?'

'Oh, we're disappointed,' Suzanne said. 'Colin, even Daddy's been crying. I've never seen Daddy cry. He never even cried at his mother's funeral, but he cried for you not winning.'

It turned out they'd all been crying. My father knew plenty about hurdling from all the years with me and they saw how awkwardly I hit the hurdle in the second round; he could see my hip come up under my ribcage and, from then on, they knew something was wrong. They knew I wasn't right in the semi-final. My mother did her old trick; she could see it in my eyes. Then they'd watched me give my best in the final, but hit all those hurdles and end up on the floor. It must have been, in a way, like watching their son and brother have a car crash.

My father had dried his tears, put a brave face on, then gone out and faced the film crews who were outside waiting for a comment. My mother and sister wouldn't go. The TV crew asked him how disappointed he was and he said: 'I'm disappointed for him because I know the kind of work he put in. Unfortunately an injury denied him victory. It's a technical event, and things like this can happen. But at least his friend won, so that's something. But I guarantee you: next year is the World Championship and he'll win that.'

I just wanted to go straight home, but Malcolm wouldn't let me, because of the injury. 'You're definitely not going. I want to see you train before you leave; I want that injury better. If you go home you'll do nothing about it; you'll sit and mope.'

That was true. I'd have flown home and the muscle could have rotted for all I cared, because my world had been shattered.

'If you stay here, it'll force you to get treatment.'

So the doctors gave me a TENS machine, which gives electrical impulses to heal pulled muscles, and I kept that on for the rest of the evening. I went out for dinner the following day with Kay and her husband and one of her friends; I couldn't even tell you where I was. I was numb.

I didn't sleep for days. When it was time to sleep, Linford would go to bed and I'd just go and sit in the kitchen. I sat in this poky kitchen, feet up on another chair, just staring outside all night. People would come in and I'd say: 'I'm cool, I'm cool', then they'd go and I'd carry on sitting there. I couldn't even close my eyes. When I did, the race immediately came flashing back, and I saw that moment with me on the floor and looking up and seeing Mark streaming away, taking his hurdles, way out in front.

Ten days later there was a meet in Monaco, a glamorous post-Olympics meet for all the new champions. Malcolm was insistent: 'I want to see you train properly here, otherwise you're not racing.'

I went to see the doctors, get my physio, massage. About six days after the final, my oblique was healing and I was ready to train. I was finally ready to sleep, too, because by then I was completely exhausted. But Malcolm wanted me running. I said: 'I'm so tired I want to die.' OK he agreed, I needn't run the high hurdles, I could lower the barriers to three feet three inches, the next level down. And he would time me. I did it, a wonderfully smooth run in a stupidly quick time. Malcolm just nodded: 'You're all right. You can go and run.'

With the oblique fixed up, I flew to Monaco. Mark was already there with Yvette. I went with them to the Hotel Abela, where we'd stayed before the Olympics. I just sat in my room, not wanting to see anybody. I told Mark to give me a knock for food. I wasn't thinking or doing anything. All I did was sit and stare out of the window at the garden outside – it's the Mediterranean, so not a bad view – waiting for the race to come round.

The hurdle line-up for the Monaco meet was the same as for the Olympic final. Everybody was in the race. Because I'd finished seventh, they put me in lane 1. All the medallists had the middle lanes. It was irrelevant that I was the fastest in the world, because the first four in the Olympics got the four middle lanes.

While I was waiting, Roger Kingdom came bouncing past. He hadn't made the Olympics because of serious knee problems. He went straight up to Mark and said: 'Hey, nice one, welcome to the club.'

Then he saw me and said: 'I'm sorry, you know.'

I shrugged. I just wanted to get the race out of the way.

I was going to run so steadily because all I was going to do was win. It was so important to win here. We went to our blocks, set ourselves up, the gun went and, no surprise, Mark shot straight out. In lane 1, I just soared past the other medal winners, then started to run Mark down, taking all the hurdles low, smooth and beautiful, not so much as clipping one; over the tenth, dip, cross the line, look across. They were all behind me. Take the flowers, thank you very much, look at the clock – and it was 13.10, two hundredths faster than Mark ran to win the Olympic final.

It was the worst possible result. I flew round my lap of honour, didn't wait for Mark, picked my gear up, took the flowers, walked back to the hotel, went into the bedroom, and cried and cried and cried. I couldn't believe that ten days after the Olympic final I'd smacked up the whole field in a time faster than the time that won it. Nor could I accept the fact that it was all for nothing, because my Olympics had gone. The despair, shame, anger and frustration, pent up inside me through those long sleepless nights in Barcelona, poured out. I was inconsolable, devastated.

I flew straight home. Mark and Yvette weren't at the house because he was touring. I walked in, chucked my bags down, went up the stairs and bumped into my mother. As soon as she saw me, she threw her arms in the air and burst into tears. She was holding me and sobbing, and then she just looked at me. 'I cannot believe it,' she cried. 'You wasted your youth for that.'

I was shaking my head, telling Mum that of course it wasn't wasted, that I'd trained hard and achieved success – and look at the money I had earned. I was happy, I told her; I wouldn't change it for the world. But I knew what she meant. She'd seen her son turn down all the normal things that everybody else did – going away, having fun, partying, getting wild, studying – so that I could commit everything in my life to track. Then she'd watched as, in front of the whole world, it was all shattered in 13 seconds.

When she left me, I went into my playroom, picked up the pool cue and started whacking some balls around the table. Then I stopped, put the cue down and I promised myself: I will never, ever let athletics make me feel like this again. I was smashed, in pieces emotionally. I felt as if my whole life had been blown apart. And up there in my room in the nice big home I had bought for myself from my rewards in track, I vowed to myself that I would never let myself be so crushed again. Not for this sport.

CHAPTER EIGHT
STUTTGART

It took me a long time to recover. I was still in really good shape, just as I had been before Barcelona, and when we started training I was very quick, but my heart wasn't in athletics. I just moped around at home, didn't want to do anything or see anyone. My misery was made worse by the way the defeat had been interpreted at home. In the press they mistook my public front, my comments about Mark, for not caring deeply enough about losing, which could hardly have been more wrong. They also seemed to take too much persuading that I had actually been injured.

I'd tell them: 'I had this bad oblique. Mark was working on it in the call room, digging into me, nearly killing me, so I could hardly even breathe with the amount of digging he was doing, to try and release this thing so that I could run.'

But people, the press, even coaches, just looked at me blankly, clearly implying: 'You just didn't win, did you? Don't make excuses.'

I didn't see why I should constantly explain myself, but it did get me down. I've always seemed to have some explaining to do, even though I was a British athlete at number one in my sport. Malcolm could see it too, that people didn't seem to believe I was injured.

He looked at Barcelona with a coach's eye. He could see the longer course of an athlete's career, and he put it to me like this: 'It feels like a tragedy now, but in the long run it will make you a better athlete.'

Obviously he knew I'd been injured, but he felt it was more complicated than that. Malcolm has observed that the most dangerous time for a top athlete is when they are at their very sharpest, as I was in Barcelona. We can be running so well that we stop thinking, and when we stop thinking we lose control, and accidents can happen. He felt I was running so well in Barcelona and was so far ahead of everybody else that

– particularly after I ran 13.10 in the heat – I became, as he puts it, 'unthinking'. That, in his view, is maybe why I got injured in the second round; I wasn't considering sufficiently what I was doing in the race. He said the experience would make me a better athlete, that having been through those experiences I wouldn't make the same mistakes again. I'd be more careful.

But, wise as he is, Malcolm's bright idea to kick-start my enthusiasm didn't turn out too well. 'Come on,' he said, 'you're fit, you're running well. You should go to the World Indoor Championships and win that. Get out there again, son.'

A decent enough idea, and I *was* in good shape. The World Indoors in March were in Toronto, Mark McKoy's home territory, and I prepared well for it. We went to Australia to train, which seriously cheered me up, because that was where I really got to know Dalton Grant, a soulmate in athletics if ever I had one. Dalton was crazy; he just didn't play anything by the same rules as me or the rest of humanity. If he wanted to do something, he did it. In Australia he just turned up one day where I was staying, because I had nice rooms, and informed me he was going to be staying with me.

That meant he had the mattress and I had the hard bed-base, for six weeks. The whole time, he stayed with me. But he was cool – a very good high-jumper, dedicated, although being in London and struggling with a training group he didn't have the coach or the facilities I had at my fingertips in Cardiff. We got up to some tricks in Australia; I can remember Dalton driving over Sydney Harbour Bridge and deciding he wasn't going to pay and just ripping through the toll booth. Linford and I were in the car looking at each other: 'Did he just do that?'

At home in Cardiff I'd get used to Dalton turning up at any hour of the day, usually early in the morning when I was asleep. He'd knock on the door and wake me up at, say, 3 a.m., I'd get to the window, bleary-eyed, chuck the keys out, he'd let himself in and I'd go back to bed. I'd wake up in the morning and think: oh, Dalton turned up last night I'll go and see how he is. Then I'd go downstairs and he would already have left. He would drive right the way across London and all the way down the M4 to my house in the middle of the night, and then he was off in the morning. When I saw him again, I never asked what it was all about, and he never mentioned it.

Dalton is married now, with children, so he has his responsibilities, although he's still a free spirit, up in the clouds in some ways, but a great person. I would look at Dalton and think I would like to be like him, in the way of being a free spirit, but I never could, because I always had too much responsibility, or felt I did.

The training with the group picked my morale up, and when I raced in the indoor season, I won every time. Around this period Samantha Farquharson came into my life, too. I had first met her when she was 16, four years earlier; she was a 100m hurdler and she came to train in the national hurdle squad. I remember thinking: Christ, she's a beautiful girl. When I got to know her a little I thought she was really funny, laughing and joking; she was lovely.

Then when she decided she wanted to train with Malcolm, she came and stayed with him, and we got to know each other better. In the end I was a bit of a weasel and gently suggested that, instead of finding a place of her own, she could come and live in our house. So she moved in and we started to spend lots of time together, going out, going for dinner, hanging out, although I was too much of a gentleman to make any move just yet.

The World Indoors was a chance to lessen the blow of Barcelona, if I could win, and particularly if I could beat Mark, which I was confident I could.

We both made it through to the final. We went down on our blocks, and Mark false-started. He was looking at disqualification if he did it again. So we went down again, set, the gun went off – or rather, it didn't, because Mark got the most incredible false start. But instead of disqualifying him, the officials (all Canadian) let the race go. We all had to run, and Mark beat me by two-hundredths of a second. He finished in 7.41 with his flyer; I recovered to run 7.43. Whether they allowed him to run because they were Canadian, they'd known him since school, we'll never know, but Mark was totally open afterwards and actually said he got a 'home-town decision'.

Again, I wanted to cry. This time I'd done all I could. I prepared well, I was the fastest in the world – there was no argument about that. But some officials let Mark get away with a false start, which cost me the race. Coming six months after the disappointment of Barcelona, it was hard to take. I questioned it all deeply: what was the point? You slog all the time, dedicate and train your whole life for these moments, and then – at the moment of the races or finals – any twist of fate can pop up and scupper your dreams.

I seriously considered giving up track. Again I was gutted; track was all I had done with my adult life and I genuinely didn't feel I could cope with this constant emotional disappointment. I had no concrete thoughts about what I'd do instead, but I was sick to my heart with it and thought I couldn't do it any more.

It took a trip to Belgium to sort me out. I went to stay with my friend Alain Cuypers, another hurdler I had known since meeting him on the circuit for the first time in 1988. I was moping around with Alain and his girlfriend, Sophie, talking through what had happened in Barcelona, then in Toronto, and how distraught I felt: 'I'm going to give up. I can't go through all this again.'

They just looked at me. Sophie said: 'You don't need to give up. Not if you don't want to, not if you have more to give.' They asked me: 'Do you think you've given everything to athletics, everything you possibly can? Can you genuinely say you've put your heart and soul into every single aspect of it?'

I thought for a moment. Athletics had been my life since I was a teenager. I'd worked hard, professionally, at it, but it had come easily, too. Perhaps I had never really had to reach inside myself and give it absolutely everything. 'Perhaps not. Maybe I could find something more to give.'

'OK. Give it everything. If it doesn't work out, then you can give up, because you will know you couldn't have done more.'

It was only a short conversation, and perhaps I wasn't deeply serious about giving up; maybe I only needed encouragement. But it was very important, a landmark, for a couple of reasons: first, it removed any thoughts of quitting; second, I consciously renewed my commitment to the sport. I reached further within myself, at times to an unhealthy extreme, giving absolutely everything to conquering the pinnacle of athletics, which I and everybody else knew I was capable of doing.

After talking with Alain and his girlfriend, I came back utterly determined to prove to the world that I was the number-one hurdler. And 1993 presented a major challenge, an absolute and immediate test: the World Championships. Malcolm and I had a goal to concentrate on through the long months of training, drummed and thumped into us: Stuttgart, the heats and semi-final, 19 August; the final the following day, 20 August.

I went back and trained hard – harder and heavier than I ever had before. Mark had gone home by then but Malcolm and I had our routine. I had done my endurance, power training in the winter, went through the fiasco of Mark's false start in the World Indoors, then began to train for speed and sharpness, preparing for the outdoor season leading up to Stuttgart. Linford, now the Olympic champion, came down to train quite often – more so, as ever, in the latter stages to get sharp before the championships.

Linford and I had gone ahead and formed our promotions company. Andy Norman was still promotions officer at the Federation, still the man with the dollars organizing the races, and the man paying the dollars, looking after our fees. These were good times commercially for top athletes and we were now commanding what might seem crazy money: £25,000 for me, and £70,000 – as much as that – for Linford, for races in the UK.

The company we were forming aimed to address the promotions side of our lives: sponsorships, endorsements. The previous year the idea had been that we would both be Olympic champions: huge figures, and very attractive for companies who wanted us to endorse their products.

For one of us, it hadn't quite worked out that way. Nevertheless, I was still only 25 and the fastest in the world and, as the businessmen would say, marketable. Linford had a massive image, attracting the fame and celebrity he'd always desperately craved. When we talked about the commercial future, Linford was initially thinking of going to the giants: IMG, the American pioneers of sports marketing who had built a sizeable stable in the UK. But I thought – and said to Linford – that he could be lost at a big agency, a small fish tucked away, and at this time in our careers we really needed to be making the most of our names.

We began to think about taking the daring step of grasping fate in our own hands and setting up our own agency, which would give us control of our image and marketing, and would also save us the commission that agents take on their deals. If there was 10 per cent of a lot of money to be had, we thought, why not keep that ourselves?

It was a big move, though, a new direction, and we were still full-time athletes. Before we went ahead, we talked very seriously to Daley Thompson about the idea of going in with him. Daley had retired, he'd made good money in athletics and was considering his business activities for the future. He wanted in effect to be our agent; he would run the company, pay the employees and we'd be his clients.

It was very tempting to let Daley take on the costs of running the company, because it would save us the major expenses up front, such as an office building and wages for staff. In the end, though, we decided to hold out and do it ourselves.

Perhaps Linford didn't know Daley well enough. Of course he knew him (Daley had done some training with Linford), but they were never close as Daley and I were. Daley had looked after me when I was young; I'd worked properly with him and saw and admired the man, and trusted him completely. With hindsight, I think Daley would have done a better job and it all might have worked out well. But at the time Linford was the Olympic champion, which perhaps made him the senior partner in this relationship, and he had to be sure that what was happening would be right for him. So the decision was that we would go on our own.

Sue Barrett was my idea. She worked for API, the promotions company run by the former 400m hurdler Alan Pascoe, a silver medallist in the British relay team at the 1972 Olympics, when John Akii-Bua had won his individual gold. Alan was very close to Andy Norman, and had built up a successful company around athletics promotions. Linford and I had worked with Sue on a campaign for the Milk Marketing Board and we'd got on well; she seemed capable and friendly.

We asked her to a meeting, and put our proposal to her. She was nervous about giving up her job and coming with us, two people she knew only as athletes, into a venture that could succeed or flop. Eventually she decided to come over, but she wanted a regular salary, not to be on commission, which was fair enough – although once we got going and she saw the amount of money coming in, perhaps she regretted not being on commission!

We set up a nice little office for Sue, in Richmond upon Thames in south London – handy enough for her because she lived in Basingstoke. Rosedale House, Rosedale Road, Richmond: a brave new world for Linford and me.

We had to consider a name, and my idea for the company was Just Us. It worked for me in a number of ways: I wanted the company to be just Linford and me, two athletes who were very recognizable – a brand if you like, easy to grasp straight away. Also it was positive, but friendly, projecting to the world: we're here to help, Just Us.

Linford was pretty stubbornly struck with another idea: Nuff Respect. He said that was what people on the streets of London were saying to us, particularly to him: Nuff Respect. He'd be walking by and people would be coming up to him: 'Nuff respect, respect is due' – recognizing his achievements.

I thought it was a bit aggressive. It was fine on the streets, but if you're not in that environment and you don't know how people talk on the streets, then it's not going to mean anything. We would be dealing with major companies – those guys weren't walking on these same streets and they'd be looking to take us on to the world market. To them, it could sound very upfront, like: respect us now, because we didn't have enough before. Also, it kind of singled us out too much as a black company, which I didn't particularly want. I wanted us to go forward and establish ourselves by being successful athletes, major personalities, and being considered good people to work and to be associated with. Black is what we are; I didn't see the need to brand that into the company. Just Us made us seem more approachable.

It became rather difficult. Linford and Sue were both keen on Nuff Respect. We had plenty of discussion about it, and I explained my side of it, but they didn't really see it. The last thing you want is to be arguing from the beginning; they were the majority and I was outvoted. So Nuff Respect it was.

They had different ideas too about how the company should go. They wanted to take on other athletes, saying that if we wanted to succeed we'd have to grow. I didn't think that was necessary. Perhaps it had something to do with the different stages we were at. Linford had won the Olympics, but he was 33 now, and looking at building a career after retiring from track. I had my disappointments burning into me, but I was still only 26, with a good chunk of my career ahead. So in this way, too, perhaps Linford was the senior partner, and his ideas held sway. Anyway, Sue always seemed to side with him, so I was outvoted.

At first it all progressed quite nicely. Then Sue felt that she was no good at writing documents such as sponsorship proposals, and she didn't want to do the accounts because she was no good at figures, so we had to employ other people on that side. I couldn't quite understand why we needed to take somebody on, because our accountant, Carmen, could have done the books. And I wasn't sure about documents either. I kind of thought if we were offering companies Linford Christie, we wouldn't necessarily need to put a huge proposal in writing, it was obvious they would be getting the Olympic sprint champion and one of the most famous athletes in the world. It seemed a bit lame to me, but I didn't harp on about it: if that was what Sue wanted, she could have it.

Personally I had some nice sponsorships, with Interflora, Tag Heuer (the watch brand), and Puma (for my kit and shoes). We also had an association with Chafford 100, a promotions company that Fatima Whitbread formed after she retired, and she organized group sponsorship deals with athletes – which did bring a spot of trouble with the BAF, which was trying to sell sponsorships too. We ended up in the middle of a battle between Gatorade and Lucozade, who eventually had to up their offer to keep us.

At that stage, the business stuff was new and exciting, but I couldn't concentrate on it because I had to focus on preparing for the World Championships, and I let our new company float on.

I didn't just train hard; I paid renewed attention to every aspect of fitness, my body, nutrition. That was a continuing lesson for me throughout my career: to tailor nutrition and my diet to performance, carefully measuring the ratio of power to weight. I have developed a whole concept of nutrition, which is essentially high protein and, it might disappoint people to know, involves eating quite sparingly, even for somebody like me, an athlete supposedly burning off energy. I also researched all the drugs that people took to enhance performance, and looked for ways to reproduce the same effects, but legally, through vitamins and supplements.

But in 1993 I was still very much learning. That, combined with my total determination to bounce back after Barcelona, drove me perhaps too far. Looking back, I would go as far as to say I was anorexic.

I have never eaten much. As a kid I was too busy. I used to run out at eight o'clock in the morning, play all day, not come in for lunch – that would waste good playing hours – come back at six o'clock and have dinner; that was it. Three meals a day was never normal for me, but in 1993 I went too far the other way.

I simply didn't eat. For two, three days at a stretch: nothing. I just drank coffee. Even when I finally ate, I would have a tomato sandwich – not even a sandwich, just one piece of bread, no butter, with some tomato on top. Not the kind of diet that would win any plaudits at a nutritionists' convention.

Looking back, I showed all the signs of anorexia. I see pictures of myself then, and I looked like a skeleton. Yet I remember waking up some days, looking at myself and thinking: Christ, I am so fat. I'd lie about my weight, because people would begin to notice I was looking thin. I remember training on the track and Colin Bovell, who is now one of the head coaches in hurdles, came up to me and said: 'Oh dear, you look terrible.'

I said: 'Why? What do you mean?'

He just pointed: 'Look at this.' You could see my hips jutting out. 'You've got nothing on there; that's just bone. You look terrible.'

I remember I didn't believe him. 'No, I'm getting into shape, just a bit more and I'll be there.'

People would get on my case and ask my weight, so I'd tell them I was 73.5 kilos, an acceptable weight, although really I was 70.5, maybe 71. Every day Malcolm would look at me and wonder: 'How much do you weigh?', looking disbelieving when I gave him a figure.

In retrospect, it was wrong, maybe even dangerous, but at the time it was all part of giving maximum commitment, heart and soul, to track. I was already training hard, so it was almost as if I was looking for the next punishment, to test myself with something else. So I didn't eat. I just drank water. Perhaps I'd have a bar of chocolate the night before a race, for a surge of energy and to feel full; that became my routine.

I can remember a feature writer describing me as 'the skinny hurdler from Wales', and I couldn't understand what he meant. When I went to Nice to run in July 1993, I can remember thinking I was fat, which was far from the reality.

How I managed to run so fast with no fuel in my body's tank is still beyond me. I was unbeaten in the season – 11 races by the time I won in Nice, beating Mark McKoy. I'd been training in Monte Carlo with Linford and Mark, but Mark wasn't going to run in the World

Championships because he would not go to the national trials. Sam did all her training with me too. She was literally my training partner, along with all the other ways we were together, and before we went to the World Championships we were an item, which was great. She came to Monaco to train with us, and when we went to Stuttgart she came along to watch me perform.

In late July, at altitude in Sestriere, a ski resort near Turin, I lowered my own European record from 13.04 to 12.97, which was now just 0.05 off the world record. It was ironic, inexplicable really, to think I could run those times in a state of practical anorexia. If I knew then what I know now about the body's fuel mechanism (how it responds to certain foods and vitamins), it's frightening to think that I might have been much better back in 1993, and run faster than I ultimately did.

I arrived in Stuttgart unbeaten, running very fast indeed, but also gaunt, edgy, under severe pressure because of what had happened in Barcelona and the comments in the press that somehow I wasn't a competitor, not a winner. Tony Dees, the American hurdler, had called me 'a bottler', and said I choked with the pressure at major champion-ships, which (besides being wrong) increased the pressure and seriously cheesed me off. I was also niggled with odd injuries. I pulled out of the Grand Prix in Zurich just a couple of weeks before the World Championships with a stiff back, the third time my back had troubled me since 1991. I bruised a foot and withdrew from a meet in Cologne at the beginning of August. I didn't want to take any risks this time.

I have one dominant memory of Stuttgart: tremendous, ever-present pressure. I didn't qualify for the final as the fastest; I ran 13.13 in the semi-final, while Jack Pierce, another American, who had won the silver just behind Greg Foster in Tokyo in 1991, ran fastest with 13.11. Tony Jarrett qualified with 13.14, his season's best – where he pulled that performance from, Lord knows. I was shocked. So I was qualifying as the second-fastest, but with other runners like Tony breathing right down my neck.

Then I really dug myself a hole, committing myself to a phenomenal performance in a BBC interview: 'I'm going under 13 seconds tomorrow, so if anybody else wants to win, they'll have to go there too.'

I wasn't sure if I believed it myself. After I said it I thought: oh God, what have I done? Then I sat in the stand to watch Sally Gunnell run her final in the 400m hurdles. She lined up, the gun went, she took off and had a tremendous battle from gun to tape with Sandra Farmer-Patrick, her great American rival. Sally pulled off the victory in a new world-record time, 52.74; she was now world champion, Olympic champion and world record holder – phenomenal. I sat in the stand and watched her do it, was so pleased for her and just wished that it had been my day, too. I was so desperate to get out there on the track, desperate to become world champion.

The night before the final, I went through my chocolate ritual, sitting in my room, wishing, hoping and praying the hours would go by. I phoned home at one point, my mother answered and I asked her: 'Where's Daddy?'

She said he was out washing the car, and I remember being so annoyed. There I was sweating and practically collapsing with the pressure, and he was so cool that he was out soaping his car.

In the morning I woke up and decided not to have breakfast but to wait for lunch before I ate. I just sat for a long time, tense, shut up in my room, concentrating, focusing, on what was to be the outcome of the most crucial 13 seconds of my life and career. Then, late morning, I could hear Dalton and Steve Smith, another high-jumper, wander out to play basketball. The sun was shining, it was a glorious day and they were dancing around the court, laughing and chatting. Oh God, I thought, why do I have to be stuck in here? Why is it my turn to run today? Why can't I be out there, free, shooting some baskets with Steve and Dalton?

Darren Campbell came to collect me for lunch. We went down to the canteen and sat there as normal. I got a piece of bread, some tomatoes and onions; that was all I was going to eat. Then Jack Pierce bounced into the lunch area. I looked at him and I felt physically sick. Jack had been very close to Greg Foster in 1991 and he looked so cool, confident, like he was sure this was his year.

'Darren,' I said, ' we've got to go. We can't stay here.' I was bent over the table. 'I'm going to vomit.'

'Are you sure?'

'I don't feel well. We've got to go back.'

We got up and left. He walked back to the room with me, and we sat there in my little garret – student accommodation as always – listening to the guys outside playing basketball. I did some deep breathing, waiting, wondering, trying to relax. I felt like I was in a hospital; it's strange to say so, but I had regular visitors. Fatima, herself a former world record holder and champion in the javelin, came in to wish me all the best and give me some words of wisdom. Tessa came by, and Linford.

Last but not least, Malcolm came and just sat with me for a long time, without talking much, until it was time to get ready to go. We had a job in hand and I tried to be cool. I showered as usual, changed, greased up my skin, shaved, tried to make myself a little bit smart. I always felt that the better I looked, the better I felt generally.

I put on my GB tracksuit and went down to catch the bus. I was oblivious to everybody. I don't remember who else we saw. It was just Malcolm Arnold and me, on a bus, on a sunny day in Stuttgart. It took about 25 minutes to get to the track. When I got there, I didn't want to warm up outside, I wanted to go inside. But it was strange; they were using the indoor stadium to do all the officials' paperwork. There were officials going backwards and forwards, but no athletes were in there warming up, so I was all alone.

I started jogging, running round, and I could feel the tension. I could feel how tense Malcolm was, because he knew how important it was for me to go and win this race. He knew what people would say if I wasn't able to perform: that I was number one in the world, but I couldn't win championships.

I told Malcolm how many hurdles I wanted to warm up with (four), and what I felt I needed to do: starts, starts, starts. I felt comfortable about everything else, but just a little unsure about my start, so I wanted to work and practise on that in the warm-up.

Malcolm put out the four hurdles. I stretched, felt very flexible and loose, very light. I put on my training tights, did some strides. I felt nimble, in condition to do something in this race. Malcolm was now looking very anxious; I could feel it. I needed to tell him something; my main job now was to relax him, tell him I was confident in what I could do. I went up to him, grabbed him by the shoulders and said: 'Malcolm, think of the race like this. You've written a letter, you've put it in the envelope, addressed the envelope, licked the stamp. My job now is just to deliver it, that's all.'

I think Malcolm felt a huge release after I said that, suddenly confident in me. In turn that helped me. We did a cracking warm-up, but

I was always unsure how I actually looked: whether it was quick enough; whether my trail leg was moving fast enough; whether I had enough leg speed; whether I was clearing the barriers too high. Malcolm usually never said much in the warm-up, just last-minute reminders, but now he was more animated than usual: 'Yep, that looks great. Yep, trail leg's moving fine. Looks good. Yep, yep.'

Then I could see that he was excited, and I realized he was looking forward to the race as much as I was. I looked at my watch: time to go. I took a deep breath, put my tracksuit on and began the longest walk of my life.

I walked with Malcolm across the bridge to the call room, went up to the door and then we had to say goodbye. From then on, I was on my own. Inside, as usual, the Americans Jack Pierce and Tony Dees were really loud, hooting and hollering. Tony Jarrett sat there silently; I just glanced at him and winked. More deep breaths, then some officials came to check our bags, to make sure we didn't have anything we shouldn't take on to the track and then we left the call room.

We were escorted down behind the back straight, still not quite on the track; we were almost locked in a cage. I could imagine this was how the gladiators must have felt: in a cage, about to go out before a packed, roaring crowd and try to kill or be killed. I remember pushing my head against the cage, looking out, hearing the gun go and seeing the women's 100m hurdles, and Gail Devers winning the race, her second world title of the championships, as she had already won the 100m flat.

God, she was great! And God, didn't I wish that was me. I thought: can't we just go? I glanced up and saw Linford. He winked at me; I couldn't respond. I put my head down. Then the gate opened and we had to walk the whole back straight before we got to where the hurdles were. I wanted to be anywhere else but there, walking down that long back straight, in the din of the crowd on a pitch-black night, illuminated by the huge stadium lights.

Finally we reached the start, where our hurdles were all laid out, ready to go. The indoor warm-up track was slightly different from the track in the stadium, so I needed to do some drills, some starts over the hurdles, to check the feel of the track into the first hurdle. I went down on my blocks for a practice start but hammered straight into the first hurdle; I had a second try and clattered into it again. So I took a chance. I said to myself: you know what? Leave it there. Don't do another start; you don't need to. The decision to leave it gave me some confidence.

They called us to our marks. The crowd went quiet. Set. I blanked my mind, waiting for nothing but that trigger. The gun went, I was out of the blocks and accelerating fast, and in my first two steps I knew instantly I'd won the race. It was an amazing feeling: two steps and I knew. But I still had to focus, not let that exhilarating feeling go, but stay in control. I just did my work, kept running and running, gliding over the hurdles, smooth as can be, until hurdle six. Suddenly my legs blew up. They were gone. I thought: oh my God, I can't feel my legs, not at all. I can't feel my sodding legs.

I kept running and taking each hurdle and, as I reached the tenth, I saw that I was still in the lead. I wanted to soar clear of this last hurdle, but my legs had zero power; I scraped over it, landed off-balance, and just ran in – an awful run-in really, not straight or powerful, just ragged.

I crossed the line with an almighty, overwhelming wave of relief. I was first. Number one. I'd won it; I'd won my first world title. It was a wonderful feeling: the pressure washing away from me, and elation surging in instead. I looked at the clock and I saw 12.91, but I ignored it. It was unofficial; I thought they'd round it down to a lesser time.

I was so pleased. I threw my hands up, then squatted down to try to take it in. Tony Jarrett, who was always such a noble rival, had come in second, beating Jack Pierce into third with a superb run of his own, and he picked me up and spun me round. I had a moment to gather my thoughts, waited, then stood up. Linford threw a T-shirt on to the track. I picked it up and opened it and it said: 'Gold at last'. I had to laugh; I just had to laugh. I put on the T-shirt and ran round the track; the cameramen were clicking away. Then I saw the sign, lit up huge, saying: '110m hurdles, a new world record, 12.91' and I was absolutely ecstatic.

It was incredible, running round the photographers, hearing people scream my name, seeing the Welsh flags waving. I couldn't stop smiling. They were asking me to stop at the clock so that they could take my picture next to the world-record time. I thought: well, you see them doing it on the TV – great, amazing athletes doing things like this, not me. And I was giggling to myself, thinking: check you out, Colin Jackson, standing there by the Seiko clock showing 12.91, a new world record. I couldn't believe it was me. That it was all happening. That my dream had come true.

I continued on my lap of honour, and I spotted Sam up there in the crowd, and Sue Barrett, both of them crying. I went back to the line, put my gear back on and now I was looking for one person: Malcolm Arnold. I just ignored everybody and headed straight for where I knew Malcolm was, but I couldn't get to him, because everybody was congratulating me; they were happy for me, and I was so happy for them, for everybody who'd kept faith in me.

And then I saw Malcolm and he had this massive smile on his face, and I was so happy for him too. Coach Arnold: he worked all his life to help other people to these moments. And now he had done it for me. We'd done it together: come back from the devastation of the year before, faced down all the doubters and critics, overcome injuries and pressures of a weight I had never experienced before. And we'd won. I'd won. I was 26; it was ten years since my father and I had seen what Malcolm could produce with athletes, and had approached him to ask him to take me into his group in Cardiff. And now here we were in Stuttgart, probably an ordinary enough German city to most people but always a magical name to me – the new world champion and world record holder.

CHAPTER NINE

GOLDEN SHOES

After finally achieving the world title in Stuttgart I was one happy bunny. Those two years encapsulate so much about the life of an athlete, not only the twin extremes of complete success and total failure, but also how the small things – particularly in a technical event like hurdling – can scupper you. You can have talent, the best coach, wholehearted dedication and the best preparation, but still you need luck, protection from some little problem, like clipping a hurdle while taking it too easy in the second round, which can rupture your whole dream.

I could never change what had happened in Barcelona, but I had devoted everything to trying to put it right the following year, and had managed to do it. Time and again in a career you have to face disappointment, then do the hard work (physically and in your own mind and heart) to come back. It is one of the great tests. But after I managed to do it in Stuttgart, I relaxed and enjoyed myself, just as I had planned to after Barcelona, blazing away on a wave of peak form. The years after Stuttgart, from 1993 to 1995, were the best of my career, when I revelled in track and fulfilled my ambitions. I won all 44 consecutive races that I competed in and never once came second. That is a record which, when I recall it now, even I find pretty startling.

Wherever I went I felt unbeatable. Victory in a World Champion-ships gave me an assured kind of confidence, on top of my natural hunger and professional self-belief. I went to the big meets knowing I could win, and the other hurdlers knew I could beat them. At the meets, in the call rooms, they were looking at me, thinking I was going to destroy the field. And I did; I used to get there, go to my room, stay there most of the time and not socialize too much; do most of my stretching there before races, go to the track, do the business, be chatty and pleasant, then get out again. I was focused.

The year of 1994 was a big championship one. Outdoors the European Championships and Commonwealth Games were coming up, both of them now my titles to defend. The highlight of my purple patch, though, came indoors. I ran quite a full indoor season, and won every race, including equalling the world record of 7.36, in front of a home crowd in Glasgow, which was pretty special. I felt a lovely warmth and affection from the British athletics fans, and I love Glasgow and Scotland anyway; I think I could live there – if the weather was just a little bit kinder. I'm sure there's an empathy between Celts; maybe we're united in laughing at the English.

A week later I competed in an indoor meet in Sindelfingen, Germany. I felt strong, at the top of my form. When the gun went, I blasted out as I had done in every race, flew out of the blocks, took the five hurdles seamlessly, gave everything at the finish, performed my trademark dip, won the race and looked at the clock: 7.30. A new world record. Another – indoors now – to go with the outdoor record I'd set just seven months earlier. It was awesome to take that much off a world record; in a race lasting just over seven seconds, six-hundredths is a major margin. I was so elated. Nearly a decade on I still hold both records, and I have to say that while one of the great hurdlers who came through in my latter years might one day better the 12.91 outdoors, it is difficult to think of that 7.30 being beaten for a long time yet. I'm so glad it's my personal best and not somebody else's.

I was in such good shape that in training, and also at several meets, I even had some epic battles with Linford over the 60m flat. That persuaded me to compete in the 60m flat at the European Indoor Championships, as well as the 60m hurdles. At the Bercy indoor arena in Paris, I came away with golds in both, and even set new championship records: 7.41 in the 60m hurdles, and 6.49 in the flat sprint. I was flying.

Around this time, Claude Moseley died. He was slashed, and bled to death at a house in Stoke Newington. In a way, that would be how Claude might have wanted to go – killed in action type of thing – but really, it was so sad. He didn't need to go like that. To me, he was a lovable rogue; he had so many opportunities and was a great natural athlete, but he couldn't quite see them or hold on to them. My mother loved Claude; she thought he needed mothering – that a bit of stability and love could tip him over on to the good side of life.

It would take me a long time to really appreciate it, but I can see how much our fortunes are dictated by our background and circumstances. I saw a lot of me in Claude, and if I hadn't had the stability of my family – with the discipline we had too – I could easily have drifted over into the stuff that sent Claude to his early grave. It wasn't worth him dying like that, stabbed to death in a hovel.

My life, so different from his, was now bang on track. Outdoors, my preparation was going awesomely well. Malcolm and I knew each other intimately, all our preparation was building on the work we'd done in the years before, and we had a training schedule mapped out to have me in optimum condition for the championship finals. Never Mr Demonstrative, Malcolm has his ways of letting you know when he's satisfied, and I knew he felt I had done him proud. He believed he had his Lyn Davies now, a Welsh athlete who could compete at the top of the world class. He'd also had John Akii-Bua, and such an intensive coaching impact on Mark McKoy and Linford Christie that they were practically his athletes, too; their Olympic golds were the fruits of his expertise. So Malcolm, as a coach, didn't have too bad a record either.

At the end of May, my lovely run of good fortune was suddenly interrupted. After preparations that were close to perfect, just as the season was starting I suffered a terrible hamstring injury. So it was back to physio and rehab work and gruelling training, which seemed to take an age. Eventually I came through, but it meant that my season started very late, in mid-July, at a Grand Prix in Gateshead – a cold blustery day, not the choicest conditions for my first race back. Thankfully I managed to win there and at last the season started to roll.

There was a certain amount of pressure on me at the championships, being the favourite, having to defend my titles and recover from this injury. The European Championships were in Helsinki, which was also just a little cold for my liking, but I was truly pleased to defend my title there, setting a new championship record of 13.04 in the semi-final, then winning the final in 13.08 for another gold medal. The Commonwealth Games were in Victoria, Canada, in August, and the British team went there and came away with plenty of medals. I won the gold, equalling the championship record I had set in Auckland (13.08 again). It was really important to hang on to those titles, to defend them. Tony Jarrett again finished second; Paul Gray, one of the training partners in our group in

Cardiff, won the bronze. So it was a very successful Commonwealth Games for the British hurdlers.

Next I moved on to a target fitting for the rich patch I was enjoying in 1994. The Golden Four was, even by the standards of the time, kind of an over-the-top prize. It was literally gold bars, worth more than US$200,000, for the athlete who could win in their event at all four Grand Prix meets in a series of Zurich, Brussels, Oslo and Berlin. It was a huge prize, but very prestigious too, with all the best athletes in the world competing.

The money pouring into athletics had made top athletes like myself and Linford rich; we were the beneficiaries. Our company, Nuff Respect, had grown almost immediately we formed it, as Linford and Sue looked to take on more people. John Regis had joined after the World Championships in Stuttgart. If it was up to me, he wouldn't have come in; nothing to do with John as a person, but simply because I wanted the company to be just for Linford and me. We would have been tight and more productive, but already, although we weren't established yet commercially, we were expanding.

Then they took on Tony Jarrett and Darren Campbell, good friends of mine in athletics, but not what I had wanted for the company. It was causing extra work, extra hassle, extra time. It didn't just double the output of phone calls and office work; it must have multiplied it by ten or fifteen times. Although I was flying on the track, Nuff Respect did start to eat into more of my time. And as the company was in London, and Sue and Linford lived there, all the meetings were held there, so I was always the one travelling. Afterwards I'd have to drive for two hours back to be home so that I could train the following morning in Cardiff. Malcolm never said much, but I can't say he ever seemed overjoyed about how much time the company was taking up. I'm sure he believed from the beginning that it was too much of a distraction; that while athletes are in their prime, they should concentrate on track and let others take care of business; that ultimately it would undermine my preparation and performance.

Sue Barrett and I had nearly fallen out for the first time in December 1993. It was winter in Britain, but a nice, hot summer where we were: Linford, me, Dalton and several others, in Australia again, training for the championships ahead.

In Sydney, everybody was overjoyed because it had just been confirmed as the host city for the 2000 Olympics. It was the year Sydney beat poor old Manchester, which memorably tried to claim that it would rain more in Sydney than in Manchester at the time of the Olympics. I don't think anybody was too surprised when the International Olympic Committee ignored the weather reports and plumped for Sydney, and parties were going on all over the place.

A friend of ours, Maurie Plant, an Australian athletics administrator whom we knew through Andy Norman, invited Linford and me to be special celebrity guests at one of these official celebrations. He offered us A$5,000 each just to go along to the party and chat to people. I told Maurie it wasn't a problem – Linford and I would be there – and he arranged everything, including a car to take us.

Just before we were due to go, Sue came up to me and said that Linford wasn't happy.

'What do you mean he's not happy?'

'He's not happy getting the same money as you. He thinks he should be getting more.'

We were only going to a dinner. We were being paid A$5,000 just to do that, not even to perform; it didn't seem to me there was too much to complain about. I was steaming with her.

We went to the dinner, no problem, shook hands and smiled, were polite. When we got back, Sue tried to confront me: 'It's my job to negotiate deals,' she said. 'When Maurie called, you should have passed him straight to me.'

'What for? Maurie is my friend; he's your friend too anyway, and Linford's. If he's giving us five grand just to go to a dinner – money which sees us through the whole trip – you take it and say thanks very much. There's nothing to negotiate.'

'I still think you're wrong,' she insisted. 'Linford thinks he should have had more money.'

I was seething. Angry with her, as she would find out, but bewildered and furious with Linford, too: if he wanted more money, why didn't he tell me? Why was he cool at the dinner and then grumbling to Sue, who came relaying messages to me? There are correct ways to do things. I don't go looking for arguments, but if somebody has a problem with me, I deal with it, pretty quickly and absolutely. Linford didn't say anything directly to me, so I couldn't bowl into him about it. If he had, I would have had it out with him. For then, with Linford, I kept quiet.

With Sue, I didn't want to mess about. I decided if she had that attitude with me, I didn't want her to represent me. A fundamental misunderstanding seemed to have occurred: I was her boss, I employed her and paid her salary, not the other way around. If I wanted to negotiate my own deal, I would do so and it had nothing to do with her. If Linford wanted more – which in this case really would have been ridiculous – he could have come to tell me. I wrote Sue an absolutely stinking letter, telling her I didn't want her to represent me, reminding her of the correct balance in this relationship.

I ran it past Linford and he said I couldn't send it: 'This'll kill her.' He shook his head. OK, I agreed, but I'll have to talk seriously to her to remind her where she stands: that it's my company, not hers. The sooner she understood that, the better.

So I pulled Sue into a room and tore a strip off her:

'If you want to know the truth, I didn't want you to work with me any more. Don't pull that stroke again, ever. I'm your boss; remember that. If I want to go above your head I will. You're an employee and your job is to work for us.'

She started crying. She said she had become caught up in Linford's grumbling about his fee and his status, and had crossed the line without thinking. 'I'm sorry,' she said, 'it won't happen again.'

'Trust me,' I said, 'it better not.'

As the company was still in its infancy, I suppose some damage was done, but I didn't let it bother me too much. I had tried to straighten it out with Sue; Linford and I didn't discuss it. But I was running well, and our race fees were phenomenal – US$27,000 for me per non-UK race; Linford was probably on US$70,000 as the Olympic champion. My sponsorships were good; to my mind, the company was still cool.

By early 1994 Andy Norman was feeling the heat from the Federation, and in March they sacked him. We didn't see that they had sufficient grounds, and we really didn't believe they could lay Cliff Temple's suicide at Andy's door. Before they took action, Peter Radford, chief executive of the Federation, came round to see several athletes with questions about Andy. We all said, or certainly I did, that we were happy with Andy, that he had always looked after us, and there was no reason to fire him.

Andy was bitter when they did. We decided he should still act as our race agent, and that helped him to build a career outside the Federation. Linford and I said we'd give him 1994, but after that we would organise our own races, through Nuff Respect. If there were 10 per cent fees to be had on the kind of money we were on, we'd rather we were keeping it than lose it to somebody else.

I was happy. When I was running well, when it came easily, when the rhythm was truly there – especially now that I was running faster than anybody else in the world – nothing bothered me. Running fast had always been my freedom.

The Golden Four introduced me to the grittier realities of athletics when the big money was there. I was a bit of a street kid and knew how the world worked. From the beginning, I knew that drug use was rife and it was something I'd have to negotiate. So when strange things that weren't exactly out of the textbook of Olympian ideals of sportsmanship and fair play began to happen, it didn't really shock me.

The Golden Four was a huge target and not only because of the gold bars. The Grand Prix are where, between World Championships and Olympics, the best athletes in the world compete. I'm proud of my European and Commonwealth titles, but the top US athletes aren't losing sleep over who's picking up those medals. Grand Prix meets are where the big beasts turn up, wanting to have you for dinner.

But in 1994 nobody was touching me. I went to Zurich, Oslo and Brussels, and won all three. That meant that if I won in Berlin, I'd reap the Golden Four. There was one other athlete who had won all three previous meets in his event: Mike Powell, the US long-jumper, Olympic silver medallist behind Carl Lewis in 1988 and 1992, who at the 1991 World Championships had broken Bob Beamon's long-jump world record set 23 years earlier at the 1968 Mexico Olympics. If Mike Powell won in Berlin, he'd win the Golden Four. If we both did it, we'd share the gold bars and the dollars.

In Brussels I'd had a row with Linford, which left him a little stunned. For me, it was significant because it exposed how fundamentally different we were in our beliefs and our approach to our whole existence as athletes. It started out of nowhere; a group of us were just hanging out and chatting in someone's room at the meet hotel, the Sheraton in Brussels. There was Linford, Sue Barrett, me, Pascal Rolling from Puma and Karen Fuchs, my favourite photographer, whom I've worked with for a long time. We were all just shooting the breeze, chatting, when Linford let go a casual remark.

'You do track to try to be famous and make money.'

I was up immediately. 'You what?'

'Yeah, of course that's why you do it. That's why everybody does it.'

I was serious. 'Not me.'

'Shut up,' he laughed. 'You're lying.'

I lost it. 'Linford, trust me. If that's what you're in it for, if that's why you're an athlete, fine. But don't you ever tell me what I think and why I'm doing it. Because that is not the reason why I do track.'

Everybody was quiet now. 'I don't care if I'm famous,' I said. 'I really don't. I train hard and I work hard to win in athletics. That's my motivation, what I care about – and that's it. So don't you ever tell me why I'm doing it, or that I'm doing it for the same reasons as you.'

I knew Linford believed that; he craved being famous, loved and needed the attention and he's very keen on the money. For me, make no mistake, the money is nice. But the attention I can honestly do without. I want to be appreciated for my performance, and if people think I'm a good person, that's cool. I became a celebrity because of my record on the track, and I enjoy many aspects of it. I like being part of a recognized crowd, meeting stars in other fields, going to parties and restaurants, and I'd like to use my celebrity to good effect in the future. But I have always worried about losing my privacy and found it difficult to be constantly on show when I'm out, especially when I don't feel up to it. I feel there is something bizarre about people wanting my autograph, although I sign it willingly. The money has been tremendous, the celebrity good and bad. I wouldn't have changed anything. But to say they were my motivation wasn't just wrong, it was offensive. It's not something you shout about in the modern world of athletics, where perhaps there is too much of Linford's attitude around, but my motivation was much deeper and more personal than the gold bars of fame and fortune. I had a hunger to take part and excel and I do believe that the sport carries within it some solid human values. I always thought everybody felt the same way as me; I'd been around quite a while before I realized that everybody was in the sport for different reasons of their own.

Perhaps it was fitting that the Golden Four Berlin decider came so soon after that little clear-the-air session. A creepy incident happened before the race, again while I was hanging around in the meet hotel. A prominent race agent came up to me and asked me how much I'd be willing to pay his client to influence the outcome of the meet.

I was dumbstruck. 'You what?'

'How much?' he repeated.

I sighed and walked away.

The meet was the following day. Of all the races that season, this was the one I felt most nervous for. The Golden Four was a prestigious target; I'd won the first three and again I was favourite, with the world watching. Then, after the agent's attempt to sully the competition, it was even more important that I performed. I lined up with my heart in my mouth. The pressure mounted, to the point where I was probably more nervous for that race in Berlin than for any other I ever ran. I had to win.

We went down to our blocks, set, the gun went and so did I. I exploded out of the blocks, blasted all ten hurdles, dipped to the finish, looked across – nobody there, the race was mine. I looked at the clock: 13.02. Pretty quick. My relief, mixed with elation, was incredible. It is one thing to win a race, even a major championship, but this was a prize for having to take the pressure and win four races in a row. It was a wonderful feeling, to compare with any of the achievements of my career.

Mike Powell won his event, so he and I shared the Golden Four fair and square. If I had won because I had paid somebody, there would have been no satisfaction, no elation, no relief or pride. It's business, then, of the most cynical kind – just about money – and you're losing any of the value of what genuine sport is about. Sleeping in my bed might suddenly have been not so easy had I paid somebody to let me win. I won the Golden Four fairly because at that time I was the best in the world in my event.

Plenty of this kind of thing goes on, no doubt. Where money is involved, the sport is bound to become corrupted, it's inevitable, but because I was successful from the beginning of my career, it has not affected me much. I was always invited to races, as Malcolm had predicted, ever since my 1987 World Championship bronze. But there is a common practice for people struggling to make the races: lane buying. Let's say eight athletes have been invited, but a senior athlete really needs to be in the race because he needs the Grand Prix points to make a championships. It's common practice for his agent to approach the agent of one of the unfancied runners and pay him to have the lane. A few grand and the underdog suddenly pulls out and the lane is available. It's been happening for years. The athlete who pulls out will normally be looked after; if he drops out of the lane they want, they'll make sure he has a place in certain meets later in the season or the following season.

The agents aren't doing it for sporting reasons – let's say, because they have an athlete who is coming back from injury and needs to race. No, they do it because they can earn from him being in the race, or earn from the championships or the next race he'll be in, if he races in this one. If their athlete gets in, he'll line their pockets. I'd think about doing somebody a favour if he really needed to race to get fit again, to compete in the World Championships or whatever. But if anybody asked me for a lane so that they could line their pockets, the answer would be the same every time: no.

To me, you don't go around moralizing, but the truth is that it is sad, humiliating for the guys dropping out, and it undermines the sport. Everyone has to decide what they are in it for: for the sport, for the essence of competing and fulfilling their human potential, or for a gold bar and a few bucks.

My last races of 1994 were in a Grand Prix in September. Because I'd started the season so late, I hadn't been at my fastest at the championships and was still reaching my very sharpest form as the season wound down. I ended up running my fastest races in these end-of-season curtain-fallers. I was still very focused, concentrated on doing well. I loved my winning streak and wasn't going to give it up. It was important for me to finish the season well, with a victory. In Tokyo I won and clocked 12.98, which was awesome; then in Madrid, in the last race, I ran 12.99, rounding off the greatest season of my life. They were to be the last times ever that I went under 13 seconds.

CHAPTER TEN
FEDERATION FALLOUT

Looking back, it is clear that while I was enjoying non-stop success on the track and was completely focused on that, other parts of my life began to slip. I was seeing a lot less of Malcolm. I had drifted away from our close relationship and, although he didn't say so at the time, I think that was a factor in him leaving the Welsh job and going to work for the British Athletic Federation, which meant a move to Birmingham. It was the top job: head coach, director of coaching and performance director, which involved Malcolm working on infrastructure again, and bringing the National Lottery in to underpin the finances of the Federation. It was a promotion, bringing more money, a better pension and all the sensible stuff Malcolm had to think about, but his first love is working directly with athletes, and I wonder whether he might have stayed if I hadn't been drifting away from him.

With Sam, I'd felt at the beginning of 1994 that I was growing and becoming more complete, and wondered if we should get married, have kids and settle down. It seemed the natural next stage. Sam was a wonderful girl and I thought it would work – obviously my mother would have been delighted – but I wasn't sure I was ready. I asked a couple of my closest friends, and they said the fact that I felt the need to ask suggested I was far from sure myself. That set me thinking: was I really ready for children in my life?

I decided I wasn't ready at all. It was funny: I always felt I was being unfair to Sam with my passion for the sport; that I couldn't give enough to her because of my love and commitment to track. I'm conscientious and believe you should look after people, and I always felt guilty when I was going to Monaco to train for four weeks, or to a meet in Paris and she was stuck at home. And because I felt guilty I couldn't fully enjoy it while I was away; then when I was at home I resented the fact that I'd felt guilty because I was only doing my job; and then it was hard to deal with being together when I was getting ready to race – it was all clouding me.

Being the type of person I am, making absolute decisions and sticking to them, once I'd decided I couldn't be ready to get married, I decided we had to finish. So I told Sam she had to move out and I couldn't give her a decent explanation as to why. It was sad, she was upset and I was cheesed off. I felt free from the guilt, but it didn't feel right that she was leaving. We still saw each other now and then afterwards, for years. The bottom line was that I thought she deserved better than I could give at the time. Materially I could give her everything, but I couldn't give her the whole of me, because my sport had the whole of me. The way I was, concentrated on my ambitions, I couldn't balance my life properly.

During this time Linford and I had been doing a lot of training together, although he was looking at retirement soon and was considering what he'd do with his future. In 1994 Jamie Baulch had emerged as a very talented 400m runner. I recognized immediately that he had the necessary hunger and application for success, and wanted to apply some of my own knowledge to help him reach the top, so I offered to coach him. Jamie was young, impressionable and pleased I wanted to take him on. Besides the coaching schedule, which I had learned from Malcolm and was now applying, I advised Jamie how he should best manage his career: I didn't think Nuff Respect should represent him for races, but that Andy Norman should do it. Andy would use his contacts and encyclopaedic knowledge of athletics to put Jamie in the right meets. Nuff Respect could do Jamie's commercial deals, and then when his racing career was really working, we could organize his races too.

With hindsight, perhaps Jamie was another distraction, although I loved working with him. Looking back, I should have gone with Malcolm to Birmingham, stayed close to him and focused on my own career. But at the time there was no way I was moving up there – simple as that. I found out later that Malcolm was cheesed off with how the company and the relationship with Linford were distracting me, and could see that my attitude was drifting and changing, although he didn't say anything. We were adults and I'm sure, at the time, I wouldn't have listened anyway.

I was still training well and in cracking shape going into 1995, but it was strange; I wasn't happy, and a kind of dissatisfaction was gnawing away at me. Partly because I was coming up to 28, had been in track full-time for ten years and had done everything I had set out to achieve,. training and even the athletics circuit had become repetitive, and I was losing the spark of motivation that lit it up.

Nuff Respect had something to do with it, too. It wasn't just the hassle, the travelling, being outvoted by Sue and Linford, or seeing the company grow into something I had never wanted. Now we were handling races as well; we had given Andy Norman his year, then told him we were leaving him. Andy never said much; there wasn't much he could say – no doubt, knowing Andy, he had plenty to say to other people. Financially times were good, but I wasn't comfortable with the way the company was developing. There was always an aggression there, probably deriving from Linford's famous prickliness, which he never had with me, but with anybody he thought was in his way or, the worst crime, not giving him due respect. The company, Sue and Linford, dealt with everything defensively, seeing arguments where there weren't any. I was always laid-back – determined to succeed, but happy, wanting to get on with people, for life to be cool. For the first time I seemed infected with restlessness, resentment, an instinct to fight the world off the track as well as on it.

I went through a long period of kicking against my nice stable life, resenting the fact that I had never moved away from quiet old Cardiff. Then I decided I would definitely move, but there was nowhere I really wanted to go, which made me even more unsettled. My sister used to launch into me, telling me to count my blessings in life, but in this frame of mind I even resented the key elements that had made me successful: why did I have such supportive parents, to whom in turn I felt such a duty and such a responsibility? Why did the best coach in the world in my event have to turn up in boring old Cardiff, meaning that I never got away? Working with Linford, a man who would hardly ever venture to Nuff Respect's offices in Richmond – or Twickenham when we moved – let alone go out of London, I was affected by that awful British parochialism which says you either live in London or you're nothing. Sulky, moody and brittle were not descriptions people would normally apply to me, but in this period I was losing some of my balance. Despite all the titles and medals cramming my father's glass cabinet, the world records on my CV, the cars purring in the drive, I was just not happy with my lot.

Still, I was training well, ranked first in the world, racking up wins in every race. The World Championships were coming up in Gothenburg, Sweden, in August, when I would be defending the title I had won in my world-record time at the high point of my athletics life in Stuttgart two years earlier.

In May, just before the season started, I went to Florida for warm-weather training. And there, just when I needed peace of mind and clarity of focus, I got ill. I felt suddenly shivery and exhausted, completely washed out. The only cause I could think of was that I had been bitten when out fishing. We used to wade into the water right up to our chests, and I'm sure that was how I picked up the virus.

My whole year went downhill from there. I was struggling with injuries; I'd had a second knee operation in 1991, but now my knees were troubling me again and I needed yet another operation. On top of that, I pulled my hamstring.

Now I was struggling to focus and my form was awful; my fastest time was around 13.15, the slowest for ages, and I lost my unbeaten record. So I was really not in an ideal frame of mind to be sucked into the argument that was brewing between Nuff Respect and the Federation.

It was all about money. When the conflict spiralled into the open and out into the athletics press, it was reported that I was in dispute with the Federation over the money I was being paid for UK meets. That wasn't true. Along with Sally Gunnell in the women's meets, Linford and I were the two biggest draws on the UK athletics scene. With Andy Norman sacked, Ian Stewart was organizing the commercial side of the Federation's UK meets, and he had agreed our fees. These were not amounts to be arguing over – this was serious money, and my fees were sorted.

The truth was that Sue Barrett and Linford had got into an argument with Ian Stewart about the fee, not for us, but for John Regis. Nuff Respect were asking for around £15,000 per race for John, and Ian Stewart wouldn't pay this. His attitude was that Linford (the Olympic champion) and I (the world champion and world record holder) were big draws to his meets. Our high fees were due reward for our achievements. But John had been unlucky. He was the best 200m runner in Europe, without question: he had won the European title in 1990, and at the 1993 World Championships in Stuttgart he won silver behind Frankie Fredericks of Namibia, with a fantastic new personal best of 19.94. In Sestriere in July 1994 he beat Fredericks and lowered his PB to 19.87, which should have set him up very nicely for the European Championships two weeks later, but unfortunately he got injured. He was out with an Achilles problem, which meant that he missed the Europeans, although he came back to get a silver in the Commonwealth Games.

Ian Stewart's view was that at that time (1995), for all John's previous achievements, he didn't have a current title and £15,000 a race was too high for the UK meets. The culture of Nuff Respect was to attack any problem head-on. Because John was one of our athletes, we all had to stand up for him. The argument was never resolved and no doubt it deepened because of the change-over from Andy Norman, who had looked after us so well, and because Peter Radford, the Federation's chief executive – not a man I had much respect for – was not one to compromise. As the meets drew nearer without a solution in sight for John's fees, it reached the point where we were refusing to run.

The bizarre thing was, I was injured anyway; I was still sick with this debilitating virus, so I couldn't run in most of the meets in any case. Out of five meets, I ran only in one that season. But the biggest UK meet was the Grand Prix in Crystal Palace in early July and we got ourselves into the position of saying we were boycotting it: Linford, John and I. That hit the newspapers. Crystal Palace was the key UK meet, and the television money was vital to the Federation, and here were the biggest names publicly boycotting it, which made the TV companies and sponsors shaky about their investments no doubt. So the row was not only embarrassing but potentially very damaging for the Federation.

Eventually we struck a deal of sorts. As a show of good faith, we agreed just to go to Crystal Palace, show our faces, talk to sponsors, as a gesture of goodwill to demonstrate there was no problem between us and the Federation. They agreed to pay us just for doing that: more than £5,000 just to turn up and do some PR, which shows what was at stake. So we went. We didn't run, but we went along, put in an appearance, went to the sponsors' tent and chatted and generally looked cheerful, to show there was no rift between the Federation and us.

Clearly, though, there was. The relationship had broken down over money and, with Linford and me on one side and Radford on the other, it was soured by a personality clash. The arguments rumbled on through the season, with the Federation (running into financial problems) on the one hand, and Nuff Respect (our stable of elite athletes) ranged against them on the other. 'A Family At War With Itself', ran one of the headlines, but with Peter Radford at the head of the table, it never felt like a family to me.

The AAA championships were in Birmingham in mid-July. I didn't have to run in them, but as they are the traditional British home meet, I decided to take part. My hamstring was constantly nagging and hurting me, and I was due to race in Padua, in Italy, the following day, so I had to be careful. I decided just to run in the 100m flat, and not risk any hurdles.

I qualified for the semi-final, but I tweaked my hamstring in the heat. It felt as if I was going to pull it, so I withdrew from the semi. Mark Zambada, my massage therapist, started to work on it, to keep it loose and make sure it suffered no further damage. No officials or anybody from the Federation came down to ask me why I'd pulled out, but as I left I did speak to one or two people. I told them my hamstring was dodgy, that I had tweaked it and wasn't sure when I'd run again. I even told Jim Rosenthal, who was covering the AAAs for ITV, that I didn't know when I would run again.

In the meantime I was in with the physio and Mark Zambada. 'Mark,' I said, 'I've got this race tomorrow: what do you think?' He told me to go over to Padua and do a long warm-up over there, with particular exercises that he set down for me to loosen the hamstring; and he told me how to check if it was at risk of pulling.

I was still far from certain that I was going to run. I said to Mark: 'Are you sure? Because we've got the World Championships coming up and I'm defending champion, so I want to be on the line then. I'm not risking it for this race.'

Mark was reassuring. 'Trust me. If you warm up as I'm setting it out for you, and you don't feel your hamstring, then you'll be OK.'

I flew out to Italy with Sue Barrett. The following day, before the race, I went through Mark's warm-up exercises. Normally for a circuit race like that I would warm up for about 40 minutes, but this was a good

Previous page A training session in Frankfurt before the Europa Cup, 1991. Linford Christie watches as John Regis helps me with stretching exercises.
Top Some words of wisdom from my long-time coach Malcolm Arnold in 1992.
Above The final at the Barcelona Olympics, 1992. I completed the race despite feeling on numerous occasions that the best idea would be to stop.
Opposite The moment of pure elation: Stuttgart World Championships. World record of 12.91 seconds. The legacy still remains.

Previous page Celebrating by throwing my vest to the crowd before my lap of honour. The extra weight of it would have killed me.

Above A lunge for the line wins me the gold in the World Championships in Seville, 1999.

Opposite The European Championships, Munich 2002. I am the only track athlete to win gold on four consecutive occasions.

Overleaf My third World Championship win. Holding the gold medal for photographers to capture my return to victory.

hour-and-a-half session, in sweltering heat, mostly leg-pulling exercises, to stretch the hamstrings and make sure they were loose. Then, gradually, I did some drive-outs from the blocks, building up the speed, driving through with some power. If my hamstrings were going to so much as tweak, I was pulling out of the race.

It was a hell of a long warm-up and it wasn't fun. I was cheesed off from running the day before, travelling and then doing this in the heat of an Italian July. On top of everything, I was tired. But, as ever, Mark's warm-up did the job. My hamstrings were intact – I'd done what I was told and I was in working order. I ran my race and beat a tasty field of athletes. Thank God for that. No worries: we picked up our money, headed for the airport and took the plane home.

When we got back, it was as if a violent storm had broken over our heads. Sue's phone was on fire, buzzing: what did we think of the furore? We didn't know what anybody was talking about. Then we read in the newspapers that Radford had said I had sold short the AAA, the sport and the fans by pulling out of the British meet, then running – apparently as fit as a fiddle – and beating a world-class field the following day. There was a clear suggestion that I hadn't been truly injured at the AAAs, and they were very happy to have it publicly known that my fee for the Padua meet was £25,000. The suggestion that I ran for money, but snubbed the domestic meets of British athletics, was outrageous and ridiculous. In fact, Radford showed no understanding of the needs and methods of modern athletics: I was preparing for the World Championships, but I'd been dogged by injury and illness. I needed to compete in the hurdles in Padua against a world-class field to continue my preparations, but I wasn't going to risk the hamstring in any race.

But Radford had the bit between his teeth and, with hindsight, I think he was looking to pay me back for the Crystal Palace row, which had embarrassed him. The British selectors had picked me for Gothenburg, provided I could prove my fitness. Next thing I knew, Peter Radford rebuked them publicly for selecting me and said disciplinary action should have been considered. Then he dragged me into the Federation offices in Birmingham for an hour-and-a-half lecture about how I'd let British athletics down, asking me how I could possibly run over hurdles the day after pulling out of the AAAs, saying: 'Don't palm me off with two-bit answers.'

I sat there and took it. Sue Barrett was there, but this wasn't her territory, and she didn't say much. I didn't say much either. I thought if Radford had some huge sense of importance that he had to express, he'd better get on and release it. But all the time I was thinking: for all the things I have done for this Federation, for British athletics, there isn't enough money you could possibly pay me in return. The work I had put in for years to reach the top, undergoing injury, operations, turmoil, and dedicating everything to track – not that I didn't want it for myself, but I didn't need anybody lecturing me about letting athletics down. My name helped to give kudos to their meets; they'd been selling TV rights and earning themselves sponsorship money off my back since 1987. Now it was 1995 and Radford was giving me a hard time for organizing my races as I needed to, in a year of injury and illness. Coming on top of everything else, this was really cheesing me off. I sat back, and he came at me: Professor Peter Radford, a one-time athlete who got a 100m bronze in the 1960 Olympics years before I was even born, previously head of PE at Glasgow University, lecturing me like the worst kind of schoolteacher. And all I had in my mind as I sat back in the chair in this dismal office was: this is absolute rubbish.

So, contrary to what his selectors had decided, Radford determined that I had to run in the Grand Prix in Sheffield, another UK Federation meet, on 23 July, to prove my fitness, or I would not be allowed to go to Gothenburg. Again, this was ridiculous. The World Championships began on 5 August, but the first heat in the 110m hurdles wasn't until 11 August, nearly three weeks after the Sheffield meet. So there was no logic, method or sound athletic thinking about me needing to race in Sheffield to prove my fitness for the World Championships. In fact, Sheffield could just as easily scupper me for Gothenburg: if it meant racing when I wasn't fit, it could put me out of the World Championships through injury.

I told Malcolm what was happening, but it was difficult for him because he was the Federation's head coach, and they employed him, so he was part of their establishment. He'd been caught up in it because he wasn't clear that I was racing in Padua, so when he was told, he seemed surprised – although his main emotion was to be pleased I'd won – and somehow that fuelled the idea that I wasn't playing straight with the Federation. I confided in Malcolm, told him the whole story. He knew that the last thing anybody could justifiably accuse me of was dishonesty, but I couldn't ask him to help really because of the position he was in, and anyway I'm not sure if there was anything he could have done.

A few days later I pulled my hamstring in training. That was it. Despite Radford's ultimatums, I couldn't run in Sheffield because I was injured. He stuck to his useless position that disqualified me from going to Gothenburg. and I had to pull out. So two years after the greatest achievement of my athletic life, I was being stopped from going to the World Championships to defend my own title. To drive home the injustice of it, by the time Gothenburg came around, I was as fit as a fiddle. I'd done all my preparations, my hamstring was fixed up, I was ready to run. And that really burned me.

Going over to Gothenburg, fit but not competing, was probably the lowest point of my career at the time. Frustrating isn't the word – it was maddening. While I was out there, I did a training session with Malcolm, and I was absolutely flying. Allen Johnson won the World Championship, taking my title away with a time of 13 dead. Tony Jarrett picked up the silver again, Roger Kingdom came in third. And I sat in the stand and burned. Then I left for a Grand Prix in Zurich and ran really quickly. I didn't win; I came second to Mark Crear, and Allen Johnson was third, but really it was a lightning-quick, even race and we all crossed the line with nothing between us.

That run demonstrated what I could have done in Gothenburg, which was both infuriating and heartbreaking. Pulling out of the Sheffield meet actually showed my commitment to the sport: I could have run and taken it easy, given the stakes Radford had raised. But instead I endured the pain of not being able to defend my title because I was professional enough to know that I wasn't fit. The press and public saw that, and Radford was humiliated again: I was injured, so what was he doing? Never had I had my integrity so questioned. To most people, the accusation that I had somehow faked an injury at the AAAs to take the money in Padua did not ring true. Certainly not those who knew me.

As for Radford, I had no respect at all for him then. He had destroyed my 1995 season for no reason. To me, he showed his complete ignorance of the demands and standards of modern athletics. The difference between modern track and athletics when he won his bronze medal in the distant past was huge; they were different worlds. Yet he didn't negotiate with me, he didn't listen, he lectured me. That's no way to go about handling anybody, but with me it was guaranteed to get my back up. To me, he had no clue about the sport and how it should be run at the top level, and I could never forgive him for wrecking 1995. After the break, I welcomed him to the preparations for 1996 by saying that I would boycott every Federation meet while Radford was in charge. Generally the press and public did not understand the roots of this argument; they thought it was about money, when it had nothing at all to do with that.

For the first time, the affair made me seriously question my involvement with Linford in Nuff Respect. Radford had handled me – us – appallingly, but equally I looked at how we (Sue, Linford, the company) had behaved and found plenty that was wrong there too. The Federation were our UK paymasters, selectors, organizers of the meets where we performed for our public. There would always be disagreements, but when I went over it in my mind, I felt this should never have escalated into such a huge battle.

We could have said: Colin is happy with his contract, but he's injured. I would have been quite happy telling the press what fee I was on – I never had a problem talking about figures. I used to say straight: this is how much we get paid, and it's this much because we've worked hard to become world-class athletes, and top people get the top dollars. If I'd been fit for Crystal Palace, I should have run. We could have made it clear that the issue was John. Or we could have made an issue of it, refused to run, but managed the PR better. We were injured after all. We could have kept it behind closed doors and negotiated. Instead, as with all things concerning Nuff Respect, we hit it head-on. Ultimately the Federation might have come out of it badly, but we did too, portrayed like a bunch of spoilt, greedy superstars.

The negotiation from Sue wasn't there and neither was the PR, which was the company's responsibility: managing our image. Then, when Radford issued his ultimatum and my world title was at risk, I was left to face it all myself. Linford was nowhere to be seen. He went to the World Championships, although he got injured in the final. But I didn't even go, as Radford's payback for a row I hadn't wanted and which had nothing to do with me. I got caught between other people's egos: Radford trying to win a war against a group of established athletes.

This kind of public war, with us painted as the aggressors, was very much not what I'd had in mind when I formed a company to represent my image. Everybody knows me as a laid-back character; I like having fun and being nice to people, and I've also learned that you get on better in business if you're liked. If people enjoy having you around, you'll be invited to meets; sponsors will want you associated with them. But Linford doesn't see life that way and everything is a battle. Derek Redmond famously said that Linford was a well-balanced guy – he had a chip on both shoulders – and this was a crack that Linford hated. But he himself admitted he was resentful, had fights he wanted to win with the media, the Federation, with everybody. Being together in Nuff Respect meant I had to adopt a similar attitude: we might disagree in private, but we had to stand together in public.

Linford's bull-in-a-china-shop attitude infected the company. From the beginning I'd go in there and hear how they talked to people on the phone and I felt it was all wrong. They were my agent, and I wanted them to project the right image for me, to be pleasant. Not to take any messing and to set clear standards, but be nice with it. If people don't like your agent, they're not going to bother to phone you. If they're dreading picking up the phone to ring your agent, you're not best placed to pull the deals in.

Instead, the attitude was: we're the best. If you want it, come and beg for it. People would phone up to ask for Linford or me to do something, and Sue would be really off-hand: 'Just send us a fax,' she'd say, and hang up. I used to wonder who it was, and think: that's not the right way to talk to people who are ringing to offer us work and money. Once I brought the subject up with her – how she was with people on the phone – and she said: 'Don't worry about it. People are going to hate me, not you. It's better that people should be upset with the agent than with the client.' That made sense of a sort, and I accepted it at the time.

After a while, though, I began to feel that Nuff Respect's image was wrong for me. I like to get on well with people, and in general people like me but now they couldn't get to me to see what sort of person I was. Sue was like a guard dog, rather than an enabler. Press interviews, for example, can run on for a while; you chat away and that's when the writers can get to know their subject, and when we can give out more considered thoughts, a bit more of ourselves. It never happened like that with Sue. She'd always be there calling time, saying we had to go. I felt that people couldn't get to me, and they were always on edge when they were with us, which was not the image of myself I wanted to portray.

We also started to lose a lot of staff. I found it puzzling; I'd go up to Nuff Respect every fortnight or more, shoot the breeze with everybody, maybe take them out for lunch, bring little presents – these people worked for me and I liked them. They seemed cool when I was there. But one by one they were trooping out of the company.

I thought at the time it wasn't right. We weren't paying them a fortune – perhaps £16,000–£17,000, as they were all young kids – but it seemed to me that it was a great job to have: working with me and Linford, travelling the world free of charge, going to track meets and celebrity dos and constantly meeting new people. I thought people would die to have this kind of job.

But I could never get a handle on why they were leaving because I wasn't there enough of the time, which was another problem. Cardiff was two and a half hours away, and I was still a full-time athlete who was supposed to be at the very top in his event. I couldn't be around to get involved in the office business – that was Sue's job.

Once, after a nice young girl had left, I asked her what the problem was because I happened to be in the office. She wouldn't tell me, she just said, 'Oh, don't worry. It's just not working out for me.'

Then Sue sat me down in a room upstairs, crying: 'Colin, am I a bad person? Am I a bad person?'

I just wanted everybody to get on and feel better. 'No,' I told her. 'Why would I think you're a bad person?'

At that stage I didn't know what was going on. Sue and I were still quite tight as friends. I'd always help her out if she needed anything. And I used to stay at her house if we had to be in London early for a meeting or a photo-shoot. She was needy, though. She used to say: 'You always do everything yourself, but Linford always makes me feel wanted.'

I just said that was me: I call you if I need something doing work-wise; I don't need to be calling you all the time. I'm self-sufficient; I spend time on my own, or hanging out, and I can look after myself. I don't need constant servicing.

Linford, on the other hand, was Mr Big; not only would he and Sue never come to Cardiff, but if we had a business meeting he wouldn't even meet us at the office, and we had to troop over to his house, which meant even more travelling for me. Whenever we were doing photoshoots there'd always be a problem. He'd be carping or complaining, making a meal of it, refusing to wear this or that. And I was always stressed, saying: 'Get on with it!' because I had a two-and-a-half-hour drive in front of me when it was finished.

At this stage I wasn't talking too much to my friends in Cardiff about things. They were just watching, seeing me change, I suppose, and become stressed and angry: getting into public rows, which was never my style. I think they were unsure what was happening. My parents were the same; they never said anything. Malcolm equally kept his thoughts to himself, but no doubt he was watching it all carefully, shaking his head. They'd all seen my fortunes sink, rapidly, from top of the world to outcast; I was constantly unhappy and barred from competing on the stage which had always been everything to me. But still, nobody realized it was going to get quite a lot worse before it got any better.

CHAPTER ELEVEN

ALAS FOR ATLANTA

The Games in Atlanta in 1996 were, realistically, my last chance to take an Olympic gold medal home for my father's glass cabinet, to decorate my career and silence any remaining doubters. The Games were early, too, starting in July, which made preparation trickier than usual. I had knee problems, as usual, so I had to consider whether to disrupt training by having an operation or risk the knee standing up to Olympic training and competition, and leave any serious medical attention until after the Games. In the winter of 1995 I tried to push aside my rising tide of problems and get down to training really hard to get in shape for the Olympics.

That renewed dedication scuppered me in itself. I still hadn't shaken off the virus I had picked up in the summer. My resistance must have been low and the training exhausted me. I was constantly tired, physically drained, and emotionally I could not dig myself out of a trough. It was probably the lowest point of my life in general. I was seriously struggling for motivation, felt I didn't want to do to much, was questioning why I was even still doing track, let alone trying to push myself for yet another massive challenge.

In this negative frame of mind, track wasn't fun any more. It had become a chore. For the first time in my life it became a grind. Malcolm was still in Birmingham and I wasn't spending enough time with him. I wasn't enjoying the people I was with, the company I was keeping; Sue and Linford and Nuff Respect were getting me down.

I brooded badly on the fact that I had fallen out with the Federation, with which I had always enjoyed good relationships. When drawn into a row, I'm not one to turn away. I had zero respect for Peter Radford, and had therefore made the decision that I was boycotting all the UK meets during the 1996 season while he was still in charge. But the role of lone rebel didn't hang well on me; I like to be liked, for things to be cool, pride myself on having loads of friends around, and I stewed on the belief that the whole row could have been avoided if we had handled it more diplomatically. I was worried that the Radford incident would make people change the affectionate way they thought of me. The idea that people could think I was a money grabber horrified me; I always felt I was overpaid anyway, although I was never embarrassed about it. But fighting over money was never my style.

It became a continuing saga, played out in the press: me criticizing the Federation; them replying, portraying me as if I thought I was too good for the UK meets, which really wasn't the case. I was dragged further into it; I felt it was damaging my years of working hard to become the fastest in the world, while always having a smile on my face.

All the while my knee was deteriorating. I'd do a training session in Cardiff, my leg would be absolutely killing me, and I would have negative, self-doubting thoughts I'd never had before: why are you doing this – what's it all for?

After training, I used to drive back home via the longest routes, not because I didn't want to go home, but to idle away some time. I'd go so many different ways, and just ponder over all the things that were bad: the row with the Federation; all the help I felt I wasn't getting, after all the things I'd done. Sulking and stewing, on and on.

I was now so lacking in motivation for athletics that I thought again about giving up. The main question was what I'd do instead. If I'd had the opportunities, in the media and elsewhere, which opened up for me towards the end of my career in 2003, I would probably have quit with relief in 1996.

Coaching Jamie Baulch was one of the brighter sparks in my life. It wasn't usual, really, for a senior athlete to be coaching a younger one, and quite a few people were telling me that I was coaching him to the detriment of my own career, spending time on Jamie that I should have been spending getting myself right. But he was so talented, and working so hard, and as I was injured, I enjoyed it and spent more energy on Jamie, developing his training and putting everything in place. He did tremendously well in 1996, and made huge progress, although he just missed out on qualifying for an Olympic place as an individual, and I was devastated for him.

I trained as hard as I could in the circumstances. I decided I hadn't time to have the knee operation and come back for the Olympics, so I would train and race through it, as I had for so long before that. During the season I missed quite a few races, but I trained extremely hard, and physically (apart from my knee) I was in good shape when the Olympics came round.

The real problem was in my head. I just didn't want to race; I couldn't be bothered. From the outside, it must be difficult to understand how an athlete can reach the Olympic Games with a chance of a medal and not be interested, especially somebody like me, who had lived his whole adult life for these great events. But that was me in Atlanta. I didn't see or appreciate the shape I was in, my potential for getting a medal, because I just didn't want to be there. There was pressure on me as the world record-holder and the memory of Barcelona constantly nagged; these were the last things I needed to feel, and the last place I wanted to be was at the Olympic Games. Far from gearing myself up for a last fling at gold, my attitude was all apathy: I've already lost in the Olympics, so what's the big issue if I lose another? All my emotions in the sport had left me; even my body seemed to have left me – this wasn't the same body I had run with in 1992. So far from being tense and sprung for the Olympics, I could quite easily have pulled out.

In Atlanta itself I didn't hang out much with the team, didn't get involved in the pranks and laughs and the holding court, which I had enjoyed so much in previous squads. I didn't hang out with Linford much at all; I was more than happy wandering around on my own. I didn't particularly need to be with anybody.

Looking back, I must have been in decent shape because I breezed into the final – I ran 13.30 in the heat, and 13.27 in the semi. In the final I tried at last to psych myself up into thinking I could perform well, but I was kidding myself. Deep down I knew I couldn't because I didn't want to, and in my frame of mind at the time there was no point anyway. I had zero care, no focus, no motivation, none of that overpowering sense of being a gladiator, of concentrating my whole being on the gun, exploding off it, hungering for the line. In the race itself I remember running down, not caring. As I reached hurdles four and five I thought: well, you know what? – I really don't give a flying monkey's whether I'm in this race at all. I'll just run down there and get it over with. So I did, took all the hurdles, came off the last one, flung my head down in a dip, looked across, and only then did I realize that I wasn't far from a medal.

Fourth: 13.19. Allen Johnson won it in 12.95, a new Olympic record. Mark Crear took silver in 13.09, and Florian Schwarthoff came in third with 13.17, two-hundredths ahead of me. Then I did have regrets: what did I think I was doing, running down without a care in the Olympic final? If I'd had just a hint of motivation, not even started better but just worked harder off hurdles eight, nine and ten, I would have picked up the bronze.

I finished my career with plenty of medals, but looking back, I threw lots of them away. In 1995 I hadn't even gone to the World Championships because of that stupid row I got myself embroiled in, and this was another medal I should have won quite easily. An Olympic medal, thrown away.

As I came off the track an official gave me my accreditation back and said, in a breezy tone: 'You were fourth? Well done, you!'

I was thinking: oh please, fourth! Don't you know I hold the world record? I'm devastated. Fourth is nothing to me.

But I didn't say anything – she was American, so you have to make allowances.

I took my accreditation and shuffled off for the bus to take us back to the warm-up track, then to the Olympic village. Only Malcolm and I were on it, sitting there in a puddle of silence. Eventually Malcolm looked at me: 'Well?'

I turned from staring out of the window and looked Malcolm in the eye: 'Well, what?'

'Well,' he repeated, 'where do we go from here?'

I knew what he was thinking. I was 29, I'd been at a low ebb for a couple of years and now we were trudging back from another defeat in an Olympic final. Was this it? Malcolm was asking. Is that you finished, son? At the time, it was difficult to foresee that I would last another seven years at the top, to imagine that I'd go on into my mid-thirties. It must have felt to Malcolm as if it was all over, and I could understand that.

Instinctively I shrugged my shoulders. 'Don't worry, Malcolm,' I shook my head. 'I ain't quitting now.'

He was very experienced. He knew, as an article of the coaching faith, that you don't try to pick over a defeat with an athlete when he's still dealing with the emotional aftermath. He was gentle really. He said I should take some time out, just go home, relax. 'When you're ready, you call me.'

Again, this was good advice. Annoyingly, Malcolm was right yet again. I hate the way he never says it, but looks at you and in his eyes you can see: I told you so. I could slap him. Anyway, that's just what I did – I took plenty of time off, more than I had done since starting out in track. I also bought my own home and moved out of the big house in Rhoose, leaving that to my parents. I bought a lovely new pad sitting right on the waterfront, looking across at Cardiff city centre, with the best of everything in terms of fittings and all my essential gadgets: TV, music, the best kitchen and coffee machine.

With hindsight, I can see that I was depressed. My life force, my emotions, my motivation were gone. I was dragged low with negative energy; I hadn't been myself for close on two years. If I were brasher, I would probably have checked myself into one of those clinics celebrities use when their lives hit the skids. I needed a radical rethink of my priorities, but being a private person I turned to my family and friends to help pick me up and put me back together.

Suzanne, my wise older sister, was around, having done very well herself and becoming a household name in *Brookside*. She'd become a Buddhist, and was full of her belief in the need for inner peace and calm. She had watched me slowly crumble from the peak – all smiles, on top of the world – to an angry young man, far too intense, brooding and unhappy. She was worried; I'd aged something chronic – even I could see that I'd aged more than a year between 1995 and 1996, because of all the pressure, hassle and difficulties.

She used to say: 'Come on, fix yourself up, boy. Fix yourself up. You have to make some decisions about the kind of person you want to be.'

She had this analogy, about some flowers in the middle of a roundabout. She said some people just drove by, or even over, them. Some might stop and look, and think they were nice. Only a few would appreciate the good things in life and have their priorities straight enough to go over and smell the flowers. Me, I'd been trampling right over them, and I had to come back to myself and appreciate my life, count my blessings.

I'd become friendly with David James, the goalkeeper who was by then playing for Liverpool, and his wife Tanya. After the Olympics I spent a lot of time staying with them, kind of like an invalid recuperating. They were great – they gave me so much space, and the pressure fell away from me. Most of the time I was just having a laugh, playing Playstation all day and night, with their kids clambering all over me, or babysitting for them. It was fun. Their house was set in grounds of around ten acres, there was a pond and a swimming pool, and it was lovely. You could get lost in the gardens, wandering around, emptying your head – just being. There were no targets, no imperative to perform: I could get up at eleven o'clock, pad around in my pyjamas all day, do what I liked. Talk, if I wanted, or sit quietly.

I did talk things over with them, a lot; they could see the turmoil I had been through. David made a huge impression on me. He was having a nightmare of his own in the full glare of the tabloid back pages. He'd had a few bad games for Liverpool, including against Manchester United, and they'd lost out in the Premier League title. The abuse heaped on him was deadly; he had the derisory name of Calamity James slapped on his head across the mass-market papers.

Yet he was so cool. He used to say: 'I know I'm going to get killed in the papers tomorrow, but do you know what? I'm not going to read them. We just won't buy a paper. Maybe we won't even leave the house at all today.'

He'd continue: 'I know I try my best. I'm not going to argue with anybody, I'm not going to hit back, I'm not going to be bitter. I try my best and it'll come right.'

After being so close to Linford, and being infected by his constant urge for a battle over the smallest slight, I recognized in David an attitude that was much healthier. His problems were huge; playing for one of the biggest football clubs in the country made our press coverage look tiny. Linford used to moan if the athletics press said he had a bad start; he'd say they were picking on him, and I'd have to pick him up and sympathize. David was being absolutely slaughtered across the national papers every day. But hanging out with him, I thought: if he can cope with criticism and keep his head, stay so balanced, under a spotlight with this much heat, it is a lesson to me in my world.

They listened to my troubles, and they said I had to change what was negative. Tanya used to say: 'We want you happy, Colin. We want our happy Colin back. You have to sort out whatever it is that is making you unhappy. It isn't right for you.'

My family were the same. They'd always seen me relish my life in track, and they used to tell me the same thing: you have to enjoy it again.

I began to think through many things that were fundamental to me and my life. I started to appreciate again some of the blessings I've had: my parents, my start in life, Malcolm, Wales, Cardiff. I came to see how wonderful Cardiff was, with facilities on hand almost placed there on purpose to help me to fulfil my potential. The years of kicking against it were coming to an end. I realized: what I've resented actually made me. Now, when I talk about Cardiff and why I have stayed, you would think I was employed by the Welsh Tourist Board. I appreciate it all: the mountains and beaches are half an hour away; the city itself has everything and is entering a new era now with the Welsh Assembly, the Millennium Stadium and so much development. I realized in a more mature way the huge advantages that fate had provided for me, with the stability and support I'd had from my family, from Malcolm and from the athletics facilities.

I compare myself to Dalton Grant, somebody I feel I have so much in common with that he is a soulmate. In London he didn't have such a good deal of the cards. Athletes struggle to find a coach they like, a decent training group, and facilities in London are all over the place; if it doesn't happen early, making it can be a difficult fight. Dalton had great talent and dedication; he was British champion for years and came fourth in the 1991 World Championships in Tokyo, but he was often battling just to sort out the basics. It becomes a spiral, too: if you are at the top and making money, then you can afford the best treatment when you have an injury; if not, you might come back before you are quite ready, your form suffers, you can have another injury, and so it goes on. Dalton had knee problems and he couldn't have the best treatment as I did. I envy him his free spirit, but I began then to see how vital my upbringing, city and environment had been. If the cookies had crumbled differently for us, Dalton could have been the world champion and I might have been like him: all the talent, but so many struggles just to compete.

In this more mature frame of mind I came to see what was important to me, and I relaxed, took some deep breaths and appreciated just who was valuable around me. I began to understand that I had to make more of the positives and strip out the negatives. At the end of 1996 I went back to Malcolm, and told him I wanted to return to track for another go with full commitment, that I wanted our former close relationship back. I'd been thinking plenty about Linford and Nuff Respect. I could see now that it was a huge distraction. The hassle and problems of being involved in any big company just weren't for me.

At the end of the year we went warm-weather training in Australia, and it was the same over there: non-stop moaning about everything – they're paying for all the petrol; Linford's buying all the food; the other people in the apartments; on and on, complaining all the time.

Linford had also had a nightmare time in Atlanta: disqualified in the final after two false starts. After that he pretty much retired; he was going to concentrate on Nuff Respect and on coaching a group of athletes, 'Team Linford'. But still he had to be in the lead in everything. Even when we were training, while I was still in serious preparation, Linford had to be in front. I used to say to him: 'You're retired! I'm damned if I'm staying behind you doing a training session. If I do that, I might as well retire.' It didn't make any sense. Even in Nuff Respect's literature, Linford was still down as an athlete. I argued, although as usual I was outvoted. To me, it was like putting Roger Bannister down as an athlete. When you're retired, that's it. But that was Linford.

He and I had been like brothers. We'd trained together and achieved so much. I'd looked up to him as a role model and admired him as an athlete – I still do – and we'd both loved being the merry pranksters in the squads in championships. But it had all soured so badly. With Linford, it was like when you are in love, and you're so overwhelmed that you think somebody is perfect, then you fall out of love and suddenly you see the real person, see their darkness.

I mulled it all over for a long time and finally decided I had to get out of Nuff Respect completely. It was a big decision to start again, but I realized I had to strip it out of my life, get rid of that negativity. I'd have to get an agent, like other athletes; let somebody else look after my affairs, leaving me free to concentrate on rebuilding my life and career on the track. I went to see Malcolm. I told him some of what had gone on, how Nuff Respect wasn't me any more, that I'd always been outvoted and marginalized in the company anyway. Although we hadn't ever discussed it, none of it seemed to come as much of a surprise to him.

Then I told him I'd decided to leave. He looked up and his face hardly moved. Deadpan, he said: 'Well,' then his face broke into the broadest smile. 'That's the best news I've heard all year.'

CHAPTER TWELVE
THE RENAISSANCE BOY

It was a big year to think about making a comeback. Lying ahead, on 1 August 1997, were the World Championships. My knee was still giving me hell, but again I decided not to have an operation, because the rehab would take too much time out of preparation. After three healing months taking stock of my life, and the trip to Australia that sealed my decision about Nuff Respect, I came back to train closely again with Malcolm.

He asked me when I was planning to leave Nuff Respect, or planning to announce it, because it would obviously hit the press when I did. I said: 'Not until after the World Championships. We don't want any more distractions. Basically, we want no more crap. We have to focus on preparing for the Worlds because I'm coming back then, as myself. After that, I'll tell them.'

I didn't call or talk to Linford and Sue about my decision, but in my own mind I'd made it. After that, my head was clear again. My spirit was free. I was very detached all year, just let all the hassle wash over me. At the age of 30 there I was, with Malcolm, concentrating on hurdling again. We went back to training, working together on the preparation schedule Malcolm had refined to a near-exact science, and the unsparing attention to my technique. I felt the motivation flood back – my head was right again. Now I just had to work on my body and my performance, but I knew I could make it back to the top.

Everything that happened with Linford or Sue after that just confirmed that my decision was right. Jamie Baulch was the first little problem. I was still organizing Jamie's training, coaching him, and his progress was superb. Although he had missed out on running as an individual in Atlanta, he'd won a silver in the 4x400m relay. My long-term goal for Jamie was 2000; I used to tell him he'd absolutely fly by then if he kept to the schedule. He'd be 27: perfect, physically strong and mature, he'd be racing really well and could have a great chance in the Olympics in Sydney.

I worked with Jamie on all his preparation for the indoor season of 1997, including getting in shape for the World Indoor Championships on the Paris Bercy track at the beginning of March. I wanted the best for him, so I'd paid for him to go to Australia with us. He was doing really well; he set a personal best for 60m, for 200m indoors and a new British record for 400m. In Lausanne, in Olympic year, he'd run 44.57 in the 400m, which was really an incredible PB, an awesome base.

In the World Indoors, I gave a little signal that I intended to be back in 1997 – I won the silver medal in the 60m hurdles. I ran 7.49, pretty quick, just one-hundredth behind Anier Garcia, the enormous Cuban who had a nice present of a gold medal for his 21st birthday. Jamie did exceptionally well too, winning the silver medal in the 400m, and we were all thrilled with that.

We returned to Cardiff and were due to start outdoor training, so I told Jamie to have himself two weeks off, then come back and we'd start strongly. I lent him my car; he was a young lad, still only 23, who'd like a spot of hot-rodding, so he went all over the city showing himself off in one of my cars.

When the two weeks were up, I was in the gym at the national sports centre in Cardiff, with Ian Mackie, a Scottish sprinter. Jamie came bouncing in.

'Hi Jamie,' I said. 'Here's your training for the next four weeks.'

He gave me a sheepish glance: 'Linford's already given me a schedule,' he said, and turned on his heels and walked out again.

I looked at Ian Mackie, he looked back at me and I shrugged. If Ian hadn't been sitting there, I might not have believed what had just happened. He was stunned. 'Right,' he said eventually, 'I guess Linford's coaching Jamie now.' I just shrugged. 'I guess he is.'

So Linford had gone behind my back and told Jamie he'd coach him, and Jamie – kid that he was – was probably more impressed with the great Linford Christie than with what I was giving him. Fine. Linford and Sue took complete commercial control of Jamie (which I hadn't wanted to happen either) from the beginning. But if Jamie thought Linford was the man, that was up to him. It was the last association I had with Jamie, and personally I think he has under-performed mostly since then, compared to what he could have been capable of. The PB he set in Lausanne when he was 23 is still his personal best outdoors today. Indoors he's done better, but I think he could have done more than he has.

As for Nuff Respect, I didn't want anything more to do with them. I started to have almost no contact; I'd never ring in, except to take my race schedule from Sue and leave it at that. There was no conversation or contact about any of the wider activities of the company. In the early years Sue used to call me all the time, but now she wasn't calling me at all. Eventually, she started telling one of the other girls, Becky Molloy, to call me, because she saw I had no interest in her whatsoever. Becky and I were always friendly in the office, laughing and joking, so she used to call to give me my races and other information I needed about sponsors and so on. We got on really well – as, in my opinion, an agent should with an athlete, client or anybody really.

In March I did an advertising campaign for the watch company Tag Heuer, which had been sponsoring me for some time. They sent the great American photographer Herb Ritts to do the shoot in Miami, and it became famous for the way he displayed my body, including some ultra-stylish naked shots. Working with him was a huge insight to me. He was a superstar, one of the most renowned photographers in the world, yet he was incredibly humble. There was not an ounce of arrogance in him and he was completely focused on me, on making sure I was comfortable.

Ritts was saying: 'You know, any time you're uncomfortable, it stops. If you want anybody gone, they can all go. It can be just me and you here, if you want; it's totally up to you. Remember: at any stage you're in charge. Nothing's a problem, you just take your time and say if you want a break.'

It was so different from the prevalent attitude that I was used to, that because you had achieved something, you had to demand respect of everybody else. Herb Ritts was concentrating on me, on his client, not on his own self-image. He was very inspirational and he opened my eyes to the way I wanted to be.

Back home I stayed increasingly in Cardiff, where I needed to be, working hard with Malcolm, like the old days. Now that I had my own place Sam moved back in. Everything was hunky-dory.

I can't say it was going fabulously well on the track; it was a hard road back when I had major problems in both knees and was overdue an operation by about a year. Then I got tonsillitis. Nice! Just what I needed. My tonsils had to come out really, but I couldn't risk going into hospital when I needed to prepare for the World Championships. I was on antibiotics for some of the time, but they're no good to athletes, because they knock the living daylights of you and wear down your immune system. My body was a long way from perfect, but my mind was still clear, and I knew what I was going to do.

I was ranked nowhere really (ninth in the world) and nobody expected me to come back and do anything in Athens. I didn't even win the UK championships – Tony Jarrett beat me. The fastest I ran all season was 13.26. With all this, I told one or two people: I'm coming back to run 13.05 in Athens. That's it. If somebody runs faster, they beat me. If not, I win. But that's what I'm going to run, dead-on: 13.05. I'm not sure if anybody believed I could do it. I'm sure Malcolm certainly had major doubts.

Linford managed to cheese me off again in the run-up. Nuff Respect had decided to promote the Welsh Games in 1997, and I ended up doing quite a bit of the running around and organizing. Things were strained with Sue, but we were talking. Then, with a couple of days to go, she said: 'Have you asked Linford if he's running?'

'Asked Linford if he's running what?'

'If he's running in the Welsh Games?'

I was just bemused. I said: 'It's his company that's promoting it. I presume he's running, because it doesn't make much sense not to turn up to a meet your own company is putting on.'

She said: 'Oh, I don't think he'll run unless you ask him.'

I was not going to plead with Linford to lower himself to take part in something that was actually taking place for the benefit of his own company. The Welsh Games came round and Linford wasn't there. He ran in a meet in Hengelo, Holland, on the same day; I don't know why. People asked me where he was and I didn't make excuses. I told them straight: he's in Hengelo. They'd read the result the next day anyway.

But, at the time, I really didn't care about all this constant game playing and I was too busy concentrating on Athens. In July, with the championships close, I went up to Birmingham to train with Malcolm for a while, and stayed with him and his wife Madelyn.

One day I was out doing some drills on the Birmingham University track. Malcolm was in the middle of the pitch on his mobile phone. I hit the second hurdle, fell, crunched on to the tarmac and seemed to slide along for ages, nearly into the third hurdle. My skin was burned raw right down my shoulder and along my thigh. I looked up in agony; Malcolm seemed not to have seen it. I thought: lovely – I've just nearly crippled myself and there's you, merrily nattering away on your mobile.

I picked myself up and thought: Lord have mercy, how many more tests do you want to send me, to prove that I'm strong? We went back to Malcolm's house and Madelyn was there, and I walked in and moaned:

'Oh Mad, I've fallen.'

She said: 'You've what? Oh God, no!'

She had a look at my shoulder. It was horrible – gory. I had to keep it moving. I couldn't let it dry because once it dried, it would tighten and then rip when I was hurdling, so I was constantly working it, injuring it really, deliberately cracking it so that it would expand and all the while I was waiting for it to get a little bit better. Hurdling is repetitive, so a big worry was that if I fell again, I would land on exactly the same place and then I'd be really gone.

I had to have four days off training before we went for final preparations in Nice. It went fine and I was in decent shape, but I really think Malcolm was with everybody else in not expecting me to do much: how could I, realistically, given everything I was contending with? Far from being in contention for a medal, the reality was that I was in danger of not even making the final, for the first time in 12 long years since I sat, gutted, in the stand at the 1985 European Indoor Championships, vowing that it would never again happen to me. Ranked ninth in the world, and with only eight lanes, if I was drawn in the wrong semi-final, I could come in fifth and not make it. If that happened, I didn't see how I could honestly carry on in track; it would be the end.

In Athens I announced myself in the first round, winning my heat in 13.19, beating Mark Crear of the US into second. The semi, the following day, I won again, beating Allen Johnson of the US, although I ran slower (13.24) easing up a little at the end to qualify.

Before the final I was truly nervous. Here I was on the big stage, facing a single race that would decide whether I was going to be there at the top or pack it all in. The night before, Becky from the office phoned me to say good luck but neither Sue nor Linford bothered to ring. I went through my usual routines and got some sleep eventually. The following day the race was in the evening. I spent the day trying to think about what I was going to be doing, trying to focus all my nerves and energy positively, not fritter my time away worrying.

It was only when I got to the warm-up area that I started to really think about my tactics. In athletics, you enter the arena on your own. Any decision you make is yours alone. That was my reason, as a teenager, for choosing track over any other sport; it is how I like it – the sole personal responsibility – although it can bring incredible pressure with it. There is nobody to depend on, no hiding place on the track. You have your lane, and you have to make your decision about how you are going to run a race, and stay with it. In high hurdles you can't change your mind. The race is too quick and too technical, and you have seven other big guys thundering down that track alongside you.

I wanted so much to win this one, to blast them all away. To make my comeback and tell the world Colin Jackson was here again, at the top of his form. To wipe out all the negatives and the hassles and arguments, which had laid me low for the past couple of years. But it was a big challenge against Allen Johnson, the defending world and Olympic champion, the favourite, and against the other best hurdlers in the world who had been picking up their medals while I'd been on my personal journey to the depths. Perhaps, I reasoned, this was one I should play safe. The most important thing was to leave with a World Championship medal; that would place me back in world class. It wasn't vital for it to be gold. And if I went all out for gold and really let rip, then I risked hitting a hurdle and ending up with nothing. You're out on a limb if you really commit yourself; you want to be at your absolute peak to take that chance.

It was the only race in my whole time in track about which, as late as the warm-up area, I was still undecided. Going for gold was so tempting and was what I really felt like doing, to blow the demons away. Eventually I decided against it. I thought: play this one safe, son. Make sure you collect the silver, and take that medal home. Do what you can do; you know yourself you can run 13.05 – stick with that. Don't try to be a hero and put everything in danger.

As I was about to go, Malcolm, his usual emotional self, said: 'Have a good one.' I was like: is that all you can say, Malcolm? I'm going out there to put my whole life on the line again, and that's all you can come out with? I started to go back; my mind still wasn't made up, and I very nearly turned round to run it past him, ask him what I should do. I think, looking back, that if I had, I wouldn't have run the race at all. My mental preparation would have been completely spiked and I'd have been gone. It was lucky that Malcolm had left. I stayed with my plan, repeating it to myself: play safe.

We went out there, out on the line. I was so nervous because it was so important, in its way the most significant race of my life. The gun went, and Allen got out before me. He had a much better start because he had a more powerful push; my knees were dodgy, so I couldn't push anywhere near as strongly or as powerfully as I wanted to. Allen was in front, but I was second and about halfway through, hurdle four or five, I started coming back at him. For a second I thought – and this goes through your mind during a race, even one that lasts only 13 seconds, for so much goes on in your mind – I could run him down. I could have him here.

Then – I stuck to my plan. You need control; perhaps this was the experience of Barcelona 1992 breathing in me. If I had gone for Allen, I would have had to really attack the barriers, and I might have made a mistake. I hadn't run anywhere near this fast all year, it was a blind experience and the risks of failing were greater than the extra reward if it all came off. So I thought: leave it there. Back off; just stay there, tucked in with the champion.

Allen went on and finished ahead of me. I was second coming off the tenth hurdle, blasted for the line and made my dip. Thank Jesus for that! I looked up at the clock and saw Allen's time: 12.93. And I thought: Christ, I've run pretty quickly here. Then I saw mine and I smiled deep, deep within myself: 13.05. You star!

I know now that my mother, back home in Cardiff, and Madelyn Arnold at her house, watched the race and afterwards they said: 'That's exactly what he said he was going to race.' I had done it, to the hundredth, and I was so, so pleased and relieved. I was back. I'd proved it to other people, but most of all I had stripped away from my life and mind all the clutter that had been pulling me back. I had concentrated again and come back, proved it to myself: I could still perform.

Running round the track afterwards, it was so funny. I think I had more congratulations than Allen, the winner. Everybody had seen me struggling since the heights of 1994, and people seemed so pleased for me to have won the silver. All the agents and coaches, everybody you see round the circuit, were coming up and congratulating me, shaking their heads. 'How did you do that?'

Malcolm was out there, really pleased for me, for both of us – kind of big-chested, pushing himself out and then, pleased as punch, doing his humble routine. 'Yeah,' he was telling people, 'we just had to sort a few little things out and then we knew we'd be back.'

Afterwards we went to the victory ceremony room. Sue and Linford were there in the crowd, thumbs up, big smiles, thinking: fantastic, we've got a medallist in Nuff Respect; we've got a little bit of kudos again, because Colin's just won a silver medal. I was looking back at them, giving them a bit of a smile and thinking: I don't know what you lot are so pleased about because, trust me, this time tomorrow you ain't going to be so happy. I was chatting away to people, top-of-the-world really. The medal ceremony went well, and I was gone, straight out with Malcolm.

My phone was humming – as it always is anyway; sometimes I feel my whole life has turned into a text message. But after a race, it's non-stop. From Sue and Linford: nothing. No congratulations, nothing, not a call. But that was cool; I wasn't expecting it, and from the following day I was going to have nothing to do with them any more.

Instead, I invited Becky out for dinner, and another guy from Nuff Respect who was out in Athens, Will Lloyd. I told them straight away in the restaurant: 'I'm leaving Nuff Respect.'

They were stunned. 'No way!'

'Yeah,' I said, 'that's it. I'm cutting all ties. I'm leaving.'

Their jaws had dropped. It was a world of its own, as all companies are to some extent, I suppose. It must have been quite shocking to them to hear that one of the partners and the senior athlete was just going to up and leave.

'When are you going to tell Sue and Linford?' they asked.

'When I see them,' I answered.

But I didn't see them that night and they didn't call, so I didn't tell them. I didn't see too much wrong with telling Will and Becky; staff are always told, so why wouldn't I tell them first? They were the first two I saw from the company and it was good that they should know. I wasn't too worried about it; I'd made the decision so long ago, although perhaps I was savouring the taste a little.

We were all staying at the Holiday Inn with the people from Puma. I knew the word would have got back to them, but decided that when I saw Sue and Linford, I'd tell them. Malcolm, being the cruel swine he is, wanted me in doing weight training at about eleven o'clock the following morning. I'd just won the silver medal and I couldn't even walk properly because my knees were killing me, and he'd got me up on the next day weight training. Typical Malcolm.

In the end, I left a message for Sue and Linford just before starting to train, then I phoned Carmen and said: 'Right, I've told them.'

'Already?' She was surprised.

'Yeah, why not?'

'I didn't think you'd have the bottle.'

I said: 'Girl, when I've made my mind up, it's got to be done. No hiding.'

I did my weight training, then came back and sat down with the Puma group. They were my main sponsors, so it was important that I told them I was planning to leave. I was presuming that because Puma worked so much with Nuff Respect, they wouldn't want to be associated with me any more.

That was when I began to discover what people really thought of the company – it became clear to me how Sue and Linford were being viewed by people who had to deal with them: my friends, family and staff. Pascal Rolling of Puma told me I had it all wrong. He said: 'When you leave Nuff Respect, you'll have more friends than you think. You don't need to leave us. Puma will be much more helpful to you. Trust me on this one.'

I felt quite reassured, having Puma under my belt as a sponsor already, now that I was out on my own. After that meeting I finally ran into Linford and Sue. They still hadn't called me the whole time. Now here they were, the two of them.

Sue said: 'Have you got something to tell us, love?'

I went: 'Yeah, I'm leaving. '

She said: 'Why?'

I didn't have the time for it and this wasn't the place. I said: 'Do you know what? I'm just leaving. It's not working for me. It's not going the way I want it, so I'm leaving.'

'And there's nothing we can say or do to change your mind?'

'No, I'm leaving. End of story.'

'Seriously?'

'Seriously. It's just not for me any more.'

That was it. They were quite cool. In my mind I had no real animosity towards them and didn't want any bitterness. I was only leaving the company because it wasn't right for me any more as the commercial image and presence of the athlete Colin Jackson. I wasn't telling them that I didn't want them as buddies any more, and I didn't feel at that stage that it had to be that way. I wanted peace, that was all.

Then I saw Malcolm. 'I've just run into them and I've told them,' I said.

He raised his eyebrows. 'How were they?'

'Cool,' I said, 'no problem. They were really cool, so cool it shocked me.'

Malcolm said nothing, just gave a doubtful: 'Hmm', as if to say: we'll see. And he walked off up to his room. He was still head coach of British athletics, and at the World Championships there was plenty for him to do and think about. It's a fraught time for a head coach and the kind of man Malcolm is, he wants no distractions.

Within minutes Linford had piled upstairs and gone bursting into his room. He just bowled in there and started absolutely laying into Malcolm. Malcolm has never told me the details of what he came out with; he can't remember them, but Linford was there for half an hour, absolutely caning him. Ranting and raving, eyeballing him, effing and blinding. He called him a 'fucking cunt' – that much Malcolm can remember.

'Weren't you frightened?' I asked him afterwards. Linford is a big guy, aggressive, not at all averse to throwing his weight around, and he does frighten people. 'Frightened of what?' Malcolm said. That was right, because Linford might be a big bad-tempered guy, but he's mostly bark and no bite. He's like a Jack Russell – yap yap yap – but give him a slap and he backs off.

Malcolm said that he barely got a word in, just asked Linford what he was on about. It seemed Linford had decided that Malcolm was to blame for me leaving the company, that he had put the idea into my mind, which was simply not true. Linford had watched me work more closely with Malcolm since the end of 1996, drift away from him and Sue, then produce the silver and tell them I was leaving, and he decided Malcolm was behind it.

As quickly as he'd come, Linford was gone again. Malcolm was bewildered, dazed, but he had a major job in the real world to be getting on with. He had had many problems to deal with as head coach in Athens, a busy week, and he was exhausted. Twenty minutes later Linford was back, starting all over again, bowling into Malcolm, ranting and raving: how Malcolm was trying to ruin everything, how he'd been against the company from the start, on and on.

So Malcolm tried to put Linford straight a little bit. Reminded him, as he puts it, that he was very lucky to have met Malcolm and me when he did, in 1987, and to have slotted into our training group and prepared for championships with us and Mark McKoy. He'd been, as Malcolm said, only too happy to join us and benefit from what we gave him: proper training, real coaching before championships.

If Linford had tried all this with me, I'd have been more direct. I'd have told him: before he met us he was nothing. If you want to work out when Linford spent time with us, just look at when he was good. Whenever he was good, he was working with us. His gold in 1992, his gold in Stuttgart the year after? Working with us. We taught him how to weight-train, the method and science that's in it. We taught him how to start. We taught him how to run. Every time we were going to a championships, Linford was always there with us, because we knew how to finish preparation, how to go into a championships sharp. At those times his coach, Ron Roddan, seemed to do nothing, just carry the starting machine and read out how fast we did 30m and 40m drills.

Malcolm gently reminded Linford of some of the contributions he'd made to Linford's success. In reply Linford, raging, said: 'Yes, and I've acknowledged that. I gave you a mention in my autobiography.'

That was it for Malcolm, and he's had no time for Linford since. He admired him hugely as an athlete; Linford was a great athlete, and the dedication he put into reaching the top at his comparatively grand age was awesome. But as a person, he's lacking a lot. Malcolm doesn't suffer fools; he's sad about Linford, because he worked so closely with him and was a good friend, but as Malcolm said: 'If somebody tells you that's what they think of you – that you're nothing, you're there to be abused and anyway you've got a mention in their book – well, there's no point continuing any relationship with them.'

I said to Malcolm: 'What was he having a go at you for? Why isn't he coming at me?'

Malcolm said: 'Well, he wouldn't, would he?'

That was true. I knew Linford inside out. I knew his life; I'd lived with him, knew everything about him. The good, and anything he might consider to be bad. So he wouldn't have a go at me, for there was too much between us, and he took it all out on poor old Malcolm, up there in his room when he was probably wanting to take 20 minutes out with a cup of tea and a copy of *Motor Racing News*.

I didn't see Linford and Sue again in Athens. I had my silver, had made my comeback and people were still buzzing round me. Then the word seeped out that I'd left Nuff Respect, and plenty of people seemed to be pretty pleased about it. The agents started touting round me, asking who was going to be representing me. But I was in no hurry.

I ran into Linford and Sue next a few weeks later at one of the end-of-season meets, the Grand Prix in Zurich. Sue asked if we could all have a meeting one evening in my hotel room, which we did. Linford asked me why I was leaving. I didn't want to have it all out; there was no point. If they really couldn't see what had gone wrong, and all the things that had happened since 1996, then that summed up what the problem was. I just wanted to move on.

'I've changed,' I said. 'The way it works isn't what I want, and I've just got to move on.'

Sue was chirping away in the background, asking me when I was going to tell them and trying to complain to me, so in the end I slapped her down: 'I don't have to tell you anything. You can shut your mouth. You work for me, that's it.'

She burst into tears then – shocked, but brought up short by reality. She was an employee and I was leaving, a decision that was beyond her. Then she said: 'Is it me? If it is, I'll leave, and you and Linford can stay.'

That was a fair gesture by Sue, who didn't want to feel she'd come between Linford and me. I sighed: 'Yes,' I nodded, 'it's partly you, but it's more than that. It's the whole environment.'

Then they started saying some strange things. 'You'll find out,' Sue said. 'You'll realize we're your true friends.'

'If you ever wanted anything from me,' Linford piped up, 'I'd still give it to you.'

'And so you should,' I said. 'Because I made you. You have to realize that.' He had no answer.

I left it there. I didn't want a huge argument, and it isn't me anyway. Linford knew that. I keep things inside – perhaps too much – and I make my own decisions. When they're made, that's it. No amount of talking was going to change the outcome – and they knew, in their hearts, what all the problems had been. They were just shocked that in the end I had the balls to stand up to them and leave. And they were doubly gutted because I had made my comeback and, with Linford retired, I was by a long way the most marketable asset they had.

Of course it hit the press. Everybody thought there must have been an argument, that Linford and I must have clashed, but we didn't. There wasn't one thing: it was the whole environment. I changed, and it wasn't right any more. I walked because it was time.

A couple of weeks later a letter dropped through the door with Malcolm's writing on the envelope. I thought: what's Malcolm writing me a letter for? He's never written to me in his life.

I opened it. It was on headed paper from the British Athletic Federation:

Dear Colin,
Just a quick, official note, to congratulate you on your fine performance in Athens. I don't know where your performance came from, or in fact where it's gone since, but it was an outstanding performance and one which brought back big memories!

Now that your life seems to be sorting itself out quite nicely for the future, I'm sure that we can recreate the greatness of 1992, '93 and '94, it just needs a bit more application from your good self before this happens.

As ever, you can count on my help to take you to places that you want to go to.

Where you actually end up is down to you!
Best wishes
Malcolm Arnold, Performance Director

I have to admit I giggled. I just thought it was so funny. He'd never written me a letter ever, and for Malcolm to sit down and do that I thought I must really have rocked him. He must have thought: Christ, that boy's done well. To me, the letter was saying: 'Not much shocks me, I'm Malcolm Arnold, Mr Imperturbable, but boy, you've shocked me now.' It was a really nice letter – my father's got it safe and sound in one of his huge piles of scrapbooks.

Malcolm hadn't believed that I'd do it in Athens. He thought I was just rabbiting on about running 13.05; never thought it was realistic. And although Linford was totally wrong that Malcolm had led me to leave Nuff Respect (he'd kept his thoughts to himself), nevertheless Malcolm had been exasperated, watching me waste time on that rubbish and seeing my performances decline from the heights of 1992–4. The row with the Federation just wasn't something the Colin Jackson that Malcolm knew would have done. Malcolm himself had felt some coach burn-out from the frustration of seeing me go the wrong way and being able to do nothing about it. And he was, as he admits, 'truly amazed, shocked' that I'd gone out there and run 13.05. He could see that I'd knuckled down and rehabilitated myself and that, even though I was now 30, there was plenty more we could do together.

In the gloom after Atlanta he'd asked me: 'Where do we go from here?' Now he had his answer: back to work. Malcolm too had made a decision, to renew his own career. Having finally managed to bring National Lottery funding to underpin the Federation's battered finances, he'd taken stock, realized he was fed up with committees and bureaucracy and wanted to get back to what he truly enjoys: working with athletes. He'd been offered a coaching job at the University of Bath, where the director of sports development, Ged Roddy, was bringing in noted coaches and performers to spearhead his ambition to become part of the English Institute of Sport. Malcolm had thought about it, then agreed to go, from January 1998.

Everything that had happened in 1997, and the rich potential of the move to Bath, motivated me to go on, to give track another big effort. Had I failed in Athens, it could have been the end, which would have been no way to go out. Instead, the World Championships offered us a great springboard for a fresh start on the road back. I must have felt inspired, because I even went and finally had my knee operations.

Previous page With Linford in 1994.
Left On a visit to Universal Studios, California. Suzanne and I meet Frankenstein.
Below Linford with my grandparents in Florida in 1995.
Bottom Neck and neck with Ross Baillie (second left) at The Lynx Indoor Championships in Birmingham, 1999. I'm on the right of the picture.

Left My family are very important to me. This recent picture shows my nephew Paris with doting Mum, grandparents and uncle Colin.
Below With my brother Gerry in a restaurant in Cardiff. He'd come over from LA to celebrate our father's sixtieth birthday.
Bottom With training partner Paul Gray, when we visited the local track on a trip to Soweto in 1996.

Opposite Leaning against a 'convenient' hurdle, I pose outside the palace after receiving my MBE in 1990.

Top left With my sister Suzanne at Cardiff Castle, receiving my OBE.

Top right Sam holding her Commonwealth Games bronze medal, Victoria, 1994.

Above At the Palace again – receiving an award from the Duke of Edinburgh, the patron of British Athletics. In the background, Peter Radford.

Top At the end of my career, with my history surrounding me.
Above The end of the road in Birmingham. Saying farewell as I retire from competitive athletics in 2003 at the age of 36.

I checked into hospital and had both knees fixed up at the same time. My sister said to me: 'Look at you, boy, you're born again.' I was the Renaissance Boy, well and truly. 'While you're at it,' I said to the doctors, 'you might as well whip my tonsils out, too.'

CHAPTER THIRTEEN

BURNING DOWN THE HOUSE

From the beginning, the move to Bath was wonderful. I have often idly wondered how different my life and career would have been if I'd had Lottery funding for living expenses and access to the superb facilities available to young athletes now, rather than my parents' generosity and the old cinder track. I'm never sure if I'd have been a better athlete or not, because we had had such a great training group when I was young. But I'm sure I would have loved the experience of the University of Bath had they had anything like it in my time.

I missed out on university, on moving away from my home city at all, and that led to me feeling trapped and unhappy during the unsettled years of my late twenties. The young athletes in Bath seemed to have everything: they were away from home, hanging out with other talented people like themselves, with the use of wonderful facilities and the expertise of coaches of the highest calibre. At the ripe old age of 31, I took to the university life myself. Because I had to split my life between Cardiff and Bath, I found myself a nice flat in Bath, where I could stay when I was up training with Malcolm.

We went back to work properly from January 1998, with our mutual understanding deepened immensely by the shock and joy of my comeback. We'd now been together for 14 years, a long journey, and had been through so much. After my operations, I took my usual care coming through rehab; I never rush back from injury, and I built my knees up properly. Then we set to work on a training schedule and preparation for the European Championships (which was my title to defend) and the Commonwealth Games in Malaysia.

Reordering my life was not too difficult – in fact it was a relief. Carmen had looked after my accounts since I was 17; she was a friend from way back, when she thought I was too cocky for my teenage bones;

and she'd asked me to be godfather to her daughter Chloe. She'd watched the relationship with Linford and the company damage my usual bouncy air and she was so relieved that I'd left. Now she helped me some more with my affairs and she would soon become my full-time PA in Cardiff.

Many of my friends suddenly felt free to tell me how much they'd wished I could leave Nuff Respect and how they'd seen me change into an angry bundle of resentment, which just wasn't me. Later, when I talked to some of the company staff I was still friendly with, they broke cover too, told me that the exodus from the company came about because the atmosphere there was so unpleasant. One of them told me that, for a while, she had cried every day before going into work. That was not what I had in mind when I formed my own company – but I hadn't known or found out about it until I left, when the people felt they could tell me.

For a race agent, I turned to Robert Wagner. He was one of the top agents, had a good stable of sprinters and you couldn't go far wrong with him. Most importantly, he made me laugh. I asked him if he fancied representing me and he said he'd love to.

I was casting around for a commercial agent to handle sponsorships, promotions and PR, and Sally Gunnell recommended I approach hers, Jonathan Marks of MTC. She said he was astute, pulled off good deals and – again importantly – was pleasant and sensible. No nonsense, but he looked after you, and you actually had a decent time working with him. 'You'll like him, you'll like him,' she kept saying.

So I talked to Jonathan and liked what I saw; he took me on and we've been together since. He's the opposite of Sue: he takes the hassle out of your life, rather than ladling it on. He understands what my needs are and works around them. If I need to work with people, he makes the introduction, then if all looks well, he leaves us to it, like adults. He looks after my PR, understands who I am, and what my qualities are, and he seeks to promote me properly. It is difficult to imagine getting into ridiculous rows and battles when I have Jonathan, and Robert, looking after me now.

All of that was good for my confidence, too. I was clearly still a bankable prospect and people wanted to do business with me. Now I was regaining my balance. I had matured a great deal, become mellower, become more the kind of person, as Suzanne said, who would stop to smell the flowers, count my blessings and not keep hurtling on.

One part of my life that didn't work out was Sam. Again, it was down to me – feeling weighed down by the responsibility of track, facing a new start, moving to Bath, and it all seemed so much of an effort. I couldn't handle being responsible for her as well. I had still felt guilty during the period when Sam was living with me again that I wasn't there enough, that I was trapped by my sport. I couldn't concentrate on two things at once. I used to be consumed by my performances so that at home I couldn't give her the attention she deserved. I was always looking for her to say just one wrong thing so that I could have a huge argument. I don't think I was running away from commitment – the typical man-thing – because it would have been easier to have married her; it was what everybody wanted and expected. I know it sounds corny when people say that you can love someone so much that you have to let them go, but it was true. I had so much respect for the person that she was, yet I could not treat her right. It cheesed me off to think that she did everything for me and I did nothing for her.

When she left the last time, it was awful. I was horrible. I had to go somewhere early the next morning and was packing. Sam had asked to talk to me – that was all she did – but I told her I had no time to talk and we had a huge argument. I just told her to pack her stuff and go. Then I phoned my father and asked him to come and get her and take her away before I left in the morning.

The next day my father pulled up. I just opened his boot, chucked her stuff into the back of his car, then took off to Birmingham. Sam ended up living with my parents at their house for about a month and then she found a flat. I didn't go to see my parents while Sam was there because she was really friendly with my mother, and of course my mother was thinking that I was a right old bastard and that it must have been my fault. Which, to be honest, it was – Sam hadn't wanted to do anything. She'd only wanted to talk to me. But I couldn't handle being with her at that time in my life – that was my problem. Eventually she moved away, to London, and it was sad. My mother was begging her not to go.

With Linford, all that remained was for me to be given back what I needed from the company, and my half of what was owed to me, which I had invested, and we could have an amicable parting of the ways.

I phoned Linford, asked him what we were going to do and he said it was cool. 'Tell me everything you want, and we'll just split it. Not a problem.'

There wasn't much I really needed. I had some private stuff there, some paperwork, and I wanted some furniture and equipment, which I'd paid for and which would be useful to me at home. The money wasn't a problem, because I had the bank details and the account was in Cardiff; I could take out what I needed. My sister was still in *Brookside*, but she was living down in Kew, so I asked her to go round to the office and pick up some stuff for me. No rush; it was just some of the paperwork, some personal stuff; just things that were mine, even some mugs. Then she could drop it round at my place when she was next in Cardiff.

Suzanne said fine, no problem. One day she went up there to collect my things. Sue Barrett told her: 'Linford said anybody who's associated with Colin is not to come in here and mustn't take anything out of this office.' My sister was stunned. Sue repeated it. So Suzanne rang me and told me: 'Colin, that's what she said. I'm not standing out on the step arguing with her. You'll have to deal with it.'

So there we were. Linford and Sue had obviously whipped themselves up into a frenzy again, just a couple of days after Linford had said that none of it would be a problem. They used to wind each other up to make a huge meal of the simplest issues, and now they were doing it over me removing my things.

I thought about whether to rip into Linford or just be cool, and again I decided I wasn't looking for a fight. I wanted it nice and easy, to run smoothly, just to get my name off their books and be disassociated from them. So I phoned Linford and said: 'Linford, let me tell you now, here is a list of the stuff I'm getting. I'm coming up Monday and I'm taking it all.'

I didn't want much. One computer – we had four, I think, but I wasn't planning to take two! There was a spare desk upstairs that I could use and we had some filing cabinets that I'd forked out a lot of money for, so I asked for two of those. And my personal stuff. That was it. I wanted to give Linford plenty of notice of when I was going to come, so that he could order more stuff if he needed it. He said it was no problem, Monday was good.

'Will someone be in the office?' I asked.

'Yeah, man, it's Monday morning, it's not a problem.'

I arranged for a removals van, and went up to London on the Sunday night, to stay with Suzanne, so that I could be in the office early the next morning, sort out the stuff, have a chat with people, then pack up and get everything back to Cardiff. I'd been training hard with Malcolm and was pretty exhausted.

Monday morning I got up early. I went to the office, but didn't see any cars. Rang the door bell: no answer. Rang the door bell again: no answer. I phoned the office: no answer. I phoned Linford's phone – off; Sue's phone – off. The removal people were arriving, and then I started to fume. I thought: they really are having a laugh now.

I'd kept everything in for so long, throughout the whole rotten business, and it is difficult to describe how mad I felt then. I was standing outside my own office, which I half-owned, just when I'd arranged to be, on a Monday morning, a long way from my home, and they were playing games like this.

I wanted to kill. I was that bad. I was shaking. I phoned my sister and I said: 'Suzanne, do you know what? You're not going to believe this. There's nobody here. There's nobody in the office.'

She said: 'You've got to be joking.'

'No, there is absolutely nobody here. Do you know what I'm going to do? I'm going to burn the place down. Trust me: I'm burning it down. That's it. It's torched. I don't give a toss.'

I just hung up the phone, took my car and drove it round to the car park. I was going to do it, no problem. I was going to put a match through the letter box and and burn the place down. If they wanted to play that daft, then nobody could have anything.

If I could have got to the door, I would have gone straight up there and done it. But there were two women with babies in pushchairs, standing outside the office, chatting away. I was boiling up inside, wanting them to leave because I was going to do it. In my head I thought nobody would know it was me; that I'd put a match through the letter box. A bit of petrol in there and the place would have gone up lovely. Nobody would have seen me because this was a residential area. They'd find the office torched and it could have been anything – an electrical fault. There wasn't a doubt in my mind.

I waited, and these women weren't moving. They were just chatting, standing around, and I was getting more vexed because they wouldn't get out of the way and let me do this thing. Just then, my sister turned up. She came over to me, looked me straight in the eye and said: 'Colin, are you sure you want to do this?'

'Suzanne,' I seethed. 'I am so angry.'

'I know,' she said. 'But do you really want to do time for these lot? That's what you're going to be doing. Are you sure you want to do time for them? They're not worth it.'

Slowly, that took the wind out of me. I heaved a deep sigh. Suzanne reasoned me out, reeled me in. 'You'll have to get your lawyers involved,' she said.

'Lawyers cost,' I snorted. 'Why do we need to fork out money for no good reason?'

'The movers will have to go,' she went on. 'You just go back to Cardiff. Get in your car and go home. Go back to Wales.'

I was steaming; and was still furious driving my car all the way home. I'd arranged everything, driven up for two hours the night before. I was trying to sort things out to make life easy for them and they'd planned it all to cause me maximum grief.

When I got home to Cardiff, I phoned Linford and this time his phone was on.

'Where were you?' I asked him. 'Where was everybody? I've been up there this morning.'

'Oh, man,' he said. 'I'm so sorry, I was stuck at the airport.' Then he came out with a line of excuses.

I couldn't even be bothered with his foolishness. Who did he think he was trying to kid? I could imagine them laughing at me – at the clever stunt they'd pulled on me.

Then I decided to play hard with them. It was my company and I was an equal partner with Linford when we had the original ill-fated idea. So I looked at the paperwork, added up every single penny that was owing to me in race fees and sponsorships, then went to the bank in the centre of Cardiff and had it all – about £55,000 – transferred to my own personal bank account.

The usual cash-flow period on most things was three months. But I just took what was owing to me, leaving only about £5,000 in the account. I knew they had bills and people to pay, but that wasn't my concern any more, if that was how they were going to play it. The company owed me and I was leaving. I didn't want them holding my money any more, so I took what was mine.

They knew soon enough, because they didn't have any money in the bank. So then Linford phoned me up: 'Colin, how come you've taken money out of the account, man?'

I was like: 'It's all the money owing to me. When the payments actually come in, you can keep them.'

Linford was complaining, saying they had bills and wages to pay, they had John Regis to pay, that I should have waited for my money. I said: 'Linford, you made the rules,' and I hung up.

He never called me back. But he did manage to bad-mouth me to everybody, telling the athletes they couldn't be paid because Colin took all the money. They didn't tell the whole truth; they didn't say why I had taken it, just that I had. Eventually Jamie Baulch mentioned it to me, saying: 'Colin, man: that was a rude one when you took the money.' So I told him: I took what was owed to me, and not a penny more.

Now they were thinking they'd better not mess too much with me because I'd get dark. That was too true. We closed the bank account, which was fine because I had nothing left in it, and Linford became the sole signatory. Then, when it came to my stuff, Linford said not to worry, he'd pay for the people to bring it to me.

When it arrived, it was all old rubbish. They sent me a computer as old as the ark. Some mashed-up filing cabinets, not the ones I'd asked for. A desk that was next to useless. Then I did get dark, and I thought they should get what was coming.

I owned half the property because we had bought outright the premises in Twickenham. My financial advisers were telling me to demand the money immediately. I was a joint owner, but Nuff Respect were paying me no rent. My advisers wanted to shut Nuff Respect down. I didn't want to be spiteful, I didn't want to waste the effort and be sucked into that negative energy any more. I said no, but I wanted the property sold and I wanted my half. So now the professionals were involved; we had valuers in to assess how much it was worth – his surveyors, my surveyors. This thing could have been sorted with an amicable parting, in a week. But it dragged on for a whole year.

To me, they seemed to be thriving on it. Finally they had a proper battle with Colin, as they had wanted, and they could tell all the athletes how awful I was. Linford was still training people who had trained with me in Cardiff and I used to see them. Paul Gray used to train with me and we were really tight; he was just a couple of years younger than me and went through the same schools; he was like a little brother. Suddenly one day he just stopped talking to me.

Then I found out from someone else that Paul had heard that I'd told Linford and Sue that he was on drugs. Paul ought to have known me well enough to realize I wouldn't say such a thing, and to come and ask me straight. Then I could have told him it was rubbish. Why would I want to bad-mouth him anyway. He was half a second slower than me, not a threat to me in any shape or form. But Paul never phoned me. He never asked me. I didn't bother with him. In fact I've had nothing much to do with Paul since that day. If he could believe such stories about me, then so be it. I'd talk to him, shoot the breeze if he was there at training, swap a few tales to keep everybody's spirits up, but as friends, that was destroyed in the fallout.

Then suddenly Jamie stopped talking to me. Eventually I did have that out with him: 'Jamie: what's up?' So I found out what his head had been filled with: apparently I laughed at him during the AAAs finals when he came in bringing up the rear. He said I was in the presentation area and, when he came down the home straight, I was laughing.

I just scoffed at him. 'Right, I was laughing. Did the same person tell you, when you were coming down the home straight, I wasn't even watching the race. I was on my mobile phone. Why would I be watching you run? I've got nothing to do with you. Why would I waste my time laughing at your weak performance?'

But then, because I actually did care a little, I said: 'I'm telling you now, I didn't laugh at you. It's up to you if you don't believe me; I'm not here to convince you. Trust me, take it from me, I wasn't. But Jay, at the end of the day, it makes no difference to me.'

Jamie was a little bit sheepish then; he must have thought of what I'd done for him – paid for his training, looked after him, given him advice, helped him through his career, even put my own career on ice while I was developing his – and then he was carrying on like that. It was the same with Paul; I couldn't understand why they fell for it. They lived with me, they knew me, and if they could believe I would be underhand with them, well, there was nothing there.

This was the sad fallout from the Nuff Respect bitterness, which I never wanted at all. Eventually my advisers started to look into making them change the name of the company; it was registered as a partnership and technically I still owned half of it. That seemed finally to worry them and Linford kicked into action and paid me for half of the property. It all took ages.

Sue I don't speak to now; I think she's embarrassed to talk to me anyway. Linford I see around: his athletes are in Cardiff, and if I saw him on the circuit, I'd always talk to him, chat. We never fell out, perhaps because there was too much there, too much history, for it to explode into the open. But it isn't the same. We aren't friends any more. I don't see him socially, I haven't got his mobile number, I've never got to know his kids at all. It's all a shame, but it happened. You have to move on. I'm so glad I changed and got out of my rut, and all the mess afterwards just confirmed that I had done the right thing. Personally, I think Linford himself should have moved on; to me, he's stuck in a rut. I can't see how that company is good for him either. I can't see, with the athletes they've got, that they can be making much money at all. An agency is only on 10 per cent; when Linford and I were competing for big money at the beginning, the money was washing through. Then we were the pay cheque. Now, I just can't see it.

In a way I feel sorry for Linford because his career fell away in recent years. How he got himself banned for nandrolone at the end, when he was already semi-retired, I'll never work out. He talked to me then and told me hadn't taken anything, and I was prepared to believe it. But people connect it to the ephedrine incident in Seoul (even though that was due to the ginseng) and his career is sullied.

Having said that, as my sister says, Linford's a big man, an adult, and he has to take responsibility for himself. He was one of the greatest and most successful athletes Britain ever produced. He's running a company and it should have huge pluses, but now I'm on the outside I know what a bad reputation it has. I shake my head in wonder that he's frittered his reputation away like that.

At its root, there is insecurity there. Linford needs to be in control, to be number one; he has to be the leader. That was the real thinking behind the name of the company in the first place; it was aggressive – he has to have respect. He's big and he scares people, but he never scared me, and because I have a side that can finally snap, Linford was a little wary of me. I used to tell him straight: 'Stop worrying about what every last person said or might think of you. Be cool. Some people will like you and some won't.' But he always had to make it an issue.

I had to leave, and now I have completely moved on. They thought I couldn't do it, that I needed them, but I didn't. I always used to laugh in subsequent years when I was successful. I used to win a race and think: this must be absolutely burning them.

I like what I hear from Suzanne of the Buddhist teachings, and her influence has been huge in helping me change, become more spiritual, understand what is important: both for me, and for the people around me whom I really do treasure. That has flowed from taking responsibility for my life, cutting away from what was bringing me down, and learning to appreciate what is valuable and good.

Later on I found out that the day I was outside the Nuff Respect office, jumping up and down with a match, somebody *was* inside, but he didn't answer the door. It could have caused some serious problems. When I look back at that awful Monday morning, I remember those two young Twickenham mums, standing outside the office doors with their pushchairs, nattering on for an age. Time, crucially, for Suzanne to get to me and calm me down, stop me doing anything crazy. Trust me, those women must have been put there for a reason. You have to believe in fate, in my book.

CHAPTER FOURTEEN

NICE WARM BATH

Bath, in a word, was nice. The facilities were so good, the university soon became an officially designated High Performance Centre, and talented young athletes were attracted down there to work under the eagle eye of Coach Arnold. We soon had a tight-knit group of people: Tatum Nelson, the sprinter; Allison Curbishley, the Scottish 400m hurdler; Melanie Neef, the 400m runner; and Ross Baillie, a fast, clean, sprint hurdler who came down from Scotland and became my training partner. Malcolm was back as a full-time coach; our time apart lay behind us and, with my knees having cleared up, I was ready to start serious work once more.

I'd first seen Ross Baillie when he was a young lad and could remember thinking he had promise, but I'd thought he was too soft with the hurdles; he never hit one, but that was because he was taking them too high, which meant he lost speed. Nevertheless he looked pretty good, and I kept an eye out for him after that. When he came down to join the group in Bath, I discovered how good he could be and, as we worked together, began to believe he would be my successor as Britain's number-one sprint hurdler.

He was only 19 when he arrived. His parents had been athletes; they're officials on the circuit still, so I suppose he was born into the life. Because he'd been a sprinter he was pretty quick. But he was soft, he'd not been pushed up in Scotland, and he needed a lot of work to learn the ethic of training: why and how hard you have to train. Malcolm and I were taking no nonsense, and it was a shock to Ross at first. But it didn't take him long to settle in and start to work really hard, and he began to see the benefits quite quickly and run fast, with his technique hugely improved.

He was a pleasure to train with – such a good athlete, laid-back but ready for hard work when required. Ross was popular with everybody.

At the weekends he used to go out drinking, unlike me – I have barely had a drink in my life apart from champagne after championship wins or on other special occasions. Ross was the gel between the athletes and Bath people in other sports, like the swimmers. I knew Mark Foster, the world champion and world record-holder at 50m freestyle and 50m butterfly, from way back, but Ross brought us and lots of other people closer together. Mark and I became very good friends and soon I was a training partner for him (as much as swimmers and athletes can train together) and eventually his coach: a fruitful relationship for us both.

Because I was recovering from my knee ops, I didn't do an indoor season in 1998. All we did was focus on preparing for the European Championships and Commonwealth Games coming up in the summer – both my titles to defend. With my mind clear and the clutter of my life sorted, the fresh start in the really good environment of Bath went very well. I began to feel something approaching true fitness and top form flow back into my limbs, like the warm embrace of an old friend. I wasn't at my absolute sharpest when the European Championships in Budapest finally came round in mid-August, but I was at least in good physical shape at last.

In the first round in Budapest I won with 13.31, then I broke the championship record in the semi-final running 13.02, which did shock me; I didn't think I would run that fast. In the final I slapped them all up. I ran 13.02 again, one-tenth of a second clear of the German hurdler Falk Balzer, to collect my third consecutive European gold medal. It felt like old times, but after the previous years' traumas, now that I had a more mature appreciation of what I was doing and why, it was even more deeply satisfying.

I ran in the World Cup in South Africa in September 1988, but when the Commonwealth Games came up in Kuala Lumpur just a few days later, I didn't feel up to competing. I had quite a severe quad injury, which was hurting, and emotionally I wasn't up for another championships at the end of the year. I had to feel that I was at my best to compete, and because I felt I couldn't really produce it, I pulled out.

Then I had the same old nonsense again, being chastized in the Welsh press for not going to Malaysia. They were trotting out that tired stuff: that I run for money, but wouldn't run for Wales. My attitude, at 31, was that I'd done my time for Wales and returned with medals: two golds and a silver in Commonwealth Games going back to 1986. Perhaps, I thought, it was time for other people to go out there and pull in some medals for Wales. Anyway, my decision was made; I didn't go.

Ross went; he was selected for Scotland, which was expected of him, and did OK, qualified for the final, but came in last. Tony Jarrett won it in 13.47, Paul Gray was fourth, and Ross came in with 13.85.

Back in Bath, I'd got myself a nice, roomy old Georgian apartment. It had a spare bedroom, and Ross was living at the university then and asked if he could come and rent the room from me. I was cool, no problem. So Ross moved in – and that was the start of my education.

Nobody likes to think of themselves as getting old and in our thirties we still consider ourselves as cool as we were in our teens, but sharing a flat with a 19-year-old smacked me in the face with the reality of the generation gap. I suppose I could almost have been his dad – and as time went on it seemed as if I was being drawn inevitably into that role. I was an established adult, and owned three homes by then; Ross was great, easy-going, but the messiest person I had ever known.

You couldn't see the carpet in his room. Cups, saucers, spoons, clothes – it used to baffle me. He'd have the place littered, but then if he wanted another cup of coffee he'd just go and get a clean mug and then leave that lying around too. So then I realized that I am a picking-things-up kind of person – no doubt going back to my mother's stern lessons to children who left mess around. I'd thought I was a slob, but Ross was in a league of his own. I used to say to him: 'Ross, I'm not your father or your mother. I'm not here to pick up after you – I've got myself to look after. If you don't pick up after yourself there's going to be war.'

I used to do everything: clean the place, cook for him, take him to training because he didn't have a car. He hadn't half landed on his feet really. Sometimes I'd get in a real strop if the flat was a total pigsty, and tell him he'd have to get out. But none of it worked. When I thought about it, it made me giggle.

Then there was the music. I never ever thought I'd hear myself tell anybody to turn their racket down, but Ross used to have MTV on, Tatum and other friends would come round, and they'd have it on full blast and just sit and watch it all day. It drove me bananas. One time I flipped and told them I couldn't take it any more, and wiped MTV off the telly completely. No music channels on there now.

I used to have a go at them: 'Listen to this music upstairs. If I watch TV, I want to watch a programme that'll entertain me or give me some information, not this noise.' Yep – that's the kind of thing I used to say to them. They'd sit on the sofa, 19-year-olds, just look at me and laugh, like I was an old fogey.

Tatum was Ross's friend from way back: they were close, like brother and sister – and they constantly bickered as if they were, too. Constantly arguing over nonsense, as far as I could see. Listening to their music at full volume and laughing at me because I was way too grown-up for them. I was the dedicated athlete: early nights, strict diet, no drink, regimented routine. They were young, talented and having fun. I remember once when it all got too much for me, trying to get an early night, I said:

'If you don't turn that music down, trust me, it's going off and you'll never see it again!'

They wouldn't, so I stomped in, ripped the hi-fi out of the wall, wound the cord round it and stomped off. Tatum was giggling so much as I did it that I marched back in.

'You think it's funny, do you?'

She shut up and I went back upstairs, thinking all the time: my God, you really did that, you did exactly what your mum and dad might have done. You ripped the hi-fi out of the wall and you're actually carrying it upstairs. You're a fully-fledged fogey now.

It was interesting, though, hanging out with them, listening to how they thought, what Ross's attitudes were, and realizing truly how far apart I was from him in age and experience. Despite all my scolding, I had so much time for Ross. In many ways, he kept me young, reconnected me with my youth, and he had a similar happy influence on so many people.

In the winter my grandfather, Dee, died. He'd been an inspiration to me all my life, a lovely man, and I'd grown up on his stories of Jamaica and him coming over to Britain to make a life for himself and his daughters. He arrived with nothing, determined just to be someone and make his mark, and he certainly did that. When he died, I was awestruck by the number of people who had loved him and would miss him. In the hospital he had 16 people around his bed. At the funeral, at Cathays Methodist Church, where all our family occasions take place – for better or for worse – it was standing room only, with crowds of people listening outside.

My parents didn't even know who many of the people were; Dee just had so many friends. I was so moved and thought it amazing that someone could be so loved by so many people.

The family was grieving, but as ever I had to go back to work: 1999 was another big year because the World Championships outdoors were coming up in Seville in the summer. We ran an indoor season too and were in serious training for the World Indoor Championships in Maebashi, Japan, in March. Malcolm told Ross that if he made the UK team, he could come to Australia with us to do some warm-weather preparation, and Ross was really excited about it. He ran 7.70 in the indoor AAA championships, which meant that he made the trip and he was so happy. But first we had to compete in an indoor Grand Prix in Birmingham. I was enjoying a little smile inside, thinking that Ross was about to discover life with the big boys; it was a hot, tough race, and I honestly thought he wouldn't stick it because he was still young and tender. But he far from cracked; he screamed out of the blocks, absolutely roared down there with everybody and ran a personal best of 7.60. I only ran 7.51, to come in second, and Ross was not too far behind. I was stunned actually, really impressed. I told him: 'Well done, son.'

We left from there and went straight to Australia to do some serious training for the World Indoors. Ross and I were joined by a good friend and training partner of mine: Elmar Lichtenegger, the Austrian champion, who would come over and train with us in Cardiff before championships, too. Preparation went really well in Australia; we worked hard, we were focused, and Ross, selected for the senior GB team, was putting in the work to run well in Maebashi.

For me, now 32, it was another important step on the way to rebuilding my career and reputation. Although I was – still am – the world record-holder indoors with a time of 7.30, which is regarded as phenomenal, and I won probably 90 per cent of my indoor races, I never really enjoyed running indoors. Over 60m, the race is so short and sharp that anybody can win it if they have a good start and a bit of luck. Experience teaches you to keep control and approach the race with some idea of tactics, but there is not the scope or skill that goes into 110m outdoors, where most of the races are won from hurdles six to ten. That's when the top guys move away from the field. Over 60m, with only five hurdles, everything is rushed. If someone else is ahead at hurdle one, already you have only four hurdles left to make up the ground;

you're hurtling into the second and it's crazy. One tiny mistake and you're gone. Athletes who aren't really a problem outdoors are suddenly a major threat indoors. It's brutal, stripped-down hurdling, and I often hated the races, especially at major championships where the tension and pressure were ladled on top.

In 1999 the major threat was a young American, Reggie Torian, a former American footballer who'd come into hurdling in 1997 and put in some decent performances, including beating Allen Johnson and me in a British Grand Prix in Sheffield in 1998. But he was over-the-top to the media. His coach was a priest or something, anyway there was some religious element, and Reggie was talking the big talk, flying around saying: 'It's mine in 1999.'

I was like: please. What's yours? Reggie might have had one decent outdoor season, but there is a long way to go before anybody can start coming on the scene and thinking they're going to rule. I thought: you might have bust up your little American mates over on that side of the Atlantic, but trust me, you're coming to hard-core competition now. We'll fight on neutral ground in Japan and see who wins.

There were no semis in Maebashi, just a heat and then the final. Ross went in the first heat; he'd have had to absolutely run his socks off to qualify, because the people in his heat were quick. He came in fifth, which was no embarrassment at all; he ran 7.69, which was remarkably good – he was making great progress.

Torian was drawn in lane 4 in my heat. I was in lane 6. We blasted down there. I started more quickly than him, faster than everybody in fact, and won the heat in 7.42, with Reggie just one-hundredth behind me. Really close, but I won.

The final was the same evening. We came out to warm up, and Reggie was grabbing the hurdles out of the way, kneeling by them, praying. I thought: he might be putting everybody else off, but he's not putting me off, he's just winding me up to the gills. I just gave Malcolm a look and I thought: Torian is having a laugh; he really is getting it from me today.

We got to the track and were on the line, preparing, and setting the blocks, doing a couple of practice starts and hurdles. Then we came to the line, and for some bizarre reason I had a false start, which I never used to do. I started to worry that maybe Reggie had got to me a little bit after all. Then the stadium announcer went and reminded everybody: 'Colin Jackson has won three silver medals at this championships,' which I had (in 1989, 1993 and 1997), but in other words, I'd never won it. This was no time to bring that up. I thought I just had to get out of the blocks hard and really go for this race – no holding back whatsoever.

I stood next to Reggie Torian, back on the line after my false start, and he jumped up in the air next to me. He jumped so high it was incredible. I couldn't believe that anybody could spring that far up from a standing start. He literally took off, and I think his legs were above my head before he landed back on earth. I was like: this guy's a freak. I thought there was no way I could win the race. I didn't have the energy.

Then, cocksure Colin, I turned it into a positive. I told myself that by springing up as high as that, old Reggie Torian had tired his legs out and he'd have nothing left. I made my mind up: rip out of the blocks and give it everything. Down we went, set, the gun went, I took off, and he got out with me; the two of us were hurtling down there. Reggie started to move away in front of me ever so slightly, then he made a tiny mistake coming off hurdle three going into hurdle four, and I flew straight in and accelerated past him. I went over four, came off hurdle five just in front and knew I had him now. I just powered myself down, threw myself on the line, looked up; I was sure I had it.

But it was very close. We had to wait. Of course there was a big screen up, so we all stood and watched the replay of the race and I thought: yep, I definitely got that. Then they took it off just as they were showing us going over the last hurdle. The announcer started: 'Ladies and gentlemen,' and our hearts were in our mouths. 'The new indoor champion, from Great Britain...' and I just wheeled away, elated. I was so happy. It was the first time I had won it, and the time was confirmed at 7.38, a new World Indoor Championship record. I allowed myself a special lap of honour.

Coming off the track, I saw Reggie Torian and smiled. 'Well done,' I said, and walked on. I was really pleased, felt a champion's pride, to have gone there, done it and picked up the gold. The following morning I went wandering down to a local shopping mall with some of the other athletes. I decided what I really fancied was a glazed doughnut, so that was how I let rip in my celebrations of my first ever World Indoor Championship title: a doughnut and a coffee in a shopping mall.

Malcolm was really pleased. Everything was back on track and going so well. The Maebashi experience was good for Ross, too. We trained together and roomed together so he could see everything that went into it, all the preparation necessary if you are going to win championships. He came to the warm-up area and saw what Malcolm and I did there; came to the track with me – everything. He was learning fast.

We went home and started to train for the outdoor season and the World Championships in Seville. We all went to Athens in April. Ross's brother, Chris, also a hurdler, came too, the first time the brothers had been away training together. It was really funny to watch Ross being offish with Chris, playing the big brother with him. Ross was an international now, he'd had some attention; plenty of people had seen what he could do and were talking about him having great potential. They were telling him: you've trained with Colin, but Colin's got to retire soon – surely – and you can be the boy to take over. I felt this was true; if Ross kept improving as he was, he definitely had it in him.

Again, we trained really well at the end of spring, and we started racing in May. At first Ross was running ridiculously slowly, then he started coming round, running very well. He raced at a meet in Nuremberg and ran 13.70, just off his personal best. As this was right at the beginning of the year, it was a great benchmark, and you knew he was going to take a chunk off that come the summer. We were all excited about it. 'You're doing all right here, son,' I told him. 'No other comment, apart from that you're doing really well.'

He said he was excited and looking forward to the season. I had a busy week ahead of me, with a race in Prague the following day, then Athens again and home on the Thursday, so I told Ross I'd see him when I was back. Then I went off to Prague with Robert, my agent. Ross was cool. The following day, I ran my race in Prague, then called him to tell him about it. I asked Ross what he was up to and he said he was playing golf with Mark Foster the following day, at a golf club I'd been meaning to join. I asked him to grab a membership form, which was lying around the flat, and take it down there for me. He said: 'Sure, I'll take it when I go down there tomorrow.'

And that was the last time I ever spoke to him.

CHAPTER FIFTEEN
ROSS

The day after I spoke to Ross, before I was due to race in Athens, I called Mark for a chat. I could hear coughing in the background. 'Is that Ross?'

'Yeah,' he said, 'he's eaten a sandwich; something must have been in it because he's coughing his guts up.'

'Well, tell him to shut up,' I joked. 'I can't hear what you're saying.'

We still didn't know what was happening. Ross went upstairs, but we could still hear him coughing violently; Mark thought he was trying to be sick. Then Ross came down the stairs and Mark said: 'He doesn't look very good. He wants me to take him to the chemist to get some antihistamine. He's had an attack like this before, and says that should sort it out.'

I couldn't see what antihistamine would do, but Mark said that Ross really wasn't looking too good and he had to go.

About 20 minutes later Mark rang me back. 'Colin, they've taken Ross to the hospital.'

'What for?'

Mark just mumbled: 'He's gone.'

I couldn't understand what was happening. I asked Mark who was with him, and he said Allison Curbishely was, so I said to put her on the phone.

'Allison,' I said, 'what's wrong with Ross?' But she made no sense either; she was just weeping away.

Eventually she managed to tell me that the doctors had given Ross adrenaline and it was serious: that he'd eaten a peanut, to which he was allergic.

'Have you phoned his mum and dad yet?'

'No.'

'Right, well, you ring his parents, I'll try to get hold of Malcolm, so we can tell them what's going on.'

181

I phoned Tatum. She started chatting and telling me some story, but I said: 'No, this is serious. Where are you?'

She had just gone back to her home in Tunbridge Wells – miles from Bath – but I told her:

'You'll have to go back down to Bath. Ross is in a bad way. He's eaten a peanut.'

She screamed and said: 'I'll get back to you, I'm going down straight away.'

I phoned Mark back. He said he'd spoken to Ross's parents and they were coming down on a flight from Scotland as soon as they could. Then I managed to get hold of Malcolm; he was on the motorway on his way home. I told him Ross was in trouble and Malcolm said he'd go straight to the hospital.

I was in Athens on a mobile phone – I didn't know any details and I couldn't understand what was going on. I thought at least if Malcolm was there, there'd be one sensible old head. Malcolm said there was nothing much I could do and that I might as well stay in Athens, run the race the next day, then come home.

I phoned my mother for her medical opinion. 'Hi, Mum,' I said. 'What happens if you have an allergic reaction and the doctors give you adrenaline?'

Her voice dropped. 'It's not good if that happens.' She started to explain, then said: 'Why? Who's this happened to?'

'Ross,' I said.

'Oh, shit.'

Now, my mother never swears. When she said that, it hit home to me how serious the situation was for Ross. She kept repeating: 'It's not good, that; it's not good at all.'

I raced the next day and ran badly, finishing fourth or fifth, because I couldn't think about anything. I flew home, jumped in a car and drove up to the hospital in Bath. Malcolm was there with Tatum. By now they'd seen Ross.

'He's not good, you know,' Malcolm said plainly.

The girls were in floods of tears. Tatum told me: 'Colin, he looks terrible. Before you go in to see him, you've got to know that.'

I walked into the room where Ross was lying. He was wired up to what seemed like so many machines. I said: 'Guess who's back in town,

Ross?' The machines went loopy, so I thought maybe he could hear me, but a nurse came rushing in and told me that would happen all the time. She looked at me. 'You do realize he's in a really bad way?'

Ross was in a coma, on a life-support machine. I started telling him about the Athens meet: Maurice Greene of the US had broken the world 100m record with a 9.79 run. Ross, being a stats man, would have loved to know that and all the details. All the time I was thinking: this makes no sense. He's only eaten a peanut.

I left the room and went outside. Everybody was in a huddle with the doctor. He was saying Ross was so far gone that when his mum and dad arrived, they would have to consider whether the life-support machine should be turned off.

The next day, Friday, we went training. It was eerily quiet and everybody was preoccupied. I was off running on my own, not thinking of anything.

Tatum came in my car on the way back. Malcolm called me.

'You're not going to like this news.'

'Why? What's going on?'

'They've turned the machines off. He's been in a coma since Tuesday. They've pronounced him dead.'

I looked at Tatum, and decided not to say anything right now, but just drive to the hospital. Allison was behind us in her car. We finally pulled in, and I had to tell Tatum. But I didn't know how to, so I just looked at her and said:

'Tate, Ross has died.'

She burst into tears. She was utterly distraught. Then I had to think about telling Allison when we got out of the car. But Allison found a parking space before I did. I dropped Tatum off, drove to a space myself, came back and Allison was literally on the floor, crying. She'd just dropped when Tatum told her.

'Come on,' I said. 'We've got to go in now, because his mum and dad and everybody are in there.'

We pulled ourselves together a bit and walked along the hospital corridor – the longest, most awful walk ever. It was an absolute nightmare because now we were going to have to face his parents, in these circumstances, and I hardly knew them. Finally we got there. As we were going in to see Ross, the nurse told us: 'He's exactly the same as you saw him yesterday; we're keeping him on the machine because we're taking donor parts from him. He won't be taken to surgery until nine o'clock this evening, so you can come in any time between now and then.'

We went in and everybody from our group was there – Mark, Melanie Neef, and Ross's mum and dad – huddled round the bed, just looking at him. I thought: how's he dead? It couldn't register that Ross was actually dead; his chest was going up and down with his breathing, hair was growing on his face. I was willing him just to move, thinking: come on, Ross, you've got till nine o'clock to do something.

Of course nothing happened. One of the hospital administrators asked me if I wanted to break the news to the press, which made me really angry. I was just there with everybody, in shock. Ross had closed down – that was it. I left really quickly, didn't hang around; just told his mum and dad I'd see them the following morning.

We all had a massive breakfast together, then I took them to the airport. I took them a really long way round because I didn't want to go past the hospital, where his body still was. That journey was a nightmare, too. Of course his parents were completely stricken with the devastation of it all. It was too much to take in. We reached the airport and off they went, back to Scotland.

Still, I'd had no time to find out what had actually happened. When I pieced it all together, by talking to Mark and everybody, I was so angry. Not at any of them – it was nobody's fault of course – but at the fates, at all the little things that had conspired to take our Ross away in such a senseless way.

They told me that at 11.30 that day Roy, our masseur, asked Ross if he wanted a massage. Ross said no, because he was playing golf with Foz at 3.30 and was just going home. As he was packing up his stuff, he ran into Allison, who said:

'Ross, will you time me in the swimming pool?'

She was only in rehab, she wasn't even a swimmer, but of course Ross agreed and did it. Then he was about to leave when Foz said that Ross might as well wait for him to finish his session, then they could grab something to eat and go straight to golf from there. Ross being Ross he liked to hang out anyway, and here was Mark offering him a lift into town, so he said fine.

As I heard all this I kept thinking: oh, Ross, why couldn't you just have gone home, man? If he'd had his massage he would have missed Allison, gone straight home, had a Slimfast as he normally would and gone round to Mark's later.

They'd never even been to that sandwich bar before. They pulled in and Ross wanted tuna, but the woman said they didn't have it; all they had was coronation chicken. Ross didn't want that but he was famished, so in the end he shrugged and bought it. Stupid little events, one after the other.

The coronation-chicken sandwich had a trace of nut in it. He only had one bite; he chewed it up and swallowed it, and Mark said as soon as he swallowed it he started coughing immediately.

I was so, so angry, thinking how every little twist and turn was a chance to step off and for Ross to just get himself home, but somehow it never happened. If he had gone home when he was originally intending to, he would still be here today. That's why I do have to believe that when your time is up, it's up, and there is nothing you can do about it.

He died on 18 June and we all fell apart. The World Championships were in Seville in August and that had been our big target: me to win it, Ross to continue his splendid progress, and now it was all meaningless. I just wandered about in a daze; nothing made any sense. I'd be somewhere and if I saw people looking sad or miserable, it made me think about Ross all over again and wonder if they could be going through something as unbearable.

Then, at other times, I'd be somewhere and think: nobody here realizes that my flatmate has gone. The person I was training with, living with, who I was with every day virtually all day – or at least until I'd finally tell him and Tatum to get out of my room and let me sleep. Dead.

To think he was never coming back – it was impossible. One of the worst things was to notice Ross's smell, still round the house. Not that he smelt bad; just that he had a distinctive smell, as everybody has, and it was still around the flat, in his bedroom, on his coat. You couldn't believe Ross wasn't just going to walk back in, flop down on the sofa and stick the music on. I remember going into the shower, thinking that when Ross had a shower in there the morning he died, he could never have realized it would be the last shower he'd ever have. It was awful, and strange.

I thought of all the nice, stupid things we'd done and all the stuff we never did. He was good at golf and was going to teach me to play, which was why I was joining the club. I thought how I'd never seen Ross drive because Tatum was always jumping in my car and asking if we could go for a drive. I'd always argue a bit, then they'd both nag and be miserable, so eventually to shut them up I'd agree and we'd go flying out on some trip or other. It felt like they were making me feel free, young again.

The training had been so good, too. I had to relearn things as I was teaching him, and that's why I'd done so well, because I had to remember the basics of good training, good technique, to lead Ross by example.

It was simply too much to take in, that the sweet life he'd had with us was over.

At his funeral Mark Foster, Tatum and I each gave a speech in turn about what Ross meant to all of us. I hadn't wanted to do it, because speaking in public really isn't me, but the girls suggested it, so I had to agree. When I was writing it, I decided that what people would most expect of me would be for me to laugh. So that's what I did. I wanted to be strong too, because I wasn't speaking last; Tatum came after me and I didn't want her to be too distraught to say her piece.

The first thing I told them was how hopeless Ross had been when he first came down, how he couldn't do anything, but within a fortnight I had him cleaning the house, cooking and making tea. I remembered how he would treat me like I was his big brother and ask me all kinds of foolish questions, and I'd treat him with little-brother contempt, telling him to shut up. How annoyed he and Tatum used to be when I called them 'the kids'. Then I told them about the time Ross had gone out wearing my clothes, and he came home plastered and throwing up. I'd put him to bed with a Nurofen and drink of water and all I could think of was: he'd better not be messing up my suit.

I said that Ross knew how to have a good time, but he also knew when it was time to work hard, and he trained so hard and was doing so well. I told them how Ross was the bond between so many different people in Bath, because everybody liked him. And how much we'd all miss him, because for me it was like losing my little brother.

My agent was there, and Robert said he'd never been to a funeral where people were laughing. Even Ross's mum was laughing. I remember his grandmother came up to me – which is bizarre, when you think how awful it must be for an old lady to have to bury her grandson. She put her arm round my waist and said: 'Thank you, very much. You know, Ross was such a lovely boy, and he loved it when he came down with you lot. He enjoyed himself so much.'

When it was all over I didn't want to train, I didn't want to do anything. It was all a waste of time: track was superficial rubbish to my eyes. Tatum went home; she was wrecked. I was on my own. I couldn't stay in Bath, so I went home to Cardiff. I haven't lived full-time in Bath since, and the whole group has broken up.

I did race in the outdoor season, but I didn't do much, didn't train properly. I had no motivation whatsoever. Athletics could hardly have made less sense. I was in decent shape, but every time I went on the line I was never focused properly because I always used to think: Ross should be here. All I ever wanted to do was sit on the patio outside my house in Cardiff and just stare across the water, thinking how unfair the world is and how we had all been robbed.

Tatum was distraught; she was so down that it was difficult to talk to her, but occasionally she was up and then we could discuss how we were.

One day Malcolm gave me a ring. 'Listen, what are you doing?'

'What do you mean: what am I doing?'

'Well, the World Championships are in three weeks. What do you want to do? Do you want to win?'

I thought for a second. 'I suppose so.'

'Well,' he said. 'You're going have to do some work if you want to win it.'

He said we didn't have to go to Bath to train; he'd come to Cardiff or we could meet halfway in Cwmbran. If we chose Bath, he said I could stay with him, not have to go back to the flat. I said I'd think about it.

The truth is, I didn't want to take it on; I couldn't face it. Then I thought: the last thing Ross would have wanted you to do would be to drop out. He'd want you to go out there and win it. So that's what I told myself: I'll do it for Ross. And if I was doing it for him, then I had to go to Seville and win, not come in some silly position down the field.

So the next morning I phoned Malcolm. 'OK, I'm coming to Bath. Why should you have to do all the driving? If I win, it won't be you who gets all the accolades.'

I went and stayed with Malcolm and Madelyn, and did all my final preparations for Seville with him in Bath.

Malcolm had been knocked for six by Ross dying, too. He just shook his head at the funeral: 'If you'd told me that Ross had been shopping on the top floor of Marks & Spencer in the middle of town, and somehow an articulated lorry ran through the shopping centre, managed to get up inside the store and hit Ross full on, I would believe it more than I can accept this. A peanut? No, sorry: I can't believe that.'

He was in shock, really, and he's never been the same since Ross died. Madelyn said that too. He's calmer really, less grumpy, as if he's been shaken into a sense of perspective and can see what is most important.

We went back to training, just Malcolm and me. I told myself I was doing it for Ross and suddenly my focus returned. I switched on, keyed into the work, and suddenly I was determined I was going to Seville to win. Malcolm and I never said anything about Ross; training gave us both something to concentrate on. In that frame of mind, the sessions were excellent – everything had to be excellent.

It was 23°C in the summer in Bath, so we stayed there until just three days before the World Championships. Then we went to Seville, I did one training session and nearly passed out it was so hot. It was 40°C; 38°C was a cool day.

The day before I was due to race I picked up a magazine, and they had a picture of the gold medal. I turned to Malcolm and said: 'That is so nice. That's what I want, not the silver, not the bronze; that one.'

'Well,' he said bluntly, 'you'd better go and get it then.'

'Trust me,' I said. 'Don't worry about it; I'll get it.'

'OK,' he sighed, 'we'll see.'

I won my heats, but unusually for me I can't remember what time I ran. Mark Crear had been the fastest in the world in 1999 and had been getting away with the most outrageous false starts all year, which had been cheesing me right off.

After the second round Kim McDonald, the renowned British agent/coach, came up to me and said: 'Did you see what happened out there?'

'What?' I hadn't been watching the other heat.

'Mark Crear's done two false starts and he's been disqualified.'

I was just smiling, thinking: there is a Lord! Ross, you are smiling down on me, son. This is ordained. Mark Crear's finally got his comeuppance.

I had Anier Garcia and Allen Johnson in my semi-finals. But Allen had an injury and he had to pull out. I was cool, did my drills in the warm-up: three side hurdles, where you go over on either side, not over the top of the hurdle; some strides, getting sharp. I was feeling good actually. The gun went, we went down there, no problems, pretty smooth, and I finished second. Garcia beat me, running 13.18. I was just behind him with 13.19. As I came off the track, Malcolm said: 'How was it?'

'Yeah,' I said, 'it was comfortable. I feel good.'

Malcolm looked at me and asked quietly: 'How much have you got left?'

I pondered: 'Hmm, about a metre.'

'Well, you'd better make it two.'

Malcolm was telling me that people were going to fly in the final the following day and I needed to find two more metres in the race, which is a hell of a lot over 110m after just one night's sleep.

I went out for dinner that night with Pascal and the people from Puma, still in my track gear. Malcolm came too. I found myself after dinner, probably around eleven o'clock, just waiting by the swimming pool, staring into it. I was thinking: I can't believe I'm going into this final on my own. Ross is dead. Even my friend and rival Tony Jarrett hasn't made the final. I'm going into a world final on my tod.

I couldn't eat in the morning; I felt so nervous and sick. I had just a tiny bit of scrambled egg and a chocolate bar. Some people from one of the British TV stations were in the hotel and when they saw me they waved, wishing me luck. I put a smile on my face, but I went up to my room thinking that I never wanted to do this again. How many times have I been through this? It's a pain; I hate this bit. When I leave here, after going through all this pressure again, I'd better be coming back with a gold medal.

Eventually Malcolm came round and knocked at the door. I told him I felt OK. He was asking me what I'd do in the warm-up because it was 41°C, so you simply couldn't do a heavy warm-up.

I did some stretching in the corridor at the hotel. Then, at the warm-up track, we did a few drills and some speed work. Malcolm said: 'You might as well leave it there.'

I didn't want to leave it there, because that would mean it was virtually time to go and I had to go through the whole process again: putting myself on the line, under tons of pressure. When Malcolm left me to go to the call room, I was on my own, and I started to think about everything and everybody – pitying myself.

Then we walked underneath a tunnel to the stadium, and it was beautifully cool under there. I pulled myself together then: this is the last time you do this; you most likely won't be going to another World Championships, so you'd better do this well. Then I felt a bit better. In the final 20 minutes in the call room I remembered my sister. I knew she would be doing her Buddhist chanting for me; wherever Suzanne was in the world (she was actually back home in Cardiff) she would be doing that for me. I know what she chants, so ten minutes before we went out, I chanted it too. Not out loud, but in my head. I definitely felt it give me some extra spirit, and after ten minutes my head felt so clear.

I felt really energized; it was amazing. Then I looked round at the other athletes and thought: you lot really are getting it today.

I was drawn in lane 6. Anier Garcia, the American Duane Ross and the other top guys were all inside me. When I went down on the blocks, I reminded myself what I was going to do: keep it simple. Get out in front and stay there. Don't complicate anything. Stick to it.

I breathed and went down, my normal ritual: touch toes, go down, set. The gun went and I got out. As soon as I started towards the first hurdle I could see I'd hit the front. I took the first hurdles and I was so careful because I didn't want to make any mistakes. Don't hit anything, I was telling myself. One more, come on now, be cool – I had to tell myself to stay cool because I was fighting my natural instinct to let rip. I could see all the big boys on my left-hand side, behind me, and I was telling myself: don't make a mistake, don't hit anything, keep cool. Closer and closer to the tenth hurdle I felt more and more anxious because I hadn't made one mistake yet. Finally I reached the tenth, took it cleanly, came off, my trail leg landed on the floor and I thought: just run! Run, run, run, run, run. I scrambled in, dipped, crossed the line.

I stood up. I didn't know who had won. Garcia had been so close over the line. Malcolm told me afterwards that he was up at the photo-finish station watching the race, and he'd been saying: 'He's won! He's won, but he doesn't realize it. The pillock doesn't know he's won.'

I was squatting down and watching the replay; they were playing every single hurdle and it seemed to take a year for this race to play out on the screen. Then I saw myself come off the last hurdle, run, dip. I could see that Garcia was just behind me and then I jumped up and thought: you've done it. I was so, so happy. I'd won, made another comeback, regained my world title after six years. The time: 13.04, my season's best. I was, aged 32, the first British athlete ever to win two World Championship golds.

Then, instantly, it was awful. Sadness flooded straight though me. I was gutted. I'd much rather have trundled in nowhere and had Ross alive. I jogged round the track and the crowd was cheering, but I was distanced, detached. I felt empty. Nice gesture, I thought: you were running it for Ross, but at the end of the day it's a race. It's eight big blokes running up a track over barriers. It's meaningless. Nothing can bring him back, certainly not a race.

Plenty of people were really happy for me, telling me what an amazing comeback I'd made in my career. Pascal was telling me he couldn't believe I'd done it after all we'd been through that year. I called Suzanne the next day and she said I was on the front of every newspaper.

I just felt dull. I called Tatum and tried to be cheery, saying: 'We all did it, the whole posse did it, not just me – I was just the deliverer.'

Tatum just said: 'Yeah.' She wasn't too moved by it. It wasn't much, really, compared to a life, or a death.

When I thought about it, I could see some meaning in the fact that I'd won. Ross had spent all his time before he died preparing with me for these championships. So my gold medal showed that the effort worked, that we'd been on the right lines, that he hadn't been completely wasting his time. At least it produced something.

As I have thought so much about Ross's death, I have come to see that there is a positive way to regard even so final a tragedy. Think of it this way: you have to go some time. Ross was young when he went; he had everything going for him. He had loads of good friends; he was loved by so many of us. He had money in his pocket, he was enjoying life, he was talented and his running was improving all the time; he was the best he'd ever been. He was never down in his life – he was always excited, always had a smile on his face and walked with a bounce in his stride because life was so good. If you have to go, perhaps it's not the worst thing to go when life is still so sweet.

Still, a lot of people felt a huge hole in the world where Ross used to be. And we all wish so much that he was still here, with us.

CHAPTER SIXTEEN

EUROPEAN RECORD-BREAKER

After I had reclaimed my World Championship, Malcolm said I should take three months out. I was back on a roll, up to where I should have been, had it not been for the disasters and disappointments of 1995 and 1996. I had a good rest and spent some time with my sister. When we started training again, I decided that if I prepared correctly I had a chance of going to the Olympics in Sydney in 2000 and of winning, which – at 33 – was going to be my last realistic chance of claiming that Olympic gold.

But me and the Olympics were never quite destined to be. One thing which had occurred to me after Atlanta was that, even though I'd been at a low ebb in those 1996 Games, my time of 13.19 was faster than my run for the silver medal in Seoul, and would have got me the silver in Barcelona, too. Yet as fate would have it, in Atlanta it wasn't even worth a medal.

In 2000 injuries began to plague me once again and I could never prepare properly. We went to Australia to train in warm weather early in the year, as we had done for nearly a decade. Weightlifting one day, I felt that my hamstring was a little awkward – not injured, just not quite right. I was going to see the unusual yet highly renowned doctor, Hans-Wilhelm Muller-Wohlfahrt, who treats athletes from lots of different sports, in Munich ten days later. He'd inject my hamstring, I thought, and then I was going straight to Ireland to see my physio-therapist, Gerard Hartmann. All I had to do was get through the following ten days of training, which were etched in the diary, vital to my preparation schedule; then, between the two of them, they'd sort my hamstring out.

It was hurting, but the massage therapist in Australia kept it under control so that I could train. We came home and I carried on training in Bath, looking forward to just a few days later when it would be fixed.

I needed to complete this period of preparation, then I could take a week off, get fixed up and start the next period of preparation, leading to racing sharpness. Yet on only my third run in training, two days later, I popped my hamstring. It was gone, seriously injured.

I couldn't believe it. I was thinking: can't you just hang on a little bit before you whack me about with injuries? But no. Immediately I knew I would be five or six weeks delayed. Now I would be going to Gerard's for rehab, not for general maintenance as planned. Surprise, surprise, I thought: I'm going to be dealt a rotten hand in Olympic year again.

The early races of the year are very important because you're sharpening up your performance and setting markers to the other athletes, announcing that they'll have to watch out for you in the major championships later in the summer. Beat people in the first week of June and you're already ahead. Delay your start because of injury and then, when you finally race, the others are more race-fit than you and they're going to kill you, which sets their markers, and you're always battling. But in 2000 I didn't race in early June because of my injury; I was over at Gerard's being treated.

Finally I ran my first race in mid-June. I ran 13.30, which wasn't too bad a start, but I strained my quad – the upper thigh muscle – so had to go back to Gerard's for yet more work. He cured that sufficiently for me to race in a meet in Chemnitz, Germany, which I won in 13.20, the second-fastest time in the world. I was cool as ice, thinking: we're back in business. Without the niggling injuries I was in tremendous shape; I'd had almost three exceptional years of solid work with Malcolm since my silver in the World Championships in 1997.

Back home, Malcolm was pleased. 'Thank God you're OK. Hamstrings feel good? Is everything good?'

'I'm fine.'

Now the schedule was to knuckle down to two weeks' speed work before racing again. With 13.20 behind me, this work in the next period would, Malcolm said, see me come out flying. That same day – just the day after the Chemnitz race – I did a session on starts, working on starting speeds. And in the last run of starts I pulled my quad.

The Olympic trials were in the first week in July, we were due to leave for Sydney in August, the Olympics were in September, and here we were in the middle of June and I'd raced twice.

I was so frustrated because I was in great shape, and I'd had all the effort of coming back from nowhere to be world champion again and now, with these awful injuries, I couldn't do what I wanted and needed to do. I sulked in my house for a while, then I realized I was being a miserable sod. Lots of people are busting their guts to help you get fixed so that you can try to fulfil a dream that you've always had. So don't be so miserable; pack your bag, listen to all the people who are trying to help you, and stop being so pig-headed.

I flew straight out to see the doctor. He examined me and I told him where it was hurting, but he couldn't feel the injury in my quad. Then he concluded it wasn't in the muscle, but in the nervous system in my back. He told me that the nerves in the back run through to the quads and he thought that was affecting it, so I had to go to the chiropractor.

So, with just weeks to go to the Olympics, I was with the German chiropractor; he was going crack, crack, crack on my back. Then I went briefly home and straight back to Gerard in Ireland so that he could try to fix my quad. Now because we were doing all this rehab to get the muscles going, the training I was having to do was endurance work, running two or three miles at a time – exactly what you don't want to be doing at the height of summer. As a sprinter, or sprint hurdler, your muscles adapt very quickly to work, and in the summer you want to be building up race sharpness, on top of all the endurance work done months before, not putting your muscles through that sort of work now. Instead, I was doing three-mile runs, rehabbing with Gerard and not racing at all. I managed only six races in the whole season, which was nothing compared to the planned schedule; I'm not used to racing so little. When I finally got to race, I was always playing catch-up with the others and was never on top of any race. The whole build-up had gone completely wrong.

I prepared as well I could in the circumstances for the Olympic trials in Birmingham, but my quad was still hurting. Even when we got to the holding camp in Brisbane it was difficult to prepare properly. I did everything accurately, but it just did not feel right, because the foundation simply wasn't there for the final sharpness work before a championships. When we left our holding camp for the Sydney Games I knew it wasn't there and the spirit went out of me. My body wasn't right, it was as simple as that. Athletics at the highest level is not a matter of effort on the day; it is about preparation which begins in the cold winter at home, a scientific programme to hone the athlete's body and technique to be in prime shape on the minute of the day of the event in the major championships in the summer ahead. In my heart, and now-experienced professional head, I knew I hadn't been able to do the work and so I knew I wasn't ready. There was huge pressure because I was world champion again and of course I had to talk the big talk in the media, but in some ways this added to the pressure because I knew it wasn't going to happen.

I qualified from the first round easily enough, then won my second round in 13.27, which felt comfortable enough and turned out to be the fastest qualifying time. The semi-final and final were the following day. Gerard was there and he was stretching and massaging me after the second round until really late – I was still in the room chatting with him until after midnight. Then he said to me: 'You'd better go to bed.'

'Why?' I asked. 'I'm not racing till late.'

He said: 'You'd better go to bed to make this special.'

'What do you mean, special?'

'Well, you know, your Olympic-final day.'

And then I realized that I didn't really give a toss. That because my preparations were all wrong, mentally and emotionally I just wasn't into it. Gerard was completely right: if I'd been focused, there was no way I'd have been up chatting to him till midnight the night before the race.

Still, I really should have won my semi-final without too much of a problem. I started behind Terence Trammell, the quick American, and Allen Johnson – the main dangers – and it felt quite comfortable, so I knew I had the measure of them. I thought I was way in front, so when I came off the last hurdle I slammed my anchors on to cruise in. Terence and Allen suddenly went right past me and I thought: where did you lot come from? I dipped and we just about crossed the line together, but I was judged to have come in third.

Malcolm was at me afterwards. 'What was that all about?'

'I swear, Malcolm, I thought I'd won the race and there was no way I would come in anything but second.'

He was in a grump. 'Now you're going to have a crap lane draw, aren't you?' The winners of the semis get the choice lanes and I thought: oh God, he's right. And sure enough when the lane draw came out, I was in lane 1, next to just the person I didn't want to be: Dudley Dorival of Haiti.

Dudley was a quick starter, which meant he would get out of the blocks with me, but he was a messy hurdler, which meant he'd be flailing across me and hampering my progress. I felt even less comfortable now. But as the final drew near, everybody around me in the team and the staff were encouraging me and wishing me luck. I began to psych myself up, thinking I really must give it some: just try to run as hard as I can, bolt out of those blocks, just go for it.

But in reality athletics doesn't work like that. I had a false start, because down on the blocks I had cramp in my feet. The starter went: 'Set', and as soon as he said it my feet pushed right out. I wasn't too anxious about it, because it wasn't due to loss of control or nerves, but because my feet were killing me. It was annoying watching the video with the commentary afterwards because they were all speculating about why I had the false start, asking whether I was too anxious. And I thought: shut up, don't paint some drama, just wait until after the race, ask me why I had a false start and I'll tell you.

We returned to the line. Set. The gun went and Allen Johnson got out really quickly but he wellied one of the hurdles in the middle. I went out hard, then I smacked hurdle four, really hard, and I practically stopped dead. I just told myself to lift myself up, keep going, keep going. I started running through and I was telling myself to try to relax. And I came in, dipped, looked across and thought: there's way too many people in front of me here for me to have got a medal. I felt a huge sense of relief; I was just so glad it was over, I wasn't devastated or anything like that. I went walking up the track and then I saw the clock stopped at the winning time of 13.00 for Anier Garcia, and I thought: if only I could have been in shape, I could have won this race, or at least claimed a medal. That cheesed me off. I was fifth, running 13.28 – even that equalled my time for the silver medal in Seoul, 12 long years ago.

But I wasn't too down. In the circumstances I had run as well as I could. It wasn't like 1992 when I should have creamed the gold medal, but made my mistake and clipped the hurdle in the second round; or 1996 when I just wasn't mentally right for it. Allen Johnson, on the other hand, was absolutely gutted; he'd finished fourth after whacking his hurdle and he was inconsolable. I gave him a hug. Although I'd finished behind him, I found myself trying to give him some reassurance: 'Don't worry about it: you'll always be an Olympic champion, they can't take that away from you. Look at the season you've had, you've been injured, you can come back next year.' I was just trying to comfort him, but he was devastated.

I left him and as I walked away I realized that Allen, a great athlete, felt he had nothing: I took his world title off him the year before; Garcia just took his Olympic title; I've still got the world record. I know Allen, know he can get down, and I could see that he really felt he had nothing. I felt for him: he was the 1996 Olympic champion and world champion in 1995 and 1997, yet here he was, feeling his whole life had crumpled. The old observations about sport being a ruthless game, and about the fine line between greatness and failure, are all too true.

I wasn't feeling sorry for myself: I was dealt the wrong set of cards, again, in Olympic year. If I'd been in shape and hadn't performed well, it would have been different. Looking back on my Olympic Games, it's strange to see how badly things went every time. I prepared the same way every year, for all major championships, but the great, injury-free years never seemed to coincide with the Olympics. Even with the emotional trauma of Ross dying the year before, I'd had a tremendous injury-free season and was in good enough shape to win the World Championships. Come the Olympics, though, I was spending more time with the physio than with my coach.

Some people see the lack of an Olympic gold as a big hole in my record. But, with my hoard of medals, and both world records still standing, how could I dare complain that the fates conspired against me in athletics? These things happen. And I made my mark. My greatest accolade was to be considered a top athlete by my peers, because they truly understood what the sport is about. And one of the proudest aspects of my career was that I was able to bounce back from adversity, make the effort again, successfully. That gave me huge satisfaction, because it came from deep within me and showed that I had what Malcolm and old-style sports coaches might call 'character'.

It's strange to reflect that although I had a long career at the very top, I never achieved that ultimate prize. In my philosophical moments since retiring, I've pondered on its meaning. Perhaps it has left me space to achieve the ultimate in whatever I do next. If I had won the Olympics, my career would have been so perfect that everything afterwards might have been an anti-climax. It must be really difficult to think – as so many sports people do – that by your early thirties you have reached the absolute pinnacle of your whole life, and it's all downhill from then on. Having missed out on that final perfection perhaps leaves me an opening to reach fulfilment in the next phase of my life.

Anyway, having my priorities right and my life in balance means that I can't complain generally about anything. I'd rather be a nice guy and not have won the Olympics than have won everything but have everybody thinking I'm a right son of a bitch. If anybody quibbles with the fact that I never won the Olympic gold, I just have to shrug and point them to everything else I achieved.

I thought quite seriously about retiring in 2001. I decided not to run in the World Championships, not to compete at that level at 34, but to have a great season racing and then perhaps go out of athletics flying. Again I wanted to prepare well, then have a good time running at the Grand Prix, with freedom from the pressures and responsibility of a major championships – just to enjoy it. The idea harked back to 1989, my CJ22 year of happiness, the last time – 12 years before – that I had a year free of those burdens.

Socially, it went according to plan; I felt free, and it was such a weight off me. My sister moved to New York and got married, and I went over there to stay with her, see my friends and have a laugh. I do love New York. Then one day we were going downtown on the subway, the doors were closing, I started running to get the train, and the doors closed just before I got there. I had to slam on my brakes, but I couldn't stop in time because I was running too fast. My front foot went down, then my trailing foot in its sturdy shoe went crashing into my front foot's Achilles. It was a completely ridiculous way to get injured. On the train, my friends were asking me if I was OK, and I said: 'I'm sure I've just damaged my Achilles.' Sure enough, in time, it really started to hurt.

On the track, that ruined the whole of my 2001. I was back in Ireland with Gerard on my own. The kneading and manipulation he put in on my Achilles were complete agony. Rehab was so slow. I can remember jogging and setting targets, like a bridge a couple of hundred metres away, trying to make it just to there. It was a slow, grim, painful ordeal – not what you're looking for in a relaxing year off.

When I came back to racing I was well below par, ranked fifth or sixth in the world, running about 13.60, which just wasn't me at all; I simply hadn't run times like that since I was a junior. It was still a relief when the World Championships came around in Edmonton, Canada, not to be there feeling all the pressure, but it had been a lousy season.

I felt I couldn't finish my years like that, so it inspired me to try again, looking ahead to 2002 with the European and Commonwealth titles to go for. Again, I steeled myself for another season, which would be my final outdoor championship year. I put my mind to another huge effort: to really work hard for those championships, focus, come back and kick ass, then be able to go out a winner.

After some good winter training and preparation, I ran in the indoor season, including the European Indoor Championship in Vienna, in March. The major threat there was my friend and training partner Elmar Lichtenegger, the Austrian champion. Elmar had hooked up with me for training for quite a while now, like Linford and Mark McKoy used to do in the old days, except that he's eight years younger than me. He's like Mark: cool, self-contained, comes to Cardiff, we train with Malcolm, he stays at my place, entertains himself for hours on end, looking at car websites most probably, playing music, watching movies, no problem at all.

Elmar's a big, strong hurdler, but his main claim to fame was when he came out with me to Nobu, the wonderful Japanese restaurant in Park Lane, London, where I like to go when the celebrity mood takes me. Robbie Williams was in there and he came over to me for a chat. We were nattering away, then he said ta-ra. When he'd gone, Elmar said: 'Who was that?' I asked: 'Heard of Robbie Williams?' He said: 'No. I thought it was the restaurant manager.' I think Elmar was about to ask Robbie to get him a clean fork.

Anyway, in 2002 we trained together, and Elmar was in great shape, a real contender in Vienna in front of his home crowd. In the first round I ran 7.55 as the fastest qualifier; Elmar won his heat comfortably with 7.66. We weren't drawn together in the semi-finals the following day. I won mine with 7.55 again, and was very pleased with that; but Elmar produced a personal best, a new Austrian record, which gave him a great reception from his crowd: 7.45, a storming run.

For Elmar, it was amazing, the fastest he'd ever run. For me, it was a challenge. He was now one-tenth of a second faster than me, a pretty wide margin indoors. I'd learned from experience to judge an indoor race, to try to retain control while blasting over the five hurdles with the rest of the field. Yet over 60m, in a race lasting just seven seconds, it takes a brave man to sit and wait, to make sure you're in the right position, to try to control a race. But you have to; panic is the last emotion you need.

Elmar is an incredibly quick starter and his semi-final run was so fast that I thought he could run 7.39 in the final. I wasn't sure if I had 7.39 in me, so I told myself I just had to get out with him and be even. Try to stay equal with him, all the way, to keep up, then win it with the dip at the end. Nobody could dip like me, and that would give me the hundredth of a second: all I needed to win it. In an athlete's later years, history and record count for a lot, psychologically, in the actual races. Athletes would feel me, see me coming level with them at the last hurdle, and they'd know I was a finisher and would dread that I was going to out-dip them at the line.

On the gun, Elmar had a tremendous start, so fast that he was ahead at the first and second hurdles. I'd have to have some heavy leg speed to catch him and I might smack hurdle five or just not have enough power. I was still playing a waiting game, concentrating on running fast, taking the barriers well, correct body posture. Then Elmar made a slight mistake – ever so slight – on hurdle three, clipping it because he was going too fast, which meant that he had to make a minor adjustment. And I pounced. Like a cat with a mouse: pounce! That fraction of a mistake, that wobble, and I was in. I crept up on him, came up to his shoulder, then had the impetus to move slightly away from him, because Elmar was still braking a little to readjust for the next hurdle. At that level, indoors, you cannot make even a fraction of a mistake.

I'd learned that long before, in Budapest in 1989, when I was the young flyer – a bit younger than Elmar actually – and Roger Kingdom was twice Olympic champion, who'd been around a while. I did the same as Elmar, got out quick, was a little bit too anxious, wobbled slightly at hurdle four, then Roger had the impetus and he flew past me. He was the same as I was now in Vienna, experienced enough to hold back and wait, just long enough to win it.

I crossed the line in 7.40: thank you very much, a gold medal. Elmar came in with 7.44. He broke his own new national record, one-hundredth quicker than in the semi-final, but the semi was his better run because he made no mistakes and was so far ahead of everybody that he eased up after the fifth hurdle and practically walked over the line.

This was one of my most important performances. It had become vital for me to go out well; I didn't want to be an athlete forced to give up because of injury or bad form, or long after it was really all over. There was some pressure because of that, and because I had all the European pretenders like Elmar wanting to whack me. Coming in just that whisker ahead of Elmar in Vienna and winning another championships, after Sydney and the wreckage of 2001, was actually emotional. It also set me up for the two outdoor titles I really wanted.

Back in Cardiff and Bath I trained well with Malcolm and the new group of young athletes who have come through under his supervision at Bath. Our group was never the same after Ross died. Tatum hardly went back to Bath, ever. Mark Foster was there – still is – and I was training with him and coaching him, but I could never live there again. Malcolm changed completely; he really smelt the flowers when Ross died. It was still very difficult to come to terms with, and I'm sure it always will be.

Linford's group trained down in Cardiff, too, Jamie and Paul Gray among them. The run-up to the Commonwealth Games in Manchester, in which we were all competing, featured an embarrassment which said so much about the ragged way British sport is administered. Here we were, preparing for a Commonwealth Games that cost over £300 million, much of it public Lottery money from Sport England. Yet at the eleventh hour, the Athletics Association of Wales could not even afford kit for their athletes. Over the years I got used to all the contradictions and to money going to the wrong places – rugby mops up millions of television money in Wales, but the game is failing and the national team is a farce. Here were some world-class athletes going to compete in one of the few champion-ships where you run under the Welsh banner, and the Association was too skint and starved of funding to pay for shorts and vests.

At the last minute Nike came in as the kit sponsor and we had our bright, shiny, new uniforms. I was desperately hoping to win the Commonwealth Games in front of a British crowd, and a British TV audience, at that cracking new stadium in Manchester, the one we had all spent our careers without – which has now been ripped up to house a football club that already had its own stadium. A crying shame and yet another sporting administrative cock-up.

I was the favourite in Manchester and also Wales's most realistic gold-medal shot, but in the final I hit the first hurdle and came to a dead-stop. I was restarting the race from hurdle two and had to catch the whole field. I went past them all, catching Tony Jarrett and Maurice Wignall of Jamaica, a young gun who'd been a mite too cocky with me round the circuit, but I just didn't have time to catch Shaun Bownes of South Africa, who got the gold. I was pleased enough with my perform-ance, really, because a silver was creditable, and my opportunity to truly shine came ten days later at the European Championships in Munich. But I felt I had let Wales down a little bit, that I was their champion and that people had really wanted me to win and I hadn't managed it. But second place felt OK, and I was up there on the rostrum.

In Munich in early August came the opportunity to make history. Nobody in track had ever won four European titles, and I was the defending champion going for that record. In field events, where you can become stronger as you get older and have greater longevity, this isn't so remarkable. But in track, where age and the wear and tear of injuries slow you down, you have to go on at a peak for a long time to be able to win four golds at consecutive tournaments four years apart. I'd won three on the trot: 1990, 1994 and 1998. And this was to be my swansong at major championships.

I had been relatively injury-free, my preparation had been good and I felt quite confident. But again there was pressure, after the silver in the Commonwealth Games, being the three-times champion and with all the young pretenders around wanting to beat me. I held my form really well; I was the fastest first-round qualifier with 13.41, fastest in the semi-final at 13.21 – Elmar went out in the semi. Then in the final I hung on in there and ran a cool race to take the title, in 13.11.

At that stage in my career, on an August evening in Munich, it was special to make history. Four European titles – the first time anybody ever did that on the track: I was so happy. It showed that for all the dramas and inevitable low points in a long career, I had a consistency of performance at the top of the sport over a long (now record-breakingly long) period of time. I could trace in my European titles a whole generation in athletics, from my first win in 1990 through to this one in

2002, at the age of 35. It was deeply satisfying and people there were so pleased for me. Most importantly, it confirmed that I could go out a winner, and I set my retirement date: the World Indoor Championships, on the home track in Birmingham, in March 2003. After that, I'd say goodbye.

CHAPTER SEVENTEEN
GOODBYE TO ALL THAT

Throughout my career, particularly after Stuttgart in 1993 when I became the world champion and world record-holder, I always had a nagging feeling that I wasn't given the recognition from the media that my status deserved. I'm not being boastful, just looking at the facts of what I achieved: the 44 races unbeaten during that period; the indoor world record; the 25 major championship medals over my career, more than any other British athlete. Although I've felt and loved the warmth and affection that glows from the home athletics fans, the media always appeared to come at me as if I had yet more to prove.

Perhaps it dated back to Barcelona in 1992 when nobody seemed quite to believe that I had injured myself in the second round, and somehow Tony Dees' ridiculous jibe that I was a bottler was not dismissed out of hand. I remember when Brendan Foster said in his commentary that he wished I was more upset to lose, I was outraged: what did he know about how hurt I was? The answer, clearly, was nothing, because if he knew me at all he'd have known how deeply winning mattered to me – that it was everything, my whole life, probably to the detriment of other aspects of me. He'd have recognized that in my performances to come back from defeat or setback, another feature of my career that I felt was not adequately appreciated.

I have wondered about which other factors might have come into play. Being Welsh, and staying in Wales, hardly put me at the forefront of the media's attention span, which struggles badly with anything outside the M25. Being black, too, makes me wonder. I am not obsessed with being black, I don't see racism everywhere, and I believe that black people have to try as hard as they can to put history behind them and make the best of the opportunities in the circumstances in which we find ourselves. We should strive to do well and fulfil our potential, not allow ourselves to be held back by prejudice or the history of it.

But that is not to say we don't recognize racism if it is there – just that I believe we can transcend it, rather than be ground down by it. I know I'm lucky to be able to say I have never faced any overt racism or abuse, ever, in my life. I do think there is much less of it in Wales, where people unite in a common defensive position against the English. Now that is taking a more positive form with the Welsh Assembly and the regeneration of Cardiff into a wonderful city, so that Welsh people can be more positive about their identity, rather than defining themselves by resentment of the English. Even my parents – immigrants from Jamaica to a country that had absorbed few black people at that time – have experienced next to no racism, except for the two isolated comments at the beginning and end of my mother's working life.

Yet I'm still vexed by wondering if my status in the media would have been different had I been white. This goes right back to my early rivalry as a junior with Jon Ridgeon, and recognizing as a fact, although nobody expressed it, that coaches and others in the athletics establishment wanted Jon to be the number-one hurdler, and not me. And that the fact of him being white, fair-haired, blue-eyed, English and at Cambridge University was altogether a more attractive package than scruffy old me, son of Jamaicans, living in Llanederyn. Latterly, after I came back in 1997 and then 1999 to become double world champion, I've compared my media profile to the attention lavished on people in other sports, like football, and wondered: if I had the looks of David Beckham, and was double world champion and double world record-holder in sprint hurdling, would I be an icon, like he is?

There is no clear answer; people will argue over the reasons. In Britain, track has a lower profile generally than football and rugby, whose clubs are supported passionately and handed down within families. So maybe it is the relative profiles of the sports. Nevertheless racism is there, even if it's unspoken. Many people haven't a trace of racism in them, but you can see it in some people's faces. It's cultural anyway, a sense in which people – and definitely the media – are more comfortable with a white face than a black one. Even though I was born in Cardiff, have lived there all my life and love it as a home, as a black person I still feel I inhabit a strange halfway zone: not fully accepted as British, but not Jamaican either. I think it will take another few generations for black people to be fully part of society in Britain. Most of the time I don't think about this; I have my family and friends and a wonderful life, but when I ponder on the status I have, compared to what it might be were I blond-haired and blue-eyed, I can't help thinking of race as a reason.

Then there has been all the fuss and speculation about my private life, the 'rumours' – which have come out in the media a couple of times – that I'm gay. To me, it's not an accusation; it's actually a sad reflection on the athletics press that they're so curious to know. I have many gay friends; I enjoy their company; they make me laugh and I like going out with them. But I have many straight friends, too; in fact the only criterion for being my friend is to be a good, kind person – although liking a laugh is also an asset. I have friends from so many different walks of life that if I had a party there would be people there from age six (Carmen's daughter, Chloe) through to 76; a great mix of people, but I bet they would all get on, because they are all good people.

So when they put it to me in an interview for *The Voice* newspaper – was I gay? – I wasn't going to deny it. First of all, it's nobody's business what I do in private. Second, it would be disrespectful to my gay friends for me to deny it. It would be as if I'm making light of it, saying that although I have many gay friends, for me there is something wrong with it, worth publicly denying. It would be offensive. Like when people say some of their best friends are black, and you know it's derogatory. So I told the interviewer that I wasn't going to deny it, because it's nothing to be ashamed of. The *Mirror* then got hold of that interview and ran – in a national newspaper – open speculation about whether or not I am gay. I was cheesed off, thinking: oh God, not this rubbish again.

Not that it has bothered me too much, but the strangest thing is that nobody in the media has ever come out and asked me: have you ever had a girlfriend? Instead, there were rumours and whispers. I can remember being on a flight back from the States, chatting to the nice middle-aged woman in the seat next to me, and she said: 'Nice-looking boy like you? Not married? Why not?' But I don't live a conventional life. It hasn't been for me to conform to other people's ideas of who I should be. I feel that most people, and broader-minded journalists (perhaps in features, rather than sport), can understand that. From the sports press all I ever wanted was for my performances to be fairly reported and for my record to be appreciated. And mostly I felt that it wasn't.

Having said all that, in the run-up to my retirement the coverage was wonderful. After the European Championships in 2002, I raced at Crystal Palace, which was my final outdoor Grand Prix in Britain. Before the race, the stadium announcer ran through my career, talking about how long I'd gone on and what medals I'd won. The crowd went bananas and I completely lost it. It was a total surprise when I was preparing to focus on the race, and my legs just turned to jelly. Listening to it, out there on the track with the other athletes, did make me think about my whole history in athletics and realize this was it; it was coming to an end. It didn't make for the send-off the crowd wanted because my mind and body were so shot that I didn't even make the first three.

I had a break and then came back in November to prepare one final time for racing, this time just the indoor season in 2003. Again, as I had for over a decade, I went to Australia for six weeks for warm-weather training. What a luxury, escaping the cold and grey of the British winter. When I came back I trained with Malcolm and the new group of Bath athletes at the indoor facility at the University of Wales Institute, Cardiff, a facility we could only dream of in my early days pounding round the cinder track in shellsuits.

At UWIC, Wales's top athletes train on a world-class indoor track, lift weights in a fine gym, alongside disabled athletes and university sports teams. Elmar and I might be about to do a training run, and a netball will roll across the lanes. It's a very democratic atmosphere, a good vibe and, among the athletes, there's always good chat and jokes amid the serious business of training. You train better in a happy environment, so I always made sure there was plenty of laughter and fun in the air.

After work on speed and sharpness, I was ready to begin the racing season. I went to compete in the international indoor meet in Glasgow in early February: Great Britain versus Italy, Russia and Sweden. It was my 70th international meet, a record – the kind of statistic which the press were more aware of than I was, and which also brought home to many people, including me, quite how long my career had been. It was also farewell to Scotland for me, where I was always made to feel so at home, on an appropriately freezing weekend, with snow carpeting Glasgow.

I won my race in 7.55 and got a lovely reception from the fans, along with nice write-ups in the Scottish and national newspapers for my caps record. It was starting to sink in, just how long I had been around, now that I was going. Other British winners at that successful meet were Jason Gardener in the 60m sprint, Marlon Devenish in the 200m, and Daniel Caines in the 400m, three good athletes who are, respectively, eight, nine and twelve years younger than me.

Elmar came over to stay with me and train in Cardiff to prepare for the next landmark, at the end of February, the Norwich Union meet in Birmingham: my final indoor Grand Prix in this country, ever. I did start to feel some pressure; now that it was dawning on me (and everybody else) that this really was it, I so much wanted to go out well, with success.

On the Monday evening, 17 February, we lifted some weights and did some short, loose runs. Paul Gray was in there, and Katherine Merry, and we shot the breeze while we were lifting, mostly recalling old laughs. Carmen turned up with Chloe, and we started to recall our early days, the ridiculous training we did – Carmen sprinting on when both Achilles heels were gone – and the pranks we played, like the time I hid Sallyanne Short's bra just before she had to go out and do a session of starts with Malcolm. Putting Sallyanne through her paces unsupported, Malcolm must have thought it was Christmas. She said afterwards: 'Malcolm had me doing so many starts today, I couldn't understand it,' and we had to bury our faces in our hands to stop from laughing. Then there was the time we were all in Florida for Sally Gunnell's wedding, and I took all Carmen and Sallyanne's underwear and put them on the overhead fans in their room, so that when they came in and turned the fans on, they were treated to windmills of lingerie. Funny, there do seem to be rather a lot of underwear stories in my account of our athletics careers!

Carmen waxed sentimental about all the years gone by, remembering my humble beginnings – in Llanederyn, just around the corner from UWIC – and where I went to from there, saying that I hadn't changed in myself all that time, which was nice. Elmar and I went for pasta in the evening at a family Italian restaurant that I go to in Cardiff, and we hung out.

The following morning we met Malcolm at the track and did a drills session; isolation drills, where we take the hurdles at the side, first with the lead leg and then with the trailing leg, with short high steps between each hurdle. We did some straight hurdles, a few starts and some sprints. 'OK?' I asked Malcolm. 'OK,' he nodded. By the end, we didn't need to say much. And as he said, he was a pair of eyes by then, watching for any necessary adjustments.

It was my birthday that day: 36 years amassed, and where was the soon-to-retire athletics superstar going to celebrate this landmark? Well, for Chloe, my six-year-old god-daughter, it just had to be her favourite place in the world: TGI Fridays, that world-famous establishment, squatting on a retail estate on the Newport Road. There, they had me standing on a chair, holding balloons and a cake with a single candle on it, while the other tables were invited to sing 'Happy Birthday dear Colin', just as we'd all done for the boy having his tenth birthday on the next table. Carmen and I teased each other mercilessly and had a good gossip about everybody; Chloe ate her ice cream, Elmar didn't say much throughout the whole do – he was probably overawed by the glamour – and then, at seven o'clock, we went home.

I went up to Birmingham on the Thursday to do a press conference for the Grand Prix and it went really well. There was none of the frostiness I have had with the athletics press at points in my career, but a genuine warmth towards me. I told them how much I wanted to win, at the meet and at the World Indoors in Birmingham in March, to end my career flying.

At the meet hotel the following day, the Marriott in Birmingham, a collage of cuttings was pinned up to a noticeboard in reception. It was all pretty much Colin Jackson – my face beaming out, and captions talking about my forthcoming retirement 'after a magnificent career'. Good stuff.

Before a race, though, that all adds to the pressure. I felt it was significant to win, and this was the run-in to the World Indoors, where I was aiming to win against a truly world-class field. I went down to the track in the afternoon and the blocks felt fine, and I knew then I would run a season's best and win the race.

Elmar was drawn on my right – not that we'd talk to each other before the race, but nevertheless there was some comfort and familiarity in it.

In a Grand Prix, there is more showbiz than in the championships, and the stadium announcer at the Birmingham Indoor Arena was none other than my old rival, Jon Ridgeon. He warned me they were going to go through the same rigmarole as they had at Crystal Palace, roaring out my past achievements to the crowd and even showing some of my races on the screen.

I wasn't going to be shocked twice. Jon announced, as we all lined up, that I was 'one of the greatest British athletes ever', with a 'fantastic career' behind me. Then they showed my win in Stuttgart – boy, I looked young – my world indoor record in Sindelfingen and my world championship in Seville in 1999. The crowd was excited, there were banners in there (one saying they were going to miss me), and this time I wasn't going to let it rock me, but would turn it psychologically to my advantage. Well, I said mentally to the other guys, we know who this is for, don't we? Be warned, this is what you're up against. I turned it all into a positive: this is me and what I have behind me, so a race like this isn't going to be a problem.

I went on the line, and I knew that my start was much better than it had been, so I was confident I could get out well. The gun went, I was at the first hurdle before anybody else and by the second I thought: I can settle down. I just kept control and ran it as if it were a heat of a championships; just stayed out there and did what I needed to do. I won it in 7.51, a season's best for me, as I had planned it.

I did a lap of honour. It was nice; I picked out a few people that I knew. Somebody had a Welsh flag so I gave them a special wave; it really was a warm and lovely reception from the crowd. I did an interview with Jon, who is a good man, then one with my old mate Sally Gunnell for the BBC. I told her it was cool, but that I was still only honing my power–weight ratio and was going to lose 4lbs before the World Indoors. Another race won, another relief. Not a month to go until it was all over.

Linford was there, and afterwards he came up to me and asked if he could have a pair of my shoes when I retired. 'Sure,' I said. It was strange. You ask for the spikes of athletes you respect; this was a mark of respect from Linford, so perhaps he would like to be involved in my life in some shape or form. I've got no axe to grind with him, and it would be nice to be friends again, although Linford would have to have changed so much for that to happen.

The following Tuesday I trained as normal in Cardiff. Jamie and Paul were there and we had a laugh while we were stretching, remembering freaking out Darren Campbell in Australia because he was petrified of spiders: while Darren was bench-pressing, Jamie unfolded a leaf; Darren thought it was a spider and practically hit the ceiling. He'd been struggling with the weights and suddenly he almost flung the bar up. Jamie himself is not too keen on insects, particularly the huge cockroaches they have in Oz, and we well remembered when Ian Mackie and I put one in his shoe out there.

Then we did some serious training: drills again, lead leg, trailing leg, short steps, then faster, building up to taking four hurdles at full pace. Then we did three hurdles at full pace, alongside Tristan Anthony, at 20 the UK junior record-holder and one of Malcolm's new hopes at Bath. Then it was training-tights off, shorts on, for some sprints with Tristan. The last time he beat me and threw his hands up for a joke. I said it all felt fine and the sprinting felt smooth – although not as smooth as Carmen looked in her leather jacket: 'Now that is smooth, girl, like Cat Slater in *EastEnders*.' She just gave me her trademark look, which says 'Shut up' without moving her lips, a curious skill she has perfected over the years of dealing with me.

Then we all suddenly realized that I had just finished my last ever training session in Cardiff. As always, the media were more aware of it than I was: BBC Wales were following me around, making a documentary, and the producer, Rich Owen, made much more of a deal about it than any of us were going to. Predictably Malcolm downplayed it: 'We'll just have to get another comedian.' But then he told Rich: 'I have plenty of memories to treasure with Colin, there is plenty to get emotional about. It's pretty much unique to last nearly twenty years in this game.'

Rich went and interviewed some of the others. Jamie told him that he and I had had our differences when he went over to Linford, but that he would always be grateful for my help in the early part of his career. Tristan, cheeky sod, said I was the life and soul of the group: 'He's always having a laugh and cracking really bad jokes, so we'll miss him. He's helped me in every aspect and I do feel privileged to have trained with him. Everybody's really surprised that I do.' Rachel King, the Welsh women's number-one hurdler, said they'd all miss me. It was a bit difficult to take in.

Bar a bit of a chat with Carmen, Malcolm and everybody else, that was it. I'd spent all my adult life training and racing in this city and now it was truly going to be over. Tristan wanted to know what I was going to do: 'Are you gonna go to the gym and get your body really ripped, now you don't have to be supple for hurdling?' Poor lad, that was his main concern.

My final warm-weather training session with Malcolm was in Tenerife. He realized then that I was getting very serious about winning the World Indoors in front of the home crowd and trying to go out a champion. Back home we had done interviews with all the newspapers, which by now had fully grasped that I was retiring. They must have looked up the statistics and come to realize that it was, all told, not a bad career.

Every paper published a glowing profile, alongside a list of my medals and achievements, stretching back to 1985. One wanted a picture of me with all my medals, so we dug them out of the cabinet in my father's office. I have never gloated over them or even looked at them much; for me, the satisfaction and relief have been in the races themselves; then I have always had to move on to the next target or championships. My father has been the chronicler of his son's career, lovingly looking after the medals, spending hours maintaining cuttings, all the way from early write-ups in the *Western Mail*, the Welsh paper, in scrapbooks that now form a pile up to my waist.

Yet when I did the photograph with the 25 medals, even I was taken aback to see them all together, spread out around me for the first time. It made me think back to many of them, and wonder at the length of time I had been competing at the top level in athletics. The coverage of my final run-in was quite different from usual, and very pleasing. As with so many things in our lives, private and public, perhaps I was being truly appreciated only now that people realized I was leaving.

At the World Indoors themselves, I did feel tremendous pressure. It was such a strange feeling to be preparing for my final race, yet I wanted badly to perform. The final was late on a Sunday afternoon, and I didn't want any distractions beforehand: no interviews, no people. I just stretched and did all my preparations in my room until as late as possible. I stretched my hamstrings and back, did some push-ups and some sit-ups, just to get the blood flowing and circulating into the larger muscle groups. I washed, shaved, changed, then got ready to go down.

When the car took me to the arena, I had that feeling of dread: you are on the line, performing again – the feeling of being exposed, which I am not going to miss. A warrior going out to kill or be killed, for the entertainment of an audience. Down to the warm-up area to practise some drills, lead leg and trailing leg, some full-blown hurdling and some starts. We probably used to surprise people, because in the warm-up area I used to really do a training session with Malcolm – we did more than most athletes do before a race. The idea is to make sure everything is absolutely sharp before a race, and the only way to make it sharp is to do some hard work. We had a final chat, and Malcolm just told me to have a go at it.

Then we had to go to the call room, the moment every athlete hates most, when there is nothing to do except be invaded by fear and nerves, and thoughts of fulfilling the expectations of everybody about to watch. There is very little glamour; we're led round the back of the seats, where the families sit munching popcorn, drinking Coke and enjoying themselves, into a holding area to wait to be called to the track. Track is still a rich sport for those with the sponsorships and meet fees at the top, but the officials are all volunteers, enthusiasts doing it for love of the sport. They can get on your nerves if you're about to give everything in a major championships and they ask for your autograph for their son or daughter, but I try not to snap: they have a job to do. In Birmingham, a middle-aged lady pinned our numbers to our vests, just like at junior county meets when I was starting out. At this stage none of the athletes look at each other, for everybody is consumed by their own thoughts. Girls are summoned forward with yellow baskets to bring out to trackside, for us to put our tracksuits and other stuff in. Then we're called out to face the lanes and the crowd.

A day earlier, I had won my heat in 7.56, not too much of a problem although I false-started, so it was a relief to come through. There was none of the razzmatazz they wrap into the Grand Prix, although when we were introduced to the crowd, Jon Ridgeon said of me: 'He has had the most incredible career; eighteen years in such a demanding event. He has always been the most professional of athletes, leaving no stone unturned in his search for excellence in performance. It would be great if he leaves with a medal.'

The crowd really rose to that. I won my semi in 7.55, smooth. But as soon as I saw the lane draw, I knew it was going to be extremely difficult for me. On form, I was fourth-fastest in the world, although Terence Trammell pulled out, giving me a slightly better chance. But I was drawn with Anier Garcia on my right, and Xiang Liu, the Chinese champion, on my left. Garcia's a champion, but he's a messy hurdler, and Liu is huge: six feet three inches.

When the gun went, we came out and Garcia hit me on the shoulder with his flailing arm. I whacked the first two hurdles and never really recovered. Liu was towering over me on my inside – I was stuck between two giants. Over 60m there isn't enough time to come back when you've clattered the first two, especially when you are 36 and it is the World Indoor final. Allen Johnson won it in 7.47, Garcia was second and Liu was third.

I came in fifth. I'd have liked to have rounded off my career by running better, but there was nothing more I could have done. I took a lap of honour anyway, my last one ever, feeling huge warmth from the crowd. Allen and I hugged each other, then went over to be interviewed by Sally Gunnell for the BBC. He'd won the race, but she asked him about me and he said: 'He's the one we all want to be like.'

Sally asked me how I felt and I said I was just pleased to go out at another world final. To finish fifth in the world wasn't too bad. Sally said she was jealous – so many athletes quit because of injury or because they just couldn't put themselves on the line again, yet here I was, injury-free, bowing out in a world final live on the BBC in front of a home crowd. I told her that's how I always wanted it, and I was thankful I could do it this way.

Quite a few people wanted to know if I might change my mind, go on until the World Championships in Paris or even the Athens Olympics in 2004, but they were seriously misunderstanding my reasons for retiring. I had planned to finish whilst I was still in good shape, and as fate would have it I had been able to do this. But fitness is no reason to carry on. Yes, I have to work out a new career that is as fulfilling as track, and which I can succeed in, but it is a relief to retire from the responsibility and relentless work of athletics. The thought of keeping fit just to enjoy being in shape – not as a profession – is deeply attractive, and it's such a relief to know I won't ever have to run fast in competition again. I wouldn't change a second of the life I've had; it was a great career, 18 incredible years, and even my mistakes and failures were valuable experiences – overcoming them made me a better athlete and person.

I have work immediately from the BBC, as a commentator at the World Championships, and I intend the media to be a major part of my new career. I am also planning to use the lessons I have learned about dedication, focus and attaining goals to lecture companies on motivation and working for success. I will also at some stage share the secrets of nutrition, diet and vitamins that I developed myself and which maintained my body at its high performance level for so long.

There is no going back, no reaching back to what I know. I could still make a decent living racing, but I wouldn't be at the top, winning. That's for younger guys: nobody could have expected me to go on beyond 36. If I were to go on longer, it'd probably get on everybody's nerves anyway. I wanted to finish nicely and cleanly, which was why I didn't quit when I was on bad form or injured. I was 18 when I went full-time into track and I did it with total dedication. I told my parents that whatever I had decided to do, I would have done it with the same commitment and been as determined to be successful. Now I feel the same way about my next career. I would like to expand my skills into wider areas, become known not just as Colin Jackson the athlete, but as somebody with a great deal to offer.

And although I have loved track and enjoyed the rewards, and made plenty of money, there were many sacrifices. I never went away, never let rip as my friends did at a young age. I've barely ever had a drink, and could rarely even have a late night. I used to be with friends in London; we'd maybe go to a club in Soho and one vodka ice would last me all night, and the night would end at eleven or twelve anyway because I had to train the following day. I've lived like that since I was 18. Not that I'm planning a life of drink and debauchery now, but to be able to have a late night and know it doesn't matter, that you're not training the next day, will be wonderful. I feel, for all the fantastic times I have had, that I lost my freedom. I was locked into a lifestyle, and the more successful you are, the more you are locked in and the greater the pressure and responsibility to live up to the standards you have set.

Now I want to experience life outside track, to be fully myself, however it works out. I need to sort out my new career and then – who knows? – now that my long marriage to track is over, perhaps I will sort something out in my private life, too. Perhaps things might blossom again with Sam, now that my life has changed completely. You never know.

The night I retired, and for the following week, my phone hummed with texts from friends and fellow athletes. I had a lovely message from Paul Gray, saying we'd had rows in our time, but I was an inspiration to him.

Jon Ridgeon sent one: 'Good luck in retirement, you deserve it. You handled yesterday brilliantly. Hope we'll stay in touch.'

My cousin Sam, who competes internationally in judo, said: 'You're an inspiration to me, cous, and I'm sure you'll be a champion in the next chapter of your life, too.'

From Ian Mackie: 'Thanks for everything, Colin; it has been great fun watching your career, but even better to be part of it. You have been a massive inspiration.'

Such messages meant a great deal, but they also made me think. People have told me this so often, that the effort and achievement they have seen me put into my life has inspired them in whatever they were doing. It is great because it's not something I have ever done deliberately, and if that is happening naturally, it's a good thing. It's nice to be liked. It made me think that if I could inspire people without trying, in track, then I can do so in the next phase of my life.

For me, the greatest achievements were not in the running of races, the training and preparation, but those of my grandfather and of Ross, both of whom had people locked out at their funerals because they were so loved. That's real achievement: standing room only at your funeral.

Tatum also texted me: 'You will always be Colin Jackson, the man, the son, the brother, the friend that's always been here.'

I got a message too from Malcolm Arnold, my coach throughout my whole career, the man whom my father and I approached when I was an ambitious 16-year-old kid and Malcolm had coached an Olympic champion. He thought then that I could be a great athlete, and we went on the journey together. He was a great coach and teacher, and very definitely a friend. The text message was Malcolm all over: 'Bad luck yesterday, but 12 out of 10 for the previous 20 years. See you soon: M. A.'

That, I thought, was pretty cool. And now: I'm free.

INDEX